The Soul Winner

or How to Lead Sinners to the Savior

Charles H. Spurgeon

The Soul Winner or How to Lead Sinners to the Savior

The present edition is a reproduction of previous publication of this classic work. Minor typographical errors may have been corrected without note, however, for an authentic reading experience the spelling, punctuation, and capitalization have been retained from the original text.

ISBN: 978-1-61895-433-6

CONTENTS

PREFATORY NOTE

This volume is issued in accordance with a plan for med by MR. SPURGEON; indeed, he had already prepared for the press the greater part of the material here published, and the rest of his manuscripts have been inserted after only slight revision. It was his intention to deliver to the students of the Pastors' College a short course of Lectures upon what he termed "that most royal employment" —SOUL-WINNING,—and, having completed the series, he purposed to collect his previous utterances to other audiences upon the same theme, and to publish the whole for the guidance of all who desired to become soul-winners, and with the hope also of inducing many more professing Christians to engage in this truly blessed service for the Saviour.

This explanation will account for the form in which the topic is treated in the present book. The first six chapters contain the College Lectures; then follow four Addresses delivered to Sunday-school teachers, open-air preachers, and friends gathered at Monday evening prayer-meetings at the Tabernacle; while the rest of the volume consists of Sermons in which the work of winning souls is earnestly commended to the attention of every believer in the Lord Jesus Christ.

For more than forty years, MR. SPURGEON was, by his preaching and writing, one of the greatest soul-winners; and by h is printed words he still continues to be the means of the conversion of many all over the world. It is believed, therefore, that thousands will rejoice to read what he spoke and wrote concerning what he called "the chief business of the Christian minister."

WHAT IS IT TO WIN A SOUL?

I purpose, dear brethren, if God shall enable me, to give you a short course of lectures under the general head of "THE SOUL-WINNER." Soulwinning is the chief business of the Christian minister; indeed, it should be the main pursuit of every true believer. We should each say with Simon Peter, "I go a fishing," and with Paul our aim should be, "That I might by all means save some."

We shall commence our discourses upon this subject by considering the question—

WHAT IS IT TO WIN A SOUL?

This may be instructively answered by describing what it is not. We do not regard it to be soul-winning to steal members out of churches already established, and train them to utter our peculiar Shibboleth: we aim rather at bringing souls to Christ than at making converts to our synagogue. There are sheep-stealers abroad, concerning whom I will say nothing except that they are not "brethren" or, at least, they do not act in a brotherly fashion. To their own Master they must stand or fall. We count it utter meanness to build up our own house with the ruins of our neighbours' mansions; we infinitely prefer to quarry for ourselves. I hope we all sympathize in the largehearted spirit of Dr. Chalmers, who, when it was said that such and such an effort would not be beneficial to the special interests of the Free Church of Scotland, although it might promote the general religion of the land, said, "What is the Free Church compared with the Christian good of the people of Scotland?" What, indeed, is any church, or what are all the churches put together, as mere organizations, if they stand in conflict with the moral and spiritual advantage of the nation, or if they impede the kingdom of Christ? It is because God blesses men through the churches that we desire to see them prosper, and not merely for the sake of the churches themselves. There is such a thing as selfishness in our eagerness for the aggrandisement of our own party; and from this evil spirit may grace deliver us! The increase of the kingdom is more to be desired than the growth of a clan. We would do a great deal to make a Paedobaptist brother into a Baptist, for we value our Lord's ordinances; we would labourearnestly to raise a believer in salvation

1

by free-will into a believe r in salvation by grace, for we long to see all religious teaching built upon the solid rock of truth, and not upon the sand of imagination; but, at the same time, our grand object is not the revision of opinions, but the regeneration of natures. We would bring men to Christ and not to our own peculiar views of Christianity. Our first care must be that the sheep should be gathered to the great Shepherd; there will be time enough afterwards to secure them for our various folds. To make proselytes, is a suitable labour for Pharisees: to beget men unto God, is the honourable aim of ministers of Christ.

In the next place, we do not consider soul-winning to be accomplished by hurriedly inscribing more names upon our church-roll, in order to show a good increase at the end of the year. This is easily done, and there are brethren who use great pains, not to say arts, to effect it; but if it be regarded as the Alpha and Omega of a minister's efforts, the result will be deplorable. By all means let us bring true converts into the church, for it is a part of our work to teach them to observe all things whatsoever Christ has commanded them; but still, this is to be done to disciples, and not to mere professors; and if care be not used, we may do more harm than good at this point. To introduce unconverted person s to the church, is to weaken and degrade it; and therefore an apparent gain may be a real loss. I am not among those who decry statistics, nor do I consider that they are productive of all manner of evil; for they do much good if they are accurate, and if men use them lawfully. It is a good thing for people to see the nakedness of the land through statistics of decrease, that they may be driven on their knees before the Lord to seek prosperity; and, on the other hand, it is by no means an evil thing for workers to be encouraged by having some account of results set before them. I should be very sorry if the practice of adding up, and deducting, and giving in the net result were to be abandoned, for it must be right to know our numerical condition. It has been noticed that those who object to the process are often brethren whose unsatisfactory reports should somewhat humiliate them: this is not always so, but it is suspiciously frequent. I heard of the report of a church, the other day, in which the minister, who was well known to have reduced his congregation to nothing, somewhat cleverly wrote, "Our church is looking up." When he was questioned with regard to this statement, he replied, "Everybody knows that the church is on its back, and it cannot do anything else but look up." When churches are looking up in that way, their pastors generally say that statistics are very delusive things, and that you cannot tabulate the work of the Spirit, and calculate the prosperity of a church by figures. The fact is, you can reckon very correctly if the figures are honest, and if all circumstances are taken into consideration if there is no increase, you may calculate with considerable accuracy that there is not much being done; and if there is a clear decrease among a growing population, you may reckon that the prayers of the people and the preaching of the minister are not of the most powerful kind.

But, still, all hurry to get members into the church is most mischievous, both to the church and to the supposed converts. I remember very well several young men, who were of good moral character, and re ligiously hopeful; but instead of searching their hearts, and aiming at their real conversion, the pastor never gave them any rest till he had persuaded them to make a profession. He thought that they would be under more bonds to holy things if they professed religion, and he felt quite safe in pressing them, for "they were so hopeful." He imagined that to discourage them by vigilant examination might drive them away, and so, to secure them, he made them hypocrites. These young men are, at the present time, much further off from the Church of God than they would have been if they had been affronted by being kept in their proper places, and warned that they were not converted to God. It is a serious injury to a person to receive him into the number of the faithful unless there is good reason to believe that he is really regenerate. I am sure it is so, for I speak after careful observation. Some of the most glaring sinners known to me were once members of a church; and were, as I believe, led to make a profession by undue pressure, well-meant but ill-judged. Do not, therefore, consider that soul- winning is or can be secured by the multiplication of baptisms, and the swelling of the size of your church. What mean these despatches from the battle-field? "Last night, fourteen souls were under conviction, fifteen were justified, and eight received full sanctification." I am weary of this public bragging, this counting of unhatched chickens, this exhibition of doubtful spoils. Lay aside such numberings of the people, such idle pretence of certifying in half a minute that which will need the testing of a lifetime. Hop e for the best, but in your highest excitements be reasonable. Enquiry-rooms are all very well; but if they lead to idle boastings, they will grieve the Holy Spirit, and work abounding evil.

Nor is it soul-winning, dear friends, merely to create excitement. Excitement will accompany every great movement. We might justly question whether the movement was earnest and powerful if it was quite as serene as a drawing-room Bible-reading. You cannot very

3

well blast great rocks without the sound of explosions, nor fight a battle and keep everybody as quiet as a mouse. On a dry day, a carriage is not moving much along the road unless there is some noise and dust; friction and stir are the natural result of force in motion. So, when the Spirit of God is abroad, and men's min ds are stirred, there must and will be certain visible signs of the movement, although these must never be confounded with the movement itself. If people imagine that to make a dust is the object aimed at by the rolling of a carriage, they can take a broom, and very soon raise as much dust as fifty coaches; but they will be committing a nuisance rather than conferring a benefit. Excitement is as incidental as the dust, but it is not for one moment to be aimed at. When the woman swept her house, she did it to find her money, and not for the sake of raising a cloud.

Do not aim at sensation and "effect." Flowing tears and streaming eyes, sobs and outcries, crowded after-meetings and all kinds of confusions may occur, and may be borne with as concomitants of genuine feeling; but pray do not plan their production.

It very often happens that the converts that are born in excitement die when the excitement is over. They are like certain insects which are the product of an exceedingly warm day, and die when the sun goes down. Certain converts live like salamanders, in the fire; but they expire at a reasonable temperature. I delight not in the religion which needs or creates a hot head. Give me the godliness which flourishes upon Calvary rather than upon Vesuvius. The utmost zeal for Christ is consistent with common-sense and reason: raving, ranting, and fanaticism are products of another zeal which is not according to knowledge. We would prepare men for the chamber of communion, and not for the padded room at Bedlam. No one is more sorry than I that such a caution as this should be needful; but remembering the vagaries of certain wild revivalists, I cannot say less, and I might say a great deal more.

What is the real winning of a soul for God? So far as this is done by instrumentality, what are the processes by which a soul is led to God and to salvation? I take it that one of its main operation s consists *in instructing a man that he may know the truth of God.* Instruction by the gospel is the commencement of all real work upon men's minds. "Go ye therefore, and teach all nations, baptizing them in the name of the Father, and of the Son, and of the Holy Ghost: teaching them to observe all things whatsoever I have commanded you: and,

4

lo, I am with you alway, even unto the en d of the world." Teaching begins the work, and crowns it, too.

The gospel, according to Isaiah, is, "Incline your ear, and come unto Me: hear, and your soul shall live." It is ours, then, to give men something worth their hearing; in fact, to instruct them. We are sent to evangelize, or to preach the gospel to every creature; and that is not done unless we teach them the great truths of revelation. The gospel is good news. To listen to some preachers, you would imagine that the gospel was a pinch of sacred snuff to make them wake up, or a bottle of ardent spirits to excite their b rains. It is nothing of the kind; it is news, there is information in it, there is instruction in it concerning matters which men need to know, and statements in it calculated to bless those who hear it. It is not a magical incantation, or a char m, whose force consists in a collection of sounds; it is a revelation of facts and truths which require knowledge and belief. The gospel is a reasonable system, and it appeals to men's understanding; it is a matter for thought and consideration, and it appeals to the conscience and the reflecting powers. Hence, if we do not teach men something, we may shout, *"Believe! Believe! Believe!"* but what are they to believe? Each exhortation requires a corresponding instruction, or it will mean nothing. *"Escape!"* From what? This requires for its answer the doctrine of the punishment of sin. *"Fly!"* But whither? Then must you preach Christ, and His wounds; yea, and the clear doctrine of atonement by sacrifice. *"Repent!"* Of what? Here you must answer such questions as, What is sin? What is the evil of sin? What are the consequences of sin? *"Be converted!"* But what is it to be converted? By what power can we be converted? What from? What to? The field of instruction is wide if men are to be made to know the truth which saves. "That the soul be without knowledge, it is not good ," and it is ours as the Lord's instruments to make men so to know the truth that they may believe it, and feel its power. We are not to try and save men in the dark, but in the power of the Holy Ghost we are to seek to turn them from darkness to light.

And, do not believe, dear friends, that when you go into revival meetings, or special evangelistic services, you are to leave out the doctrines of the gospel; for you ought then to proclaim the doctrines of grace rather more than less. Teach gospel doctrines clearly, affectionately, simply, and plainly, and especially those truths which have a present and practical bearing upon man's condition and God's grace. Some enthusiasts would seem to have imbibed the notion that, as soon as a minister addresses the un converted, he should deliberately contradict his usual doctrinal discourses, because it is supposed that there will be no conversions if he preaches the whole counsel of God. It just comes to this, brethren, it is supposed that we are to conceal truth, and utter a half-falsehood, in order to save souls. We are to speak the truth to God's people because they will not hear anything else; but we are to wheedle sinners into faith by exaggerating one part of truth, and hiding the rest until a more convenient season. This is a strange theory, and ye t many endorse it. According to them, we may preach the redemption of a chosen n umber to God's people, but universal redemption must be our doctrine when we speak with the outside world; we are to tell believers that salvation is all of grace, but sinners are to be spoken with as if they were to save themselves; we are to inform Christians that God the Holy Spirit alone can convert, but when we talk with the unsaved, the Holy Ghost is scarcely to be named. We have not so learned Christ. Thus others have done; let them be our beacons, and not our examples. He who sent us to win souls neither permits us to invent false-hoods, nor to suppress truth. His work can be done without such suspicious methods.

Perhaps some of you will reply, "But, still, God has blessed half-statements and wild assertions." Be not quite so sure. I venture to assert that God does not bless falsehood; He may bless the truth which is mixed up with error; but much more of blessing would have come if the preaching h ad been more in accordance with His own Word. I cannot admit that the Lord blesses evangelistic Jesuitism, and the suppression of truth is not too harshly named when I so describe it. The withholding of the doctrine of the total depravity of man has wrought serious mischief to many who have listened to a certain kind of preaching. These people do not get a true healing because they do not know the disease under which they are suffering; they are never truly clothed because nothing is done towards stripping them. In many ministries, there is not enough of probing the heart and arousing the conscience by the revelation of man's alienation from God, and by the declaration of the selfishness and the wickedness of such a state. Men need to be told that, except divine grace shall bring them out of their enmity to God, they must eternally perish; and they must be reminded of the sovereignty of God, that He is not obliged to bring them out of this state, that He would be right and just if He left them in such a condition, that they have no merit to plead before Him, and no claims upon Him, but that if they are to be saved, it must be by grace, and by grace alone. The preacher's work is to throw sinners down in utter helplessness, that they may be compelled to look up to Him who alone can help them.

To try to win a soul for Christ by keeping that soul in ignorance of any truth, is contrary to the mind of the Spirit; and to endeavour to save men by mere claptrap, or excitement, or oratorical display, is as foolish as to hope to hold an angel with bird-lime, or lure a star with music. The best attraction is the gospel in its purity. The weapon with which the Lord conquers men is the truth as it is in Jesus. The gospel will be found equal to every emergency; an arrow which can pierce the hardest heart, a balm which will heal the deadliest wound. Preach it, and preach nothing else. Rely implicitly upon the old, old gospel. You need no other nets when you fish for men; those your Master has given you are strong enough for the great fishes, and have meshes fine enough to hold the little ones. Spread these nets and no others, and you need not fear the fulfilment of His Word, "I will make you fishers of men."

Secondly, to win a soul, it is necessary, not only to instruct our hearer, and make him know the truth, but *to impress him so that he may feel it*. A purely didactic ministry, which should always appeal to the understanding, and should leave the emotions untouched, would certainly be a limping ministry. "The legs of the lame are not equal," says Solomon; and the unequal legs of some ministries cripple them. We have seen such an one limping about with a long doctrinal leg, but a very short emotion al leg. It is a horrible thing for a man to be so doctrinal that he can speak coolly of the doom of the wicked, so that, if he does not actually praise God for it, it costs him no anguish of heart to think of the ruin of millions of our race. This is horrible! I hate to hear the terrors of the Lord proclaimed by men whose hard visages, harsh tones, and unfeeling spirit betray a sort of doctrinal desiccation: all the milk of human kindness is dried out of them. Having no feeling himself, such a preacher creates none, and the people sit and listen while he keeps to dry, lifeless statements, until they come to value him for being "sound", and they themselves come to be sound, too; and I need not ad d, sound asleep also, or what life they have is spent in sniffing out heresy, and making earnest men offenders for a word. Into this spirit may we never be baptized! Whatever I believe, or do not believe, the command to love my neighbour as myself still retains its claim upon me, and God forbid that any views or opinions should so contract my soul, and harden my heart as to make me forget this law of love! The love of God is first, but this by no means lessens the obligation of love to man; in fact, the first command includes the second. We are to seek our neighbour's conversion because we love him, and we are to speak to him in loving terms God's loving gospel, because our heart desires his eternal good.

A sinner has a heart as well as a head; a sinner has emotions as well as thoughts; and we must appeal to both. A sinner will never be converted until his emotions are stirred. Unless he feels sorrow for sin, and unless he has some measure of joy in the reception of the Word, you cannot have much hope of him. The Truth must soak into the soul, and dye it with its own colour. The Word must be like a strong wind sweeping through the whole heart, and swaying the whole man, even as a field of ripening corn waves in the summer breeze. Religion without emotion is religion without life.

But, still, we must mind how these emotions are caused. Do not play upon the mind by exciting feelings which are not spiritual. Some preachers are very fond of introducing funerals and dying children into their discourses, and they make the people weep through sheer natural affection. This may lead up to something better, but in itself what is its value? What is the good of opening up a mother's griefs or a widow's sorrows? I do not believe that our merciful Lord has sent us to make men weep over their departed relatives by digging anew their graves, and rehearsing past scenes of bereavement and woe. Why should He? It is granted that you may profitably employ the death-bed of a departing Christian, or of a dying sinner, for proof of the rest of faith in the one case, and the terror of conscience in the other; but it is out of the fact proved, and not out of the illustration itself, that the good must arise. Natural grief is of no service in itself; indeed, we look upon it as a distraction from higher thoughts, and as a price too great to exact from tender hearts, unless we can repay them by engrafting lasting spiritual impressions upon the s tock of natural affection. "It was a very splendid oration, full of pathos," says one who heard it. Yes, but what is the practical outcome of this pathos? A young preacher once remarked, "Were you not greatly struck to see so large a congregation weeping?" "Yes," said his judicious friend, "but I was more struck with the reflection that they would probably have wept more at a play." Exactly so; and the weeping in both cases may be equally valueless. I saw a girl on board a steamboat reading a book, and crying as if her heart would break; but when I glanced at the volume, I saw that it was only one of those silly yellow-covered novels which load our railway bookstalls. Her tears were a sheer waste of moisture, and so are those which are produced by mere pulpit tale-telling and death-bed painting.

If our hearers will weep over their sins, and after Jesus, let their tears flow in rivers; but if the object of their sorrow is merely natural, and not at all spiritual, what good is done by setting them weeping? There might be some virtue in making people joyful, for there is sorrow enough in the world, and the more we can promote cheerfulness, the better; but what is the use of creating needless misery? What right have you to go through the world pricking everybody with your lancet just to show your skill in surgery? A true physician only makes incisions in order to effect cures, and a wise minister only excites painful emotions in men's minds with the distinct object of blessing their souls. You and I must continue to drive at men's hearts till they are broken; and then we must keep on preaching Christ crucified till their hearts are bound up; and when this is accomplished, we must continue to proclaim the gospel till their whole nature is brought into subjection to the gospel of Christ. Even in these preliminaries you will be made to feel the need of the Holy Ghost to work with you, and by you; but this need will be still more evident when we advance a step further, and speak of the new birth itself in which the Holy Spirit works in a style and manner most divine.

I have already insisted upon instruction and impression as most needful to soul-winning; but these are not all,—they are, indeed, only means to the desired end. A far greater work must be done before a man i s saved. A wonder of divine grace must be wrought upon the soul, far transcending anything which can be accomplished by the power of man. Of all who m we would fain win for Jesus it is true, "Except a man be born again, he cannot see the kingdom of God." The Holy Ghost must work regeneration in the objects of our love, or they never can become possessors of eternal happiness. They must be quickened into a new life, and they must become new creatures in Christ Jesus. The same energy which accomplishes resurrection and creation must put forth all its power upon them nothing short of this can meet the case. They must be born again from above. This might seem at first sight to put human instrumentality altogether out of the field; but on turning to the Scriptures we find nothing to justify such an inference, and much of quite an opposite tendency. There we certainly find the Lord to be all in all, but we find no hint that the use of means must therefore be dispensed with. The Lord's supreme majesty and power are seen all the more gloriously because He works by means. He is so great that He is not afraid to put honour upon the instruments He employs, by speaking of them in high terms, and imputing to them great influence. It is sadly possible to say too little of the Holy Spirit;

indeed, I fear this is one of the crying sins of the age; but yet that infallible Word, which always rightly balances truth, while it magnifies the Holy Ghost, does not speak lightly of the men by whom He works. God does not think His own honour to be so questionable that it can only be maintained by decrying the human agent. There are two passages in the Epistles which, when put together, have often amazed me. Paul compares himself both to a father and to a mother in the matter of the new birth: he says of one convert, "Whom I have begotten in my bonds," and of a whole church he says, "My little children, of whom I travail in birth again until Christ be formed in you." This is going very far; indeed, much further than modern orthodoxy would permit the most useful minister to venture, and yet it is language sanctioned, yea, dictated, by the Spirit of God Himself; and therefore it is not to be criticised. Such mysterious power doth God infuse into the instrumentality which He ordain s that we are called "labourers together with God" ; and this is at once the source of our responsibility and the ground of our hope.

Regeneration, or the new birth, works a change in the whole nature of man, and, so far as we can judge, its essence lies in the implantation and creation of a new principle within the man. The Holy Ghost create sin us a new, heavenly, and immortal nature, which is known in Scripture as "the spirit" , by way of distinction from the soul. Our theory of regeneration is that man in his fallen nature consists only of body and soul, and that when he is regenerated there is created in him a new and higher nature—" the spirit" —which is a spark from the everlasting fire of God's life and love; this falls into the heart, and abides there, and makes its receiver a partaker of the divine nature." Thenceforward, the man consists of three parts, body, soul, and spirit, and the spirit is the reigning power of the three. You will all remember that memorable chapter upon the resurrection, I Corinthians xv., where the distinction is well brought out in the original, and may even be perceived in our version. The passage rendered, "It is sown a natural body," etc., might be read, "It is sown a soulish body; it is raised a spiritual body. There is a soulish body, and there is a spiritual body. And so it is written, The first man Adam was made a living soul; the last Adam was made a quickening spirit. Howbeit, that was not first which is spiritual, but that which is soulish; and afterward that which is spiritual." We are first in the natural or soulish stage of being, like the first Adam, and then in regeneration we enter into a new condition, and we become possessors of the life-giving "spirit." Without this spirit, no man can see or enter the kingdom of heaven. It must therefore be our intense desire that the Holy Spirit should visit our hearers, and create them anew,—that He would co me down upon these dry bones, and breathe eternal life into the dead in sin. Till this is done, they can never receive the truth, "for the natural man receiveth not the things of the Spirit of God: for they are foolishness unto him: neither can he know them, because they are spiritually discerned." "The carnal mind is enmity against God: for it is not subject to the law of God, neither in deed can be." A new and heavenly mind must be created by omnipotence, or the man must abide in death. You see, then, that we have before us a mighty work, for which we are of ourselves totally incapable. No minister living can save a soul; nor can all of us together, nor all the saints on earth or in heaven, work regeneration in a single person. The whole business on our part is the height of absurdity unless we regard ourselves as used by the Holy Ghost, and filled with His power. On the other hand, the marvels of regeneration which attend our ministry are the best seals and witnesses of our commission. Whereas the apostles could appeal to the miracles of Christ, and to those which they wrought in His name, we appeal to the miracles of the Holy Ghost, which are as divine and as real as those of our Lord Himself. These miracles are the creation of a new life in the human bosom, and the total change of the whole being of t hose upon whom the Spirit descends.

As this God-begotten spiritual life in men is a mystery, we shall speak to more practical effect if we dwell upon the signs following and accompanying it, for these are the things we must aim at. First, regeneration will be shown in conviction of sin. This we believe to be an indispensable mark of the Spirit's work; the new life as it enters the heart causes in tense inward pain as one of its first effects. Though nowadays we hear of persons being healed before they have been wounded, and brought into a certainty of justification without ever having lamented their condemnation, we are very dubious as to the value of such healings and justifyings. This style of things is not according to the truth. God never clothes men until He has first stripped t hem, nor does He quicken them by the gospel till first they are slain by the law. When you meet with persons in whom there is no trace of conviction of sin, you may be quite sure that they have not been wrought upon by the Holy Spirit; for "when He is come, He will reprove the world of sin, and of righteousness, and of judgment." When the Spirit of the Lord breathes on us, He withers all the glory of man, which is but as the flower of grass, and then He reveals a higher and abiding glory. Do not be astonished if you find this conviction of sin to be very acute and alarming; but, on the other hand, do not condemn those in whom it is less intense, for so long as sin is mourned over, confessed, forsaken, and abhorred, you have an evident fruit of the Spirit. Much of the horror and unbelief which goes with conviction is not of the Spirit of God, but comes of Satan or corrupt nature; yet there must be true and deep conviction of sin, and this the preacher must labour to produce, for where this is not felt the new birth has not taken place.

Equally certain is it that true conversion may be known by the exhibition of a *simple faith in Jesus Christ*. You need not that I speak unto you of that, for you yourselves are fully persuaded of it. The production of faith is the very centre of the target at which you aim. The proof to you that you have won the man's soul for Jesus is never before you till he has done with himself and his own merits, and has closed in with Christ. Great care must be taken that this faith is exercised upon Christ for a complete salvation, and not for a part of it. Numbers of persons think that the Lord Jesus is available for the pardon of past sin, but they cannot trust Him for their preservation in the future. They trust for years past, but not for years to come; whereas no such sub-division of salvation is ever spoken of in Scripture as the work of Chris t. Either He bore all our sins, or none; and He either saves us once for all, or not at all. His death can never be repeated, and it must have made expiation for the future sin of believers, or they are lost, since no further atonement can be supposed, and future sin is certain to be committed. Blessed be His name, "by Him all that believe are justified from all things." Salvation by grace is eternal salvation. Sinners must commit their souls to the keeping of Christ to all eternity; how else are they saved men? Alas! according to the teaching of some, believers are only saved in part, and for the rest must depend upon their future endeavours. Is this the gospel? I trow not. Genuine faith trusts a whole Christ for the whole of salvation. Is it any wonder that many converts fall away, when, in fact, they were never taught to exercise faith in Jesus for eternal salvation, but only for temporary conversion? A faulty exhibition of Christ begets a faulty faith; and when this pines away in its own imbecility, who is to blame for it? According to their faith so is it unto them: the preacher and possessor of a partial faith must unitedly bear the blame of the failure when their poor mutilated trust comes to a break-down. I would the more earnestly insist upon this because a semi-legal way of believing is so common. We must urge the trembling sinner to trust wholly and alone upon the Lord Jesus forever, or we shall have him inferring that he is to begin in the Spirit and be made perfect by the flesh: he will surely walk by faith as to the past, and then by works as to the future, and this will be fatal. True faith in Jesus receives eternal life, and sees perfect salvation in Him, whose one sacrifice hath sanctified the people of God once for all. The sense of being saved, completely saved in Christ Jesus, is not, as some suppose, the source of carnal security and the enemy of holy zeal, but the very reverse. Delivered from the fear which makes the salvation of self a more immediate object than salvation from self; and inspired by holy gratitude to his Redeemer, the regenerated man becomes capable of virtue, and is filled with an enthusiasm for God's glory. While trembling under a sense of insecurity, a man gives his chief thought to his own interests; but planted firmly on the Rock of ages, he has time and heart to utter the new song which the Lord has put into his mouth, and then is his moral salvation complete, for self is no longer the lord of his being. Rest not content till you see cl ear evidence in your converts of a simple, sincere, and decided faith in the Lord Jesus.

Together with undivided faith in Jesus Christ there must also be *unfeigned repentance of sin*. Repentance is an old-fashioned word, not much used by modern revivalists. "Oh!" said a minister to me, one day, "it only means a change of mind." This was thought to be a profound observation. "Only a change of mind" ; but what a change! A change of min d with regard to everything! Instead of saying, "It is only a change of mind," it seems to me more truthful to say it is a great and deep change— even a change of the mind itself. But whatever the literal Greek word may mean, repentance is no trifle. You will not find a better definition of it than the one given in the children's hymn:—

> "Repentance is to leave
> The sins we loved before
> And show that we in earnest grieve,
> By doing so no more."

True conversion is in all men attended by a sense of sin, which we have spoken of under the head of conviction; by a sorrow for sin, or holy grief at having committed it; by a hatred of sin, which proves that its dominion is ended; and by a practical turning from sin, which shows that the life within the soul is operating upon the life without. True belief and true repentance are twins: it would be idle to attempt to say which is born first. All the spokes of a wheel move at once when the wheel moves, and so all the g races commence action when regeneration is wrought by the Holy Ghost.

Repentance, however, there must be. No sinner looks to the Saviour with a dry eye or a hard heart. Aim, therefore, at heart-breaking, at bringing home condemnation to the conscience, and weaning the mind from sin, and be not content till the whole mind is deeply and vitally changed in reference to sin.

Another proof of the conquest of a soul for Christ will be found in a real change of life. If the man does not live differently from what he did before, both at home and abroad, his repentance needs to be repented of; and his conversion is a fiction. Not only action and language, but spirit and temper must be changed. "But," says someone, "grace is oft en grafted on a crab-stock." I know it is; but what is the fruit of the grafting? The fruit will be like the graft, and not after the nature of the original stem. "But ," says another, "I have an awful temper, and all of a sudden it overcomes me. My anger is soon over, and I feel very penitent. Though I cannot control myself; I am quite sure I am a Christian." Not so fast, my friend, or I may answer that I am quite as sure the other way. What is the use of your soon cooling if in two or three moments you scald all around you? If a man stabs me in a fury, it will not heal my wound to see him grieving over his madness. Hasty temper must be conquered, and the whole man must be renewed, or conversion will be questionable. We are not to hold up a modified holiness before our people, and say, You will be all right if you reach that standard. The Scripture says, "He that committeth sin is of the devil." Abiding under the power of any known sin is a mark of our being the servants of sin, for "his servants ye are to whom y e obey." Idle are the boasts of a man who harbours within himself the love of any transgression. He may feel what he likes, and believe what he likes, he is still in the gall of bitterness and the bonds of iniquity while a single sin rules his heart and life. True regeneration implants a hatred of all evil; and where one sin is delighted in, the evidence is fatal to a sound hope. A man need not take a dozen poisons to destroy his life, one is quite sufficient.

There must be a harmony between the life and the profession. A Christian professes to renounce sin and if he does not do so, his very name is an imposture. A drunken man came up to Rowland Hill, one day, and said, "I am one of your converts, Mr. Hill." "I daresay you are ," replied that shrewd and sensible preacher; "but you are none of the Lord's, or you would not be drunk." To this practical test we must bring all our work.

In our converts we must also see *true prayer*, which is the vital breath of godliness. If there is no prayer, you may be quite sure the soul is dead. We are not to urge men to pray as though it were the great gospel duty, and the one prescribed way of salvation; for our chief message is, "Believe on the Lord Jesus Christ." It is easy to put prayer into its wrong place, and make it out to be a kind of work by which men are to live; but this you will, I trust, most carefully avoid. Faith is the great gospel grace; but still we cannot forget that true faith always prays, and when a man professes faith in the Lord Jesus, and yet does not cry to the Lord daily, we dare not believe in his faith or his conversion. The Holy Ghost's evidence by which He convinced Ananias of Paul's conversion was not, "Behold, he talks loudly of his joys and feelings," but, "Behold, he prayeth," and that prayer was earnest, heart-broken confession and supplication. Oh, to see this sure evidence in all who profess to be our converts!

There must also be a willingness to obey the Lord in all His commandment s. It is a shameful thing for a man to profess discipleship and yet refuse to learn his Lord's will upon certain points, or even dare to decline obedience when that will is known. How can a man be a disciple of Chris t when he openly lives in disobedience to Him?

If the professed convert distinctly and deliberately declares that he knows his Lord's will but does not mean to attend to it, you are not to pamper his presumption, but it is your duty to assure him that he is not saved. Has not the Lord said, "He that taketh not up his cross, and co meth after Me, cannot be My disciple"? Mistakes as to what the Lord's will may be are to be tenderly corrected, but anything like wilful disobedience is fatal; to tolerate it would be treason to Him that sent us. Jesus must be received as King as well as Priest; and where there is any hesitancy about this, the foundation of godliness is not yet laid.

> "Faith must obey her
> Maker's will As well as trust
> His grace A pardoning God is jealous still
> For His own holiness."

Thus, you see, my brethren, the signs which prove that a soul is won are by no means trifling, and the work to be done ere those signs can exist is not to be lightly spoken of. A soul-winner can do nothing without God. He must cast himself on the Invisible, or be a laughing-stock to the devil, who regards with utter disdain all who think to subdue human nature with mere words and arguments. To all who hope to succeed in such a lab our by their own strength, we would address the words of the Lord to Job, "Canst thou draw out leviathan with a hook? or his tongue with a cord which thou lettest down? Wilt thou play with him as with a bird? or wilt thou bind him for thy maidens? Lay thine hand upon him, remember the battle, do no more. Behold, the hope of him is in vain: shall not one be cast down even at the sight of him?" Dependence upon God is our strength, and our joy: in that dependence let us go forth, and seek to win souls for Him.

Now, in the course of our ministry, we shall meet with many failures in this matter of soul-winning. There are many birds that I have thought I had caught; I have even managed to put salt on their tails, but they have gone flying off after all. I remember one man, whom I will call Tom Careless. He was the terror of the village in which he lived. There were many incendiary fires in the region, and most people attributed them to him. Sometimes, he would be drunk for two or three weeks at a spell, and then he rave d and raged like a madman. That man came to hear me; I recollect the sensation that went through the little chapel when he came in. He sat there, and fell in love with me; I think that was the only conversion that he experienced, but he pro fessed to be converted. He had, apparently, been the subject of genuine repentance, and he became outwardly quite a changed character, gave up his drinking and swearing, and was in many respects an exemplary individual. I rem ember seeing him tugging a barge, with perhaps a hundred people on board, whom he was drawing up to a place where I was going to preach; and he was glorying in the work, and singing as gladly and happily as any one of them. I f anybody spoke a word against the Lord or His servant, he did not hesitate a moment, but knocked him over. Before I left the district, I was afraid that there was no real work of grace in him; he was a wild Red Indian sort of a man. I have heard of him taking a bird, plucking it, and eating it raw in the field. This is not the act of a Christian man, it is not one of the things that are comely, and of good repute. After I left the neighborhood, I asked after him, and I could h ear nothing good of him; the spirit that kept him outwardly right was gone, and he became worse than he was before, if that was possible; certainly, he was no better, he was unreachable by any agency. That work of mine did not stand the fire; it would not bear even ordinary temptation, you see, after the person who had influence over the man was gone away. When you move from the village or town where you have been preaching, it is very likely that some, who did run well, will go back. They have an affection for you, and your words have a kind of mesmeric influence over them; and when you are gone, the dog will return to his vomit,

16

and the sow that was washed to her wallowing in the mire. Do not be in a hurry to count these supposed converts; do not take them into the church too soon; do not be too proud of their enthusiasm if it is not accompanied with some degree of softhening, and tenderness, to show that the Holy Spirit has really been at work within them.

I remember another case of quite a different sort. I will call this person *Miss Mary Shallow*, for she was a young lady, who was never blessed with many brains; but living in the same house with several Christian young ladies she also professed to be converted. When I converse d with her, there was apparently everything that one could wish for. I thought of proposing her to the church; but it was judged best to give her a little trial first. After a while, she left the associations of the place where she had lived, and went where she had nothing much to help her; and I never heard anything more of her except that her whole time was spent in dressing herself as smartly as she could, and in frequenting gay society. She is a type of those who have not much mental furniture; and if the grace of God does not take possession of the empty space, they very soon go back into the world. I have known several like a young man whom I will c all Charlie Clever, uncommonly clever fellows at anything and everything, very clever at counterfeiting religion when they took up with it. They prayed very fluently; they tried to preach, and did it very well; whatever they did, they did it off-hand, it was as easy to them as kissing their hand. Do not be in a hurry to take such people into the church; they have known no humiliation on account of sin, no brokenness of heart, no sense of divine grace. They cry, "All serene!" and away they go; but you will find that they will never rep ay you for your labour and trouble. They will be able to use the language of G od's people as well as the best of His saints, they will even talk of their doubts and fears, and they will get up a deep experience in five minutes. They are a little too clever, and they are calculated to do much mischief when they get into the church; so keep them out if you possibly can.

I remember one who was very saintly in his talk, I will call him John Fair speech. Oh! how cunningly he could act the hypocrite, getting among our young men, and leading them into all manner of sin and iniquity, and yet he would call and see me, and have half-an-hour's spiritual conversation! An abominable wretch, who was living in open sin at the very time that he was seeking to come to the Lord's table, and joining our societies, and anxious to be a leading man in every good work. Keep your weather eye open, brethren! They will come to you with money in their hands, Peter's fish with the silver in its mouth; and they will be so helpful in the work! They speak so softly, and they are such perfect gentlemen! Yes, I believe Judas was a man exactly of that kind, very clever at deceiving those around him. We must mind that we do not get any of these into the church if we can anyhow keep them out. You may say to yourself; at the close of a service, "Here is a splendid haul of fish!" Wait a bit. Remember our Saviour's words, "The kingdom of heaven is like unto a net, that was cast into the sea, and gathered of every kind; which, when it was full, they drew to shore, and sat down, and gathered the good into vessels, but cast the bad away." Do not number your fishes before they are broiled; nor count your converts before you have tested and tried them. This process may make your work somewhat slow; but then, brethren, it will be sure. Do your work steadily and well, so that those who come after you may not have to say that it was far more trouble to them to clear the church of those who ought never to have been admitted than it was to you to admit them. If God enables you to build three thousand bricks into His spiritual temple in one day, you may do it; but Peter has been the only bricklayer who has accomplished that feat up to the present. Do not go and paint the wooden wall as if it were solid stone; but let all your building be real, substantial, and true, for only this kind of work is worth the doing. Let all your building for God be like that of the apostle Paul, "According to the grace of God which is given unto me, as a wise master builder, I have laid the foundation, and another buildeth thereon. But let every man take heed how he buildeth thereup on. For other foundation can no man lay than that is laid, which is Jesus Christ. Now if any man build upon this foundation gold, silver, precious stones, wood, hay, stubble; every man's work shall be made manifest: for the day shall declare it, because it shall be revealed by fire; and the fire shall try every man's work of what sort it is. If any man's work abide which he hath built thereupon, he shall receive a reward. If any man's work shall be burned, he shall suffer loss but he himself shall be saved; yet so as by fire."

QUALIFICATIONS FOR SOUL-WINNING— GODWARD

Our main business, brethren, is to win souls. Like the shoeing-smiths, we need to know a great many things; but, just as the smith must know about horses, and how to make shoes for them, so we must know about souls, and how to win them for God. The part of the subject on which I shall speak to you this afternoon is—

QUALIFICATIONS FOR SOUL-WINNING,

keeping myself to one set of those qualifications, namely, the Godward ones, and I shall try to treat the subject in somewhat of a common-sense style, asking you to judge for yourselves what those qualifications would be which God would naturally look for in His servants, what qualifications He would be likely to approve, and most likely to use. You must know that every workman, if he be wise, uses a tool that is likely to accomplish the purpose he has in view. There are some artists who have never been able to play except upon their own violin, nor to paint except with their own favourit e brush and palette; and certainly, the great God, the mightiest of all the workers, in His great artistic work of soul-winning, loves to have His own special tools. In the old creation, He used none but His own instruments, "He spake, and it was done;" and in the new creation, the efficient agent is still His powerful Word. He speaks through the ministry of His servants, and therefore they must be fit trumpets for Him to speak through, fit instruments for Him to use for conveying His Word to the ears and hearts of men. Judge ye, then, my brethren, whether God will use you; imagine yourselves in His place, and think what kin d of men those would be whom you would be most likely to use if you were in the position of the Most High God .

I am sure you would say, first of all, that a *man who is to be a Soul-winner must have holiness of character*. Ah! how few who attempt to preach think sufficiently of this! If they did, it would strike them at once that the Eternal would never use dirty tools, that the thrice-holy Jehovah would only select holy instruments for the accomplishment of His work. No wise man would pour his wine into foul bottles; no kind and good parent would allow his children to go

19

to see an immoral play; and God will not go to work with instruments which would compromise His own character. Suppose it were well known that, if men were only clever, God would use them, whatever their character and conduct might be; suppose it were understood that you could get on as well in the work of God by chicanery and untruthfulness as by honest y and uprightness, what man in the world, with any right feeling, would not be ashamed of such a state of affairs? But, brethren, it is not so. There are many in the present day who tell us that the theatre is a great school for morals. that must be a strange school where the teachers never learn their own lessons. I n God's school, the teachers must be masters of the art of holiness. If we teach one thing by our lips and another by our lives, those who listen to us will say, "Physician, heal thyself." "Thou sayest, 'Repent.' Where is thine own repentance? Thou sayest, 'Serve God, and be obedient to His will.' Do you serve Him? Are you obedient to His will?" An unholy ministry would be the derision of the world, and a dishonour to God. "Be ye clean, that bear the vessels of the Lord." He will speak through a fool if he be but a holy man. I do not, of course, mean that God chooses fools to be His ministers; but let a man once become really holy, even though he has but the slenderest possible ability, he will be a m ore fit instrument in God's hand than the man of gigantic acquirements, who is not obedient to the divine will, nor clean and pure in the sight of the Lord God Almighty.

Dear brethren, I do beg you to attach the highest importance to your own personal holiness. Do live unto God. If you do not, your Lord will not be with you; He will say of you as He said of the false prophets of old, "I sent them not, nor commanded them: therefore they shall not profit this people at all, saith the Lord." You may preach very fine sermons, but if you are not yourselves holy, there will be no souls saved. The probability is that you will not come to the conclusion that your want of holiness is the reason for your non-success; you will blame the people, you will blame the age in which you live, you will blame anything except yourself; but there will be the root of the whole mischief. Do I not myself know men of considerable ability and industry, who go on year after year without any increase in their churches? The reason is, that they are not living before God as they ought to live. Sometimes, the evil is in the family of the minister; his sons and daughters are rebels against God, bad language is allowed even amongst his own children, and his reproofs are simply like Eli's mild question to his wicked sons, "Why do ye such things?" Sometimes, the minister is worldly, greedy after gain, neglectful of his work. That is not according to

God's mind, and He will not bless such a man. When I listened to Mr. George Müller, as he was preaching at Mentone, it was just such an address as might be given to a Sunday-school by an ordinary teacher, yet I never heard a sermon that did me more good, and more richly profited my soul. It was George Müller in it that made it so useful. There was no George Müller in it in one sense; for he preached not himself but Christ Jesus the Lord; he was only there in his personality as a witness to the truth, but he bore that witness in such a manner that you could not help saying, "That man not only preaches what he believes, but also what he lives." In every word he uttered, his glorious life of faith seemed to fall upon both ear and hear t. I was delighted to sit and listen to him; yet, as for novelty or strength of thought, there was not a trace of it in the whole discourse. Holiness was the preacher's force; and you may depend upon it that, if God is to bless us, our strength must lie in the same direction.

This holiness ought to show itself in communion with God. If a man delivers his own message, it will have such power as his own character gives to it; but if he delivers his Master's message, having heard it from his Master's lips, that will be quite another thing; and if he can acquire something of the Master's spirit as He looked upon him, and gave him the message, if he can reproduce the expression of his Master's face, and the tone of his Master's voice, that also will be quite another thing. Read McCheyne's Memoir, read the whole of it, I cannot do you a better service than by recommending you to read it; there is no great freshness of thought, there is nothing very novel or striking in it, but as you read it, you must get good out of it, for you are conscious that it is the story of the life of a man who walked with God. Moody would never have spoken with the force he did if he had not lived a life of fellowship with the Father, and with His Son, Jesus Christ. The greatest force of the sermon lies in what has gone before the sermon. You must get ready for the whole service by private fellowship with God, and real holiness of character.

You will all confess that, if a man is to be used as a winner of souls, he must have *spiritual life to a high degree.* You see, brethren, our work is, under God, to communicate life to others. It would be well to imitate Elisha when he stretched himself upon the dead child, and brought him back to life. The prophet's staff was not sufficient, because it had no life in it: the life must be communicated by a living instrument, and the man who is to communicate the life must have a great deal of it himself. You remember the words of Christ,

21

"He that believeth on Me, as the Scripture hath said, out of his belly shall flow rivers of living water," that is, the Holy Spirit, when He dwells within a living child of God, afterwards rises out of the very midst of him as a fountain or a river, so that others may come and participate in the Spirit's gracious influences. I do not think there is one of you who would wish to be a dead minister. God will not use dead tools for working living miracles ; He must have living men, and men that are all alive. There are many who are alive, but they are not altogether alive. I remember once seeing a painting of the resurrection, which was one of the queerest pictures I ever saw. The artist had attempted to depict the moment when the work was only half done: there were some who were alive down as far as their waists, some had one arm alive, some had part of their heads alive. The thing is quite possible in our day. There are some men who are only about half alive; they have a living j aw, but not a living heart; others have a living heart, but not a living brain; others have a living eye, they can see things pretty plainly, but their hearts are not alive, they can give good descriptions of what they see, but there is no warmth of love in them. There are some ministers who are one half angel, and the other half—well, let us say, maggots. It is an awful contrast; but there are many instances of it. Are there any such here? They preach well, and you say, as you listen to one of them, "That is a good man." You feel that he is a good ma n; you hear that he is going to such-and-such a person's house to supper, and you think that you will go in to supper there, too, that you may hear what gracious words will fall from his lips; and as you watch, out they come—maggots! It was an angel in the pulpit; now come the worms! It is so often, but it ought never to be so; if we want to be true witnesses for God, we must be all angel and no worms. God deliver us from this state of semi-death! May we be all alive from the crown of our head to the sole of our foot! I know some such ministers ; you cannot come into contact with them without feeling the power of the spiritual life which is in them. It is not merely while they are talking upon religious topics, but even in the commonplace things of the world, you are conscious that there is something about the men which tells you that they are all alive unto God. Such men will be used by God for the quickening of others.

Suppose it were possible for you to be exalted into the place of God, do you not think, next, that you would employ a man who thought little of himself, *a man of humble spirit*? If you saw a very proud man, would you be likely to use him as your servant? Certainly, the great God has a predilection for those who are humble. "For thus saith the high and lofty One that inhabiteth eternity, whose name is

Holy; I dwell in the high and holy place, with him also that is of a contrite and humble spirit, to revive the spirit of the humble, and to revive the heart of the contrite ones." He loatheth the proud; and whenever He sees the high and mighty, He passes them by; but whenever He finds the lowly in heart, He takes pleasure in exalting them. He delights especially in humility amongst His ministers. It is an awful sight to see a proud minister. There are few things that can give the devil more joy than this, whenever he takes his walks abroad. Here is something that delights him, and he says to himself, "Here are all the preparations for a great fall before long." Some ministers show their pride by their style in the pulpit; you can never forget the way in which they announced their text: "It is I: be not afraid." Others manifest it in their attire, in the silly vanity of their dress; or else in their common talk, in which they continually magnify the deficiencies of others, and dilate on their own extra-ordinary excellences. There are two sorts of proud people, and it is difficult sometimes to say which of the two is the worse. There is, first of all, the kind that is full of that vanity which talks about itself, and invites other people to talk about it, too, and to pat it on the back, and stroke its feathers the right way. It is all full of its little morsel of a self, and goes strutting about, and saying, "Praise me, please, praise me, I want it," like a little child who goes to each one in the room, and says, "See my new dress; isn't it a beauty?" You ma y have seen some of these pretty dears; I have met many of them. The other kind of pride is too big for that sort of thing. It does not care for it; it despises people so much that it does not condescend to wish for their praises. It is so supremely satisfied with itself that it does not stoop to consider what others thin k of it. I have sometimes thought it is the more dangerous kind of pride spiritually, but it is much the more respectable of the two. There is, after all, something very noble in being too proud to be proud. Suppose those great donkeys did bray at you, do not be such a donkey as to notice them. But this other poor little soul says, "Well, everybody's praise is worth something," and so he baits his mousetraps, and tries to catch little mice of praise, that he may cook them for his breakfast. He has a mighty appetite for such things. Brethren, get rid of both kinds of pride if you have anything of either of them about you. The dwarf pride and the ogre pride are both of them abominations in the sight of the Lord. Never forget that you are disciples of Him who said, "Learn of Me; for I am meek and lowly in heart."

Humility is not having a mean opinion of yourself. If a man has a low opinion of himself; it is very possible that he is correct in his estimate. I have known some people, whose opinion of themselves, according to what they have said, was very low indeed. They thought so little of their own powers that they never ventured to try to do any good; they said the y had no self-reliance. I have known some so wonderfully humble that they have always liked to pick an easy place for themselves; they were too humble to do anything that would bring any blame upon them: they called it humility, but I thought "sinful love of ease" would have been a better name for their conduct. True humility will lead you to think rightly about yourselves, to think the truth about yourselves.

In the matter of soul-winning, humility makes you f eel that you are nothing and nobody, and that, if God gives you success in the work, you will be driven to ascribe to Him all the glory, for none of the credit of it could properly belong to you. If you do not have success, humility will lead you to blame your own folly and weakness, not God's sovereignty. Why should God give blessing, and then let you run away with the glory of it? The glory of the salvation of souls belongs to Him, and to Him alone. Then why should you try to steal it? You know how many attempt this theft. "When I was preaching at such-and-such a place, fifteen persons came into the vestry at the close of the service, and thanked me for the sermon I had preached." You and your blessed sermon be hanged,—I might have used a stronger word if I had liked, for really you are worthy of condemnation whenever you take to yourself the honour which belongeth unto God only. You remember the story of the young prince, who came into the room where he thought his dying father was sleeping, and put the king's crown on his head to see how it would fit him. The king, who was watching him, said, "Wait a little while, my son, wait till I am dead." So, when you feel any inclination to put the crown of glory on your head, just fancy that you hear God saying to you, "Wait till I am dead, before you try on My crown." As that will never be, you had better leave the crown alone, and let Him wear it to whom it rightfully belongs. Our song must ever be, "Not unto us, O Lord, not unto us, but unto Thy name give glory, for Thy mercy, and for Thy truth's sake."

Some men, who have not had humility, have been sent adrift from the ministry, for the Lord will not use those who will not ascribe the honour entirely to Himself. Humility is one of the chief qualifications for usefulness; many have passed away from the roll of useful men because they have been lifted up with pride, and so have fallen into the snare of the devil. Perhaps you feel that, as you are only poor students, there is no fear of your falling into this sin; but it is quite possible that with some of you there is all the more danger, for this very reason, if God should bless you, and put you in a prominent position. A man who is brought up in a good circle of society all his life, does not feel the change so much when he reaches a posit ion which to others would be a great elevation. I always feel that, in the case of certain men whom I could name, a great mistake was made. As soon as they were converted, they were taken right out of their former associations, and put before the public as popular preachers. It was a great pity that many made little kings of them, and so prepared the way for their fall, for they could not bear the sudden change. It would have been a good thing for them if everybody had pitched into them, and abused them, for ten or twenty years; for it would have probably saved them from much after-misery. I am always very grateful f or the rough treatment I received in my earlier days from all sorts of people. The moment I ever did any good thing at all, they were at me like a pack of hounds. I had not time to sit down and boast what I had done, for they were raving and roaring at me continually. If I had been picked up all of a sudde n, and placed where I am now, the probability is that I should have gone down again just as quickly. When you go out of the College, it will be well for you if you are treated as I was. If you have great success, it will turn your head if God does not permit you to be afflicted in some way or other. If you are ever tempted to say, "Is not this great Babylon, that I have built?" just remember Nebuchadnezzar, when he was "driven from men, and did eat grass as oxen, and his body was wet with the dew of heaven, till his hairs were grown like eagle s' feathers, and his nails like birds' claws." God has many ways of fetching proud Nebuchadnezzars down, and He can very easily humble you, too, if you are ever lifted up with conceit. This point of the need of deep humility in a soul-w inner does not need any proof; everyone can see, with half an eye, that God is not likely to bless any man much unless he is truly humble.

The next essential qualification for success in the work of the Lord, and it is a vital one, is a *living faith*. You know, brethren, how the Lord Jesus Christ could not do many mighty works in His own country because of the unbelief of the people; and it is equally true that, with some men, God cannot do many mighty works because of their unbelief. If ye will not believe, neither shall ye be used of God. "According to your faith be it unto you," is one of the unalterable laws of His kingdom. "If ye have faith as a grain of mustard seed, ye shall say unto this mountain, Remove hence to yonder place, and it shall remove, and nothing shall be impossible unto you;" but if the question has to be put, "Where is your faith?" the mountains will not move for you, nor will even a poor sycamore tree be stirred from its place.

You must have faith, brethren, about your call to the ministry; you must believe without question that you are really chosen of God to be ministers of the gospel of Christ. If you firmly believe that God has called you to preach the gospel, you will preach it with courage and confidence; and you will feel that you are going to your work because you have a right to do it. If you have an idea that possibly you are nothing but an interlope r, you will do nothing of any account; you will be only a poor, limping, diffident, half-apologetic preacher, for whose message no one will care. You had better not begin to preach until you are quite sure that God has called you to the work. A man once wrote to ask me whether he should preach or not. When I do not know what reply to send to anyone, I always try to give as wise an answer as I possibly can. Accordingly, I wrote to this man, "Dear Friend,—If the Lord has opened your mouth, the devil cannot shut it; but if the devil has opened it, may the Lord shut it up!" Six months afterwards, I met the man, and he thanked me for my letter, which, he said, greatly encouraged him to go on pre aching. I said, "How was that?" He replied, "You said, 'If the Lord has opened your mouth, the devil cannot shut it.'" I said, "Yes, I did so; but I also put the otherside of the question." "Oh!" said he, at once, "that part did not relate to me." We can always have oracles to suit our own ideas if we know how to interpret them. If you have genuine faith in your call to the ministry, you will be ready, with Luther, to preach the gospel even while standing with in the jaws of the leviathan, between his great teeth.

You must also believe that the message you have to deliver is God's Word. I had sooner that you believed half-a-dozen truths intensely than a hundred only feebly. If your hand is not large enough to hold a great deal, hold firmly what you can; because, if it came to a regular push and shove, and we all of us were allowed to carry away as much gold as we could take from a heap, it might not be much use to have a very big purse, but he would come off best in the scuffle who should close his hand tightly on as much as he could conveniently hold, and not let it go. We may sometimes do well to imitate the boy mentioned in the ancient fable. When he put his hand into a narrow-necked jar, and grasped as many nuts as he could hold, he could not get even one of them out; but when he let half of them go, the rest came out with ease. So must we do; we cannot hold everything, it is impossible, our hand is not big enough; but when we do get anything in it, let us hold it fast, and grip it tightly. Believe what you do believe, or else you will never persuade anybody el se to believe it. If you adopt this style, "I think this is a truth, and as a young man I beg to ask your kind attention to what I am about to say; I am merely suggesting," and so on, if that is your mode of preaching, you will go to work the easiest way to breed doubters. I would rather hear you say, "Young as I am, what I have to say comes from God, and God's Word says so-and-so and so-and-so; there it is, and you must believe what God says, or you will be lost." The people who hear you will say, "That young fellow certainly believes something;" and very likely some of them will be led to believe, too. God uses the faith of His ministers to breed faith in other people. You may depend upon it that souls are not saved by a minister who doubts; and the preaching of your doubts and your questions can never possibly decide a soul for Christ. You must have great faith in the Word of God if you are to be winners of souls to those who hear it.

You must also believe in the power of that message to save people. You may have heard the story of one of our first students, who came to me, and said, "I have been preaching now for some months, and I Do not think I have had a single conversion." I said to him, "And do you expect that the Lord is going to bless you and save souls every time you open your mouth?" "No, sir," he replied. "Well, then," I said, "that is why you do not get souls saved. If you had believed, the Lord would have given the blessing." I had caught him very nicely; but many others would have answered me in just the same way as he did. They tremblingly believe that it is possible, by some strange mysterious method, that once in a hundred sermons God might win a quarter of a soul. They have hardly enough faith to keep them standing upright in their boots; how can they expect God to bless them? I like to go to the pulpit feeling, "This is God's Word that I am going to deliver in His name; it cannot return to Him void; I have asked His blessing upon it, and He is bound to give it, and His purposes will be answered, whether my message is a savour of life unto life, or of death unto death to those who hear it."

Now, if this is how you feel, what will be the result if souls are not saved? Why, you will call special prayer-meetings, to seek to know why the people do not come to Christ; you will have enquirers' meetings for the anxious; you will meet the people with a joyful countenance, so that they may see that you are expecting a blessing, but, at the same time, you will let them know that you will be grievously disappointed unless the Lord gives you conversions. Yet, how is it in many places? Nobody prays much about the matter, there are no meetings for crying to God for a blessing, the minister never encourages the people to come and tell him about the work of grace in their souls; verily, verily, I say unto you, he has his reward he gets what he asked f or, he receives what he expected, his Master gives him his penny, but nothing else. The command is, "Open thy mouth wide, and I will fill it;" and here we sit, with closed lips, waiting for the blessing. Open your mouth, brother, with a full expectation, a firm belief, and according to your faith so shall it be unto you.

That is the essential point, you must believe in God and in His gospel if you are to be a winner of souls; some other things may be omitted, but this matter of faith must never be. It is true that God does not always measure His mercy by our unbelief, for He has to think of other people as well as of us; but, looking at the matter in a common-sense way, it doe s seem that the most likely instrument to do the Lord's work is the man who expects that God will use him, and who goes forth to labour in the strength of that conviction. When success comes, he is not surprised, for he was looking for it. He sowed living seed, and he expected to reap a harvest from it; he cast his bread upon the waters, and he means to search and watch till he finds it again.

Once more, if a man is to succeed in his ministry, and win many souls, he must be characterized by thorough earnestness. Do we not know some men, who preach in such a lifeless manner that it is highly improbable that anybody will ever be affected by what they say? I was present when a good man asked the Lord to bless to the conversion of sinners the sermon that he was about to deliver. I do not wish to limit omnipotence, but I do not believe that God could bless to any sinner the sermon that was then preached unless He had made the hearer misunderstand what the minister said. It was one of those "bright poker sermons" , as I call them. You know that there are pokers that are kept in drawing-rooms to be looked at, but never used. If you ever tried to poke the fire with them, would not you catch it from the lady of the house? These sermons are just like those pokers, polished up, bright, and cold; they seem as if they might have some relation to the people in the fixed stars, they certainly have no connection with anyone in this world. What good could come of such discourses, no one can tell; but I feel sure there is not power enough in them to kill a cockroach, or a spider; certainly, there is no power in them to bring a dead soul to life. There are some sermons of which it is quite true that, the more you think of them, the less you think of them; and if any poor sinner goes to hear them with the hope of getting saved, you can only say that the minister is more likely to stand in the way of his going to heaven than to point him to the right road.

You may depend upon it that you may make men understand the truth if you really want to do so; but if you are not in ear nest, it is not likely that they will be. If a man were to knock at my door in the middle of the night, and when I put my head out of the window to see what was the matter, he should say, in a very quiet, unconcerned way, "There is a fire at the back part of your house," I should have very little thought of any fire, and should feel inclined to empty a jug of water over him. If I am walking along, and a man comes up to me, and says, in a cheerful tone of voice, "Good afternoon, sir, do you know that I am starving? I have not tasted food for ever so long, indeed, I have not;" I should reply, "My good fellow, you seem to take it very easy; I do not believe you want for much, or you would not be so unconcerned about it." Some men seem to preach in this fashion:—" My dear friends, this i s Sunday, so here I am; I have been spending my time in my study all the week, and now I hope you will listen to what I have to say to you. I do not know that there is anything in it that particularly concerns you, it might have some connection with the man in the moon; but I understand that some of you are in danger of going to a certain place which I do not wish to mention, only I hear that it is not a nice place for even a temporary residence. I have especially to preach to you that Jesus Christ did something or other, which, in some way or other, has something to do with salvation, and if you mind what you do" —and so on—" it is possible that you will" —and so on, and so on. That is, in a nutshell, the full report of many a discourse. There is nothing in that kind of talk that can do anybody any good; and after the man has kept on in that style for three-quarters of an hour, he closes by saying, "Now it is time to go home," and he hopes that the deacons will give him a couple of guineas for his services. Now, brethren, that sort of thing will not do. We did not come into the world to waste our own time, and other people's, in that fashion.

I hope we were born for something better than to be mere chips in the porridge, like the man I have described. Only fancy God sending a man into the world to try to win souls, and that is the style of his mind, and the whole spirit of his life. There are some ministers who are constantly being knocked up with doing nothing; they preach two sermons, of a sort, on Sunday, and they say the effort almost wears their life out; and they go and give little pastoral visitations, which consist in drinking a cup of tea and talking small gossip; but there is no vehement agony for souls, no "Woe! woe!" on their hearts and lips, no perfect consecration, no zeal in God's service. Well, if the Lord sweeps them away, if He cuts them down as cumberers of the ground, it will not be a matter for surprise. The Lord Jesus Christ wept over Jerusalem, and you will have to weep over sinners if they are to be saved through you. Dear brethren, do be earnest, put your whole soul into the work, or else give it up.

Another qualification that is essential to soul-winning is great simplicity of heart. I do not know whether I can thoroughly explain what I mean by that, but I will try to make it clear by contrasting it with something else. You know some men who are too wise to be just simple believers; they know such a lot that they do not believe anything that is plain and simple. their souls have been fed so daintily that they cannot live on anything but Chinese birds'-nest, and such luxuries. There is no milk that ever came fresh from a cow that is good enough for them, they are far too superfine to drink such a beverage as that. Everything they have must be incomparable. Now God does not bless these exquisite celestial dandies, these spiritual aristocrats. No, no; as soon as you see them, you feel ready to say, "They may do well enough as Lord So-and-so's servants, but they are not the men to do God's work. He is not likely to employ such grand gentlemen as they are." When they select a text, they never explain its true meaning; but they go round about to find out something that the Holy Ghost never intended to convey by it, and when they get hold of one of their precious "new thoughts "— oh, dear! what a fuss they make over it! Here is a man who has found a stale herring! What a treat! It is so odoriferous! Now we shall hear of this stale herring for the next six months, when somebody else will find another one. What a shout they set up! "Glory! Glory! Glory! Here is a new thought!" A new book comes out about it, and al l these great men go sniffing round it to prove what deep thinkers and what wonderful men they are. God does not bless that kind of wisdom.

By simplicity of heart, I mean, that a man evidently goes into the ministry for the glory of God and the winning of souls, and nothing else. There are some men who would like to win souls and glorify God if it could be done with due regard to their own interests. They would be delighted, oh, yes! certainly, very pleased indeed, to extend the kingdom of Christ, if the kingdom of Christ would give full play to their amazing powers. They would go in for soul-winning if it would induce people to take the horses out of their carriage, and drag them in triumph through the street; they must be

30

somebody, they must be known, they must be talked about, they must hear people say, "What a splendid man that is!" Of course, they give God the glory after they have sucked the juice out of it, but they must have the orange themselves first. Well, you know, there is that sort of spirit even among ministers; and God cannot endure it. He is not going to have a man's leavings; He will have all the glory, or none at all. If a man seeks to serve himself, to get honour to himself, instead of seeking to serve God and honour Him alone, the Lord Jehovah will not use that man. A man who is to be used by God must just believe that what he is going to do is for the glory of God, and he must work from no other motive. When outsiders go to hear some preachers, all that they remember i s that they were capital actors; but here is a very different kind of man. After they have heard him preach, they do not think about how he looked, or how he spoke, but about the solemn truths he uttered. Another man keeps rolling out what he has to tell in such a fashion that those who listen to him say to one another, "Do you not see that he lives by his preaching? He preaches for his living." I would rather hear it said, "That man said something in his sermon that made many of the people think less of him, he uttered most distasteful sentiments, he did nothing but drive at us with the Word of the Lord all the while that he was preaching, his one aim was to bring us to repentance and faith in Christ." That is the kind of man whom the Lord delights to bless.

I like to see men, like some before me here, to whom I have said, "Here you are, earning a good salary, and likely to rise to a position of influence in the world; if you give up your business, and come into the College, you will very likely be a poor Baptist minister all your life;" and they have looked up, and said, "I had sooner starve and win souls than spend my life in any other calling." Most of you are that kind of men, I believe you all are. There must never be an eye to the glory of God and the fat sheep; it must never be God's glory and your own honour and esteem among men. It will not do; no, not even if you preach to please God and Jemima it must be God's glory alone, nothing less and nothing else, not even Jemima. As the limp et to the rock, so is she to the minister; but it will not do for him even to think of pleasing her. With true simplicity of heart, he must seek to please God, whether men and women are pleased or not.

Lastly, there must be *a complete surrender of yourself to God*, in this sense, that from this time you wish to think, not your own thoughts, but God's thoughts; and that you determine to preach, not

31

anything of your own invention, but God's Word; and further, that you resolve not even to give out that truth in your own way, but in God's way. Suppose you read your sermons, which is not very likely, you desire not to write anything but what shall be entirely according to the Lord's mind. When you get hold of a fine big word, you ask yourself whether it is likely to be a spiritual blessing to your people; and if you think it would not, you leave it out. Then there is that grand bit of poetry that you could not understand, you felt that you could not omit that; but when you asked whether it was likely to be instructive to the rank and file of your people, you were obliged to reject it. You must stick those gems, that you found on a literary dust-heap, into the coronet of your discourse, if you want to show the people how industrious you have been; but if you desire to leave yourself entirely in God's hands, it is probable that you will be led to make some very simple statement, some trite remark, something with which everyone in the congregation is familiar. If you feel moved to put that into the sermon, put it in by all means, even if you have to leave out the big words, and the poetry, and the gems, for it may be that the Lord will bless that simple statement of the gospel to some poor sinner who is seeking the Saviour.

If you yield yourself thus unreservedly to the mind and will of God, by- and-by, when you get out into the ministry, you will sometimes be impelled to use a strange expression or to offer an odd prayer, which at the time may have a queer look even to yourself; but it will be all explained to you afterwards, when someone comes to tell you that he never understood the truth until you put it that day in such an unusual way. You will be more likely to feel this influence if you are thoroughly prepared by study and prayer for your work in the pulpit, and I urge you always to make all due preparation, and even to write out in full what you think you ought to say; but not to go and deliver it memoriter, like a poll parrot repeating what it has been taught, for if you do that, you will certainly not be leaving yourself to the guidance of the Holy Spirit.

I have no doubt you will sometimes feel that there is a passage that you must put in, a fine piece by one of the British poets, or a choice extract from some classic author. I do not suppose you would like it to be known; but you did read it to a College friend. Of course, you did not ask him to praise it, because you felt sure that he could not help doing so. There was one particular piece in it that you have very seldom heard equalled; you are sure that Mr. Punshon or Dr. Parker could not have done better than that. You are quite certain that, when the people hear that sermon, the y will be obliged to feel that there is something in it. It may be, however, that the Lord will consider that it is too good to be blessed, there is too much in it; it is like the host of men that were with Gideon, they were too many for the Lord, He could not give the Midianites into their hands, lest they should vaunt themselves against Him, saying, "Our own might hath gotten us the victory." When twenty-two thousand of them had been sent away, the Lord said to Gideon, "The people are yet too many," and all of them had to be sent home except the three hundred men that lapped, and then the Lord said to Gideon, "Arise, get thee down unto the host; for I have delivered it into thine hand." So the Lord says about some of your sermons," I cannot do any good with them, they are too big." There is that one with the fourteen subdivisions; leave seven of them out, and then perhaps the Lord will bless it. Someday it may hap pen, just when you are in the middle of your discourse, that a thought will come across your mind, and you will say to yourself; "Now, if I utter this, that old deacon will make it hot for me; and there is a gentleman just come in who keeps a school, he is a critic, and will be sure not to be pleased if I say this; and besides, there is here a remnant according to the election of grace, and the 'hyper' up in the gallery will give me one of those heavenly looks that are so full of meaning." Now, brother, feel ready to say just anything that God gives you to say, irrespective of all the consequences, and utterly regardless of what the "hypers" or the lowpers or anybody else will think or do.

One of the principal qualifications of a great artist's brush must be its yielding itself up to him so that he can do what he likes with it. A harpist will love to play on one particular harp because he knows the instrument, and the instrument almost appears to know him. So, when God puts His hand upon the very strings of your being, and every power within you seems to respond to the movements of His hand, you are an instrument that he can use. It is not easy to keep in that condition, to be in such a sensitive state that you receive the impression that the Holy Spirit desires to convey, and are influenced by Him at once. If there is a great ship out at sea, and there comes a tiny ripple on the waters, it is not moved by it in the least. Here comes a moderate wave, the vessel does not feel it, the Great Eastern sits still upon the bosom of the deep. But just look over the bulwarks; see those corks down there, if only a fly drops into the water, they feel the motion, and dance upon the tiny wave. May you be as mobile beneath the power of God as the cork is on the surface of the sea! I am sure this self-surrender is one of the essential qualifications for a preacher who is to be a winner of souls. There is a something that must be said if you are to be the means of saving that man in the corner; woe unto you if you are not ready to say it, woe unto you if you are afraid to say it, woe unto you if you are ashamed to say it, woe unto you if you do not dare to say it lest somebody up in the gallery should say that you were too earnest, too enthusiastic, too zealous!

These seven things, I think, are the qualifications, Godward, which would strike the mind of any of you if you tried to put yourself into the position of the Most High, and considered what you would wish to have in those whom you employed in the winning of souls. May God give all of us these qualifications, for Christ's sake! Amen.

QUALIFICATIONS FOR SOUL-WINNING— MANWARD

You remember, brethren, that on the last occasion I gave you a lecture on soul-winning, I spoke of the qualifications, Godward, that would fit a man to be a soul-winner; and I tried to describe to you the kind of man that the Lord was most likely to use in the winning of souls. This afternoon, I propose to take as my subject—

THE CHARACTERISTICS OF A SOUL-WINNER, MANWARD.

I might almost mention the very same points that I enumerated before as being those which will best tell manward, for I do think that those qualities that commend themselves to the notice of God, as being most adapted to the end He desires, are also likely to be approved by the object acted upon, that is, the soul of man.

There have been many men in the world who have not been at all adapted for this work; and, first, let me say that *an ignoramus is not likely to be much of a soul-winner.* A man who only knows that he is a sinner, and that Christ is a Saviour, may be very useful to others in the same condition as himself, and it is his duty to do the best he can with what little knowledge he possesses; but, on the whole, I should not expect such a man to be very largely used in the service of God. If he had enjoyed a wider and deeper experience of the things of God, if he had been in the highest sense a learned man because taught of God, he could have used his knowledge for the good of others; but being to a great extent ignorant of the things of God himself, I do not see how he can make them known to other people. Truly, there must be some light in that candle which is to lighten men's darkness, and there must be some information in that man who is to be a teacher of his fellows. The man who is almost or altogether ignorant, whatever will he has to do good, must be left out of the race of great soul-winners; he is disqualified from even entering the lists, and therefore, let us all ask, brethren, that we may be well instructed in the truth of God, that we may be able to teach others also.

Granted that you are not of the ignorant class to which I have been referring, but supposing that you are well instructed in the best of all wisdom, what are the qualities that you must have towards m en if you are to win them for the Lord? I should say, there must be about us an evident sincerity; not only sincerity, but such sincerity that it shall be manifest at once to anyone who honestly looks for it. It must be quite clear to your hearers that you have a firm belief in the truths that you are preaching; otherwise, you will never make them believe them. Unless they are convinced, beyond all question, that you do believe these truths yourselves, there will be no efficacy and no force in your preaching. No one must suspect you of proclaiming to others what you do not fully believe in yourself; if it should ever be so, your work will be of no effect. All who listen to you ought to be conscious that you are exercising one of the noblest crafts, and performing one of the most sacred functions that ever fell to the lot of man. If you have only a feeble appreciation of the gospel you profess to deliver, it is impossible for those who hear you r proclamation of it to be greatly influenced by it. I heard it asked, the other day, of a certain minister, "Did he preach a good sermon?" and the reply to the enquiry was, "What he said was very good." "But did you not profit by the sermon?" "No, not in the slightest degree." "Was it not a good sermon?" Again came the first answer, "What he said was very good." "What do you mean? Why did you not profit by the sermon if what the preacher said was very good? " This was the explanation that the listener gave, "I did not profit by the discourse because I did not believe in the man who delivered it; he was simply an actor performing a part; I did not believe that he felt what he preached, nor that he cared whether we felt or believed it or not."

Where such a state of things as that exists, the hearers cannot be expected to profit by the sermon, no matter what the preacher may say; they may try to fancy that the truths he utters are precious, they may resolve that they will feed upon the provision whoever may set the dish before them; but it is no use, they cannot do it, they cannot separate the heartless speaker from the message he delivers so carelessly. As soon as a man lets his work become a matter of mere form or routine, it sinks into a performance in which the preacher is simply an actor. He is only acting a part, as he might in a p lay at the theatre; and not speaking from his inmost soul, as a man sent from G od. I do beseech you, brethren, speak from your hearts, or else do not speak at all. If you can be silent, be silent; but if you must speak for God, be thoroughly sincere about it. It would be better for you to go back to business, and weigh butter or sell reels of cotton, or do anything rather than pretend to be ministers of the gospel unless God has called you to the work. I believe that the most damnable thing a man can do is to preach the gospel merely as an actor, and to turn the worship of God into a kind of theatrical performance. Such a caricature is more worthy of the devil than of God. Divine truth is far too precious to be made the subject of such a mockery. You may depend upon it that, when the people once suspect that you are insincere, they will never listen to you except with disgust, and they will not be at all likely to believe your message if you give them cause to think that you do not believe it yourselves.

I hope I am not wrong in supposing that all of us are thoroughly sincere in our Master's service; so I will go on to what seems to me to be the next qualification, manward, for soul-winning, and that is, evident earnestness. The command to the man who would be a true servant of the Lord Jesus Christ is, "Thou shalt love the Lord thy God with all thy hear t, and with all thy soul, and with all thy strength, and with all thy mind." If a man is to be a soul-winner, there must be in him intensity of emotion as well as sincerity of heart. You may preach the most solemn warnings, and the most dread fulthreatenings, in such an indifferent or careless way that no one will be in the least affected by them; and you may repeat the most affectionate exhortations in such a half-hearted manner that no one will be moved either to love or fear. I believe, brethren, that for soul-winning there is more in this matter of earnestness than in almost anything else. I have seen and heard some who were very poor preachers, who yet brought many souls to the Saviour through the earnestness with which they delivered their message. There was positively nothing in their sermons (until the provision merchant used them to wrap round his butter), yet those feeble sermons brought many to Christ. It was not what the preachers said, so much as how they said it, that carried conviction to the he arts of their hearers. The simplest truth was so driven home by the intensity of the utterance and emotion of the man from whom it came that it told with surprising effect. If any gentleman here would present me with a cannon-ball, say one weighing fifty or a hundred pounds, and let me roll it across the room; and another would entrust me with a rifle-ball, and a rifle out of which I could fire it, I know which would be the more effective of the two. Let no man despise the little bullet, for very often that is the one that kills the sin, and kills the sinner, too. So, brethren, it is not the bigness of the words you utter; it is the force with which you deliver them that decides what is to come of the utterance. I have heard of a ship that was fired at by the cannon in a fort, but no impression was made upon it until the general in command gave the order for the balls to be made red-hot, and then the vessel was sent to the bottom of the sea i n three minutes. That is what you must do with your sermons, make them red-hot; n ever mind if men do say you are too enthusiastic, or even too fanatical, give them red-hot shot, there is nothing else half as good for the purpose you have in view. We do not go out snow-balling on Sundays, we go fire-balling; we ought to hurl grenades into the enemy's ranks.

What earnestness our theme deserves! We have to tell of an earnest Saviour, an earnest heaven, and an earnest hell. How earnest we ought to be when we remember that in our work we have to deal with soul s that are immortal, with sin that is eternal in its effects, with pardon that is infinite, and with terrors and joys that are to last for ever and ever! A man who is not in earnest when he has such a theme as this,—can he possess a heart at all? Could one be discovered even with a microscope? If he were dissected, probably all that could be found would be a pebble, a heart of stone, or some other substance equally incapable of emotion. I trust that, when God gave us hearts of flesh for ourselves, He gave us hearts that could feel for other people also.

These things being taken for granted, I should say, next, that it is necessary for a man who is to be a soul-winner, that he should have an evident love to his hearers. I cannot imagine a man being a winner of souls when he spends most of his time in abusing his congregation, and talking as if he hated the very sight of them. Such men seem happy only when they are emptying vials of wrath over those who have the unhappiness of listening to them. I heard of a brother preaching from the text, "A certain man went down from Jerusalem to Jericho, and fell among thieves." He began his discourse thus, "I do not say that this man came to the place where we are, but I do know another man who did come to this place, and fell among thieves." You can easily guess what would be the result of such vitriol-throwing. I know of one who preached from the passage, "And Aaron held his peace," and one who heard him said that the difference between him and Aaron was, that Aaron held his peace, and the preacher did not; but, on the contrary, he raved at the people with all his might.

You must have a real desire for the good of the people if you are to have much influence over them. Why, even dogs and cats love the people who love them, and human beings are much the same as these dumb animals. People very soon get to know when a cold man gets into the pulpit, one of those who seem to have been carved out of a block of marble. There have been one or two of our brethren of that kind, and they have never succeeded anywhere. When I have asked the cause of their failure, in each case the reply has been, "He is a good man, a very good man; he preaches well, very w ell, but still we do not get on with him." I have asked, "Why do you not like him?" The reply has been, "Nobody ever did like him." "Is he quarrelsome?" "O h! dear no, I wish he would make a row." I try to fish out what the drawback is, for I am very anxious to know, and at last someone says, "Well, sir, I do not think he has any heart; at least, he does not preach and act as if he had any."

It is very sad when the failure of any ministry is caused by want of heart. You ought to have a great big heart, like the harbour at Portsmouth or Plymouth, so that all the people in your congregation could come and cast anchor in it, and feel that they were under the lee of a great rock. Do you not notice that men succeed in the ministry, and win souls for Christ, just in proportion as they are men with large hearts? Think, for instance, of Dr. Brock; there was a mass of a man, one who had bowels of compassion; and what is the good of a minister who has not? I do not hold up the accumulation of flesh as an object worthy of your attainment; but I do say that you must have big hearts, if you are to win men to Jesus; you must be Great-hearts if you are to lead many pilgrims to the Celestial City. I have seen some very lean men who said that they were perfectly holy, and I could almost believe that they could not sin, for they were like old bits of leather, there did not appear to be anything in them that was capable of sinning. I met one of these "perfect" brethren once, and he was just like a piece of sea-weed, there was no humanity in him. I like to see a trace of humanity somewhere or other about a man, and people in general like it, too; they get on better with a man who has some human nature in him. Human nature, in some aspects, is an awful thing; but when the Lord Jesus Christ took it, and joined His own divine nature to it, He made a grand thing of it, and human nature is a noble thing when it is united to the Lord Jesus Christ. Those men who keep themselves to themselves, like hermits, and live a supposed sanctified life of self-absorption, are not likely to have any influence in the world, or to do good to their fellow-creatures. You must love the people, and mix with them, if you are to be of service to t hem. There are some ministers who really are much better men than others, yet they do not accomplish so much good as those who are more human, those who go and sit down with the people, and make themselves as much as possible at home with them. You know, brethren, that it is possible for you to appear to be just a wee bit too good, so that people will feel that you are altogether transcendental beings, and fitter to preach to angels, and cherubim, and seraphim, than to the fallen sons of Adam. Just be men among men; keeping yourselves clear of all their faults and vices, but mingling with them in perfect love and sympathy, and feeling that you would do anything in your power to bring them to Christ, so that you might even say with the apostle Paul, " Though I be free from all men, yet have I made myself servant unto all, that I might gain the more. And unto the Jews I became as a Jew, that I might gain the Jews; to them that are under the law, as under the law, that I might gain them that are under the law; to them that are without law, as without law, (being not without law to God, but under the law to Christ,) that I might gain them that are without law. To the weak became I as weak, that I might gain the weak: I am made all things to all men, that I might by all means save some."

The next qualification, manward, for soul-winning i s evident unselfishness. A man ceases to bring men to Christ as soon as he becomes known as a selfish man. Selfishness seems to be ingrained in some people; you see it at the table at home, in the house of God, everywhere. When such individuals come to deal with a church and congregation, their selfishness soon manifests itself; they mean to get all they can, although in the Baptist ministry they do not often get much. I hope each of you, brethren, will be willing to say, "Well, let me have but food and raiment, and I will be therewith content." If you try to put the thought of money altogether away from you, the money will often come back to you doubled; but if you seek to grab and grasp all, you will very likely find that it will not come to you at all. Those who are selfish in the matter of salary, will be the same in everything else; they will not want their people to know anybody who can preach better than themselves; and they cannot bear to hear of any good work going on anywhere except in their own chapel. If there is a revival at another place, and souls are being saved, they say, with a sneer, "Oh! yes, there are many converts, but what are they? Where will they be in a few months' time?" They think far more of their own gain of one new member per year than of their neighbour's hundred at one time. If your people see that kind of selfishness in you, you will soon lose power over them; if you make up your mind that you will be a great man, whoever has to be thrust on one side, you will go to the cats as sure as you are alive. What are you, my dear brother, that people should all bow down and worship you, and think that in all the world there is none beside you? I tell you what it is; the less you think of yourself, the more will

40

people think of you; and the more you think of yourself, the less will people think of you. If any of you have any trace of selfishness about you, pray get rid of it at once, or you will never be fit instruments for the winning of souls for the Lord Jesus Christ.

Then I am sure that another thing that is wanted in a soul-winner is holiness of character. It is no use talking about "the higher life" on Sundays, and then living the lower life on week days. A Christian minister must be very careful, not only to be innocent of actual wrong-doing, but not to be a cause of offence to the weak ones of the flock. All things are lawful, but all things are not expedient. We ought never to do anything that we judge to be wrong, but we ought also to be willing to abstain from things which might not be wrong in themselves, but which might be an occasion of stumbling to others. When people see that we not only preach about holiness, but that we are ourselves holy men, they will be drawn towards holy things by our character as well as by our preaching.

I think also that, if we are to be soul-winners, there must be about us a *seriousness of mann*er. Some brethren are serious by nature. There was a gentleman in a railway carriage, some time ago, who overheard a conversation between two of the passengers. One of them said, "W ell, now, I think the Church of Rome has great power, and is likely to succeed with the people, because of the evident holiness of her ministers. There is, for instance, Cardinal _, he is just like a skeleton; through his long fasting and prayers, he has reduced himself almost to skin and bone. Whenever I hear him speak, I feel at once the force of the holiness of the man. Now, look at Spurgeon, he eats and drinks like an ordinary mortal; I would not give a pin to hear him preach." His friend heard him very patiently, and then said quit e quietly, "Did it ever strike you that the Cardinal's appearance was to be accounted for by the fact of his liver being out of order? I do not think it is grace that makes him as lean as he is, I believe it is his liver." So, there are some brethren who are naturally of a melancholy disposition, they are always very serious; but in them it is not a sign of grace, it is only an indication that their livers are out of order. They never laugh, they think it would be wicked to do so ; but they go about the world increasing the misery of human kind, which is dreadful enough without the addition of their unnecessary portion. Such people evidently imagine that they were predestinated to pour buckets of cold water upon all human mirth and joy. So, dear brethren, if any of you are very serious, you must not always attribute it to grace, for it may be all owing to the state of your liver.

The most of us, however, are far more inclined to that laughter which doeth good like medicine, and we shall need all our cheerfulness, if we are to comfort and lift up those who are cast down; but we shall never bring many souls to Christ, if we are full of that levity which characterises some men. People will say, "It is all a joke; just hear how those young fellows jest about religion, it is one thing to listen to them when they are in the pulpit, but it is quite another matter to listen to them when they are sitting round the supper table." I have heard of a man who was dying, and he sent for the minister to come and see him. When the minister came in, the dying man said to him, "Do you remember a young man walking with you one evening, some years ago, when you were going out to preach?" He said, he did not. "I recollect it very well," replied the other. "Do you not remember preaching at such-and-such a village, from such- and-such a text, and after the service a young man walked home with you?" "Oh, yes, I remember that very well!" "Well, I am the young man who walked home with you that night; I remember your sermon, I shall never forget it." "Thank God for that," said the preacher. "No," answered the dying man, "you will not thank God when you have heard all I have to say. I walked with you to the village, but you did not say much to me on the way there, for you were thinking over your sermon; you deeply impressed me while you were preaching, and I was led to think about giving my heart to Christ. I wanted to speak to you about my soul on the way home; but the moment you got out you cracked a joke, and all the way back you made such fun upon serious subjects, that I could not say anything about what I felt, and it thoroughly disgusted me with religion, and all who professed it, and now I am going to be damned, and my blood will lie at your door, as sure as you are alive:" and so he passed out of the world. One would not like anything of that sort to happen to himself; therefore, take heed, brethren, that you give no occasion for it. There must be a prevailing seriousness about our whole lives, otherwise we cannot hope to lead other men to Christ.

Finally, if we are to be much used of God as soul-w inners, there must be in our hearts a great deal of tenderness. I like a man to have a due amount of holy boldness, but I do not care to see him brazen-faced and impudent. A young man goes into a pulpit, apologises for attempting to preach, and hopes the people will bear with him; he does not know that he has anything particular to say, if the Lord had sent him he might have had some message for them, but he feels himself so young and inexperienced that he cannot s peak very positively about anything. Such talk as that will never save a mouse, much less an immortal soul. If the Lord has sent you to preach the gospel, why should you make any apologies? Ambassadors do not apologise when they go to a foreign court; they know that their monarch has sent them, and they deliver their message with all the authority of king and country at their back. Nor is it worthwhile for you to call attention to your youth. You are only a trumpet of ram's horn; and it does not matter whether you were pulled off the ram's he ad yesterday, or five-and- twenty years ago. If God blows through you, there will be noise enough, and something more than noise; if He does not, nothing will come of the blowing. When you preach, speak out straight, but be very tender about it; and if there is an unpleasant thing to be said, take care that you put it in the kindest possible form. Some of our brethren had a message to deliver to a certain Christian brother, and when they went to him they put it so awkwardly that he was grievously offended. When I spoke to him about the same matter, he said, "I would not have minded your speaking to me; you have a way of putting an unpleasant truth so that a man cannot be offended with you however much he may dislike the message you bring to him." "Well, but," I said, "I put the matter just as strongly as the other brethren did." "Yes, you did," he replied, "but they said it in such a nasty kind of a way that I would not stand it. Why, sir, I had rather be blown up by you than praised by those other people!" There is a way of doing such things so that the person reproved feels positively grateful to you. One may kick a man downstairs in such a fashion that he will rather like it; while another may open a door in such an offensive way that you do not want to go through till he is out of the way. Now, if I have to tell anyone certain unpalatable truths which it is necessary that he should know if his soul is to be saved, it is a stern necessity for me to be faithful to him; yet I will try so to deliver my message that he shall not be offended at it. Then, if he does take offence, he must; the probability is that he will not, but that what I say will take effect upon his conscience.

I know some brethren who preach as if they were prize-fighters. When they are in the pulpit, they remind me of the Irishman a t Donnybrook Fair; all the way through the sermon they appear to be calling up on someone to come up and fight them, and they are never happy except when they are pitching into somebody or other. There is a man who often preache son Clapham Common, and he does it so pugnaciously that the infidels whom he assails cannot endure it, and there are frequent fights and rows. There i s a way of preaching so as to set everybody by the ears; if some men were allowed to preach in heaven, I am afraid they would set the angels fighting. I know a number of ministers of this stamp. There is one who, to my certain knowledge, has been at over a dozen places during his not very long ministerial life. you can tell where he has been by the ruin he leaves behind him. He always finds the churches in a sad state, and he straightway begins to purify them, that is, to destroy them. As a general rule, the first thing, out goes the principal deacon, and the next, away go all the leading families, and before long, the man has purified the place so effectually that the few people who are left cannot keep him. Off he goes to another place, and repeats the process of destruction. He is a kin d of spiritual ship-scuttler, and he is never happy except when he is boring a hole through the planks of some good vessel. He says he believes the ship is unsound; so he bores, and bores, until just as she is going down, he slips off, and gets aboard another vessel, which very soon sinks in the same manner. he feels that he is called to the work of separating the precious from the vile, and a preciously vile mess he makes of it. I have no reason to believe it is the condition of the liver in this brother, it is more likely that there is something wrong with his heart; certainly, there is an evil disease upon him that always makes me get into a bad temper with him. It is dangerous to entertain him above three days, for he would quarrel in that time with the most peaceably disposed man in the world. I never mean to recommend him to a pastorate again; let him find a place for himself if he can, for I believe that, where-ever he goes, the place will be like the spot where the foot of the Tartar's horse is put down, the grass will never again grow there. If any of you brethren have even a little of this nasty, bitter spirit about you, go to sea that you may get rid of it. I hope it may happen to you according to the legend which is told concerning Mahomet. "In every human being," so the story runs, "there are two black drops of sin. The great prophet himself was not free from the common lot of evil; but an angel was sent to take his heart, and squeeze out of it the two black drops of sin." Get those black drops out somehow while you are in College; if you have any malice, or ill-will, or bad temper in you, pray the Lord to take it out of you while you are here; do not go into the churches to fight as others have done.

"Still," says a brother, "I am not going to let the people tread on me. I shall take the bull by the horns." You will be a great fool if you do. I never felt that I was called to do anything of the kind. Why not let the bull alone, to go where he likes? A bull is a very likely creature to project you into space if you get meddling with his horns. "Still," says another, "we must set things right." Yes, but the best way to set things right is not to make them more wrong than they are. Nobody

44

thinks of putting a mad bull into a china shop in order to get the china cleaned, and no one can by a display of evil temper set right anything that is wrong in our churches. Take care always to speak the truth in love, and especially when you are rebuking sin.

I believe, brethren, that soul-winning is to be done by men of the character I have been describing; and most of all will this be the case when they are surrounded by people of a similar character. You want to get the very atmosphere in which you live and labour permeated with this spirit before you can rightly expect the fullest and richest blessing s. Therefore, may you and all your people be all that I have pictured, for the Lord Jesus Christ's sake! Amen.

SERMONS LIKELY TO WIN SOULS

This afternoon, brethren, I am going to speak to you about—

THE KIND OF SERMONS THAT ARE MOST LIKELY TO CONVERT PEOPLE,

the sort of discourses we should deliver if we really want our hearers to believe in the Lord Jesus Christ, and to be saved. Of cours e, we are all perfectly agreed that the Holy Spirit alone can convert a soul; none can enter into the kingdom of God except they are born again from above. All the work is done by the Holy Spirit; and we must not take to ourselves any part of the credit for the result of the work, for it is the Spirit who new-creates and works in man according to the eternal purpose of God.

Still, we may be instruments in His hands, for He chooses to use instruments, and He chooses them for wise reasons. There must be an adaptation of means to the end, as there was with D avid when he went forth with the sling and stone to slay Goliath of Gath. Goliath was a tall fellow, but a stone from a sling can mount; and, besides, the giant was armed and protected, and scarcely vulnerable except in his forehead, so that was the very place to hit him. Though David took a sling, it was not so much because he had no other weapon as that he had practised slinging, as most boys do in some form or other; and then he chose a smooth stone because he knew it would fit the sling. He took the right kind of stone to enter Goliath's head, so, when he slung it at the giant, it struck him in the forehead, penetrate d his brain, and he sank down to the ground.

You will find that this principle of adaptation run s through the whole work of the Holy Spirit. If a man is wanted to be the apostle of the Gentiles, the Holy Spirit selects the large-minded, well-trained, highly-educated Paul, for he was more fit for such work than was the somewhat narrow though strong-minded Peter, who was better suited for preaching to the Jews, and who was of far more use to the circumcision than he ever could have been among the uncircumcision. Paul in his place is the right man, and Peter in his place is the right man. You may see in this principle a lesson f or yourselves, and seek to adapt your means to your end. God the Holy Spirit can convert a soul by any text of Scripture apart from your paraphrase, your comment, your exposition; but there are certain Scripture passages, as you know, that are the best to bring before the minds of sinners, and if this is true about your texts, much more is it so in your discourses to your hearers. As to which sermons are most likely to be blessed to the conversion of those to whom they are preached, I should say,—

First, they are *those sermons which are distinctly aimed at the conversion of the hearers.* I heard a prayer, some time ago, from a minister who asked the Lord to save souls by the sermon he was about to deliver. I do not hesitate to say that God Himself could not bless the sermon to that end unless He made the people misunderstand all that the preacher said to them, because the whole discourse was rather calculated to harden the sinner in his sin than to lead him to renounce it, and to seek the Saviour. There was not hing in it that could be blessed to any hearer unless he turned it inside out or bottom upwards. The sermon did me good on the principle that was applied by a good old lady to the minister she was obliged to hear. When asked, "Why do you go to such a place?" she replied," Well, there is no other place of worship to which I can go." "But it must be better to stay at home than to hear such stuff," said her friend. "Perhaps so," she answered, "but I like to go out to worship even if I get nothing by going. You see a hen, sometimes, scratching all over a heap of rubbish to try to find some corn; she does not get any, but it shows that she is looking for it, and using the means to get it, and then, too, the exercise warms her." So the old lady said that scratching over the poor sermons she heard was a blessing to her because it exercised her spiritual faculties, and warmed her spirit.

There are sermons of such a kind that, unless God takes to ripening wheat by means of snow and ice, and begins to illuminate the world by means of fogs and clouds, He cannot save souls under them. Why, the preacher himself evidently does not think that anybody will be converted by them! If a hundred persons or if half-a-dozen were converted by them, nobody would be so astonished as the preacher himself; in fact, I know a man who was converted, or at least convicted, under the preaching of a minister of that kind. In a certain parish church, as the result of the clergyman's pre aching, there was a man who was under deep conviction of sin. He went down to see his minister, but the poor man did not know what to make of him, and said to him, "I am very sorry if there was anything in my sermon to make you uncomfortable; I did not mean it to be so." "Well, sir," answered the troubled ma n, "you said that we must

47

be born again." "Oh!" replied the clergyman, "that was all done in baptism." "But, sir," said the man, who was not to be put off, "you did not say so in your sermon; you spoke of the necessity of regeneration. " "Well, I am very sorry I said anything to make you uncomfortable, for really I think all is right with you. You are a good sort of a fellow; you were never a poacher, or anything else that is bad." "That may be, sir, but I have a sense of sin , and you said we must be new creatures." "Well, well, my good man," at last said the perplexed parson, "I do not understand such things; I never was born again." He sent him to the Baptist minister, and the man is now himself a Baptist minister, partly as the result of what he learned from the preacher who did not himself understand the truth he had declared to others.

Of course, God can convert a soul by such a sermon as that, and by such a ministry as that, but it is not likely; it is more probable that, in His infinite sovereignty, He will work in a place where a warmhearted man is preaching to men the truth that he has himself received, all the while earnestly desiring their salvation, and ready to guide them further in the ways of the Lord as soon as ever they are saved. God does not usually lay His new-born children down amongst people where the new life will not be under stood, or where it will be left without any proper nurture or care so, brethren, if you want your hearers to be converted, you must just see that your preaching aims directly at conversion, and that it is such as God will be likely to bless to that end. When that is the case, then look for souls to be saved, and look for a great number of them, too. Do not be satisfied when a single soul is converted. Remember that the rule of the kingdom is, "According to your faith be it unto you." I said last night, in my sermon in the Tabernacle, that I was glad it was not written, "According to thine unbelief, so be it unto thee." If there be in us a great faith, God will give us blessing according to our faith. Oh, that we were altogether rid of unbelief, that we believed great things of God, and with hear t and soul so preached that men were likely to be converted by such discourses, proclaiming truths likely to convert them, and declaring them in a manner that would be likely to be blessed to the conversion of our hearers. Of course, all the while we must be trusting to the Holy Spirit to make the work effectual, for we are but the instruments in His hands.

But coming a little closer to our subject, if the people are to be saved, it must be by *sermons that interest them.* You have first to get them to come under the sound of the gospel, for there is, at all events in London, a great aversion to a place of worship, and I am

48

not much surprised that it is so concerning many churches and chapels. I think, in many instances, the common people do not attend such services because they do not understand the theological "lingo" that is used in the pulpit; it is neither English, nor Greek, but Double-dutch; and when a working-man goes once and listens to these fine words, he says to his wife, " I do not go there again, Sal; there is nothing there for me, nor yet for you; there may be a good deal for a gentleman that's been to College, but there is nothing for the likes of us." No, brethren, we must preach in what White-field used to call "market language" if we would have all classes of the community listening to our message.

Then, when they do come in, we must preach interestingly. The people will not be converted while they are asleep; and if they go to sleep, they had better have been at home in bed, where they would sleep much more comfortably. We must have the minds of our hearers awake and active if we are to do them real good. You will not shoot your birds unless you get them to fly, you must get them started up from the long grass in which they are hiding. I would sooner use a little of what some very proper preachers regard as a dreadful thing, that wicked thing called humour,—I would sooner wake the congregation up that way than have it said that I droned away at them until we all went to sleep together. Sometimes, it may be quite right to have it said of us as it was said of Rowland Hill, "What does that man mean? He actually made the people laugh while he was preaching." "Yes," was the wise answer, "but did you not see that he made them cry directly after?" That was good work, and it was well done. I sometimes tickle my oyster until he opens his shell, and then I slip the knife in. He would not have opened for my knife, but he did f or something else; and that is the way to do with people. They must be made to open their eyes, and ears, and souls, somehow; and when you get them open, you must feel, "Now is my opportunity; in with the knife." There is one vulnerable spot in the hides of those rhinoceros sinners that come to hear you but take care that, if you do get a shot through that weak spot, it shall be a thorough gospel bullet, for nothing else will accomplish the work that needs to be done.

Moreover, the people must be interested to make the m remember what is said. They will not recollect what they hear unless the subject interests them. They forget our fine perorations, they cannot recall our very pretty pieces of poetry,—I do not know that they would do them any good if they did remember them; but we must tell our hearers something they will not be likely to forget. I believe

49

in what Father Taylor calls "the surprise power of a sermon" ; that is, something that is not expected by those who are listening to it. Just when they reckon that you are sure to say something very precise and straight, say something awkward and crooked, because they will re member that, and you will have tied a gospel knot where it is likely to remain. I remember reading of a tailor, who had made his fortune, and he promised to tell his brother-tailors how he had done it. They gathered around his bed when he was dying, and he said, as they all listened very attentively, "Now I am to tell you how you tailors are to make your fortunes; this is the way, always put a knot in your thread." I give that same advice to you preachers, always put a knot in your thread; if there is a knot in the thread, it does not come out of the material. Some preachers put in the needle all right, but there is no knot in their thread, so it passes through, and they have really done nothing after all. Put a good many knots in your discourses, brethren, so that there may be all the greater probability that they will remain in your people's memories. You do not your preaching to be like the sewing done by some machines, for, if one stitch breaks, the whole will come undone. There ought to be plenty of "burrs" in a sermon,—Mr. Fergusson will tell you what "burrs" are, I'll warrant you that he has often found them clinging to his coat in his bonnie Scotland. Put these "burrs" all over the people; say something that will strike them, something that will stick to them for many a day, and that will be likely to bless them. I believe that a sermon, under God's smile, is likely to be the means of conversion if it has this peculiarity about it, that it is interesting to the hearers as well as directly aimed at their salvation.

The third thing in a sermon that is likely to win souls to Christ is, *it must be instructive.* If people are to be saved by a discourse, it must contain at least some measure of knowledge. There must be light as well as fire. Some preachers are all light, and no fire, and others are all fire and no light; what we want is both fire and light. I do not judge those brethren who are all fi re and fury; but I wish they had a little more knowledge of what they talk about, and I think it would be well if they did not begin quite so soon to preach what the y hardly understand themselves. It is a fine thing to stand up in the street, and cry, "Believe! Believe! Believe! Believe! Believe! Believe!" Yes, my dear soul, but what have we to believe? What is all this noise about? Preachers of this sort are like a little boy who had been crying, and something happened that stopped him in the middle of his cry, and presently he said, "Ma, please what was I crying about?" Emotion, doubtless, is a very proper thing in the pulpit, and the feeling, the pathos, the power of heart, are good and grand things in the right place; but do also use your brains a little, do tell us something when you stand up to preach the everlasting gospel.

The sermons that are most likely to convert people seem to me to be those that are full of truth, truth about the fall, truth about the law, truth about human nature, and its alienation from God, truth about Jesus Christ, truth about the Holy Spirit, truth about the Everlasting Father, truth about the new birth, truth about obedience to God, and how we learn it, and al l such great verities. Tell your hearers something, dear brethren, whenever you preach, tell them something, tell them something!

Of course, some good may come, even if your hearers do not understand you. I suppose it might be so, for there was a very esteemed lady speaking to the Friends gathered at the Devonshire House meeting. She was a most gracious woman, and was addressing the English Friends in Dutch, and she asked one of the brethren to translate for her, but the hearers said there was so much power and spirit about her speaking, though it was in Dutch, that they did not want it translated, for they were getting as much good out of it as was possible. Now, these hearers were Friends, and they are men of different mould from me, for I do not mind how good a woman the esteemed lady was, I should have liked to know what she was talking about, and I am sure I should not have been in the least degree profited unless it had been translated; and I like ministers always to know what they are talking about, and to be sure that there is something in it worth saying. Do try, therefore, dear brethren, to give your hearers something beside a string of pathetic anecdotes that will set them crying. Tell the people something; you are to teach them, to preach the gospel to your hearers, to make them understand as far as you can the things which should make for their peace. We cannot expect people to be saved by our sermons, unless we try really to instruct them by what we say to them.

Fourthly, *the people must be impressed by our sermons, if they are to be converted.* They must not only be interested, and instructed, but they must be impressed; and, I believe, dear friends, there is a great deal more in impressive sermons than some people think. In order that you may impress the Word upon those to whom you preach, remember that it must be impressed upon yourself first. You must feel it yourself, and speak as a man who feels it; not as if you feel it, but because you feel it, otherwise you will not make it felt by others. I wonder what it must be to go up into the pulpit, and read somebody else's sermon to the congregation. We read in the

Bible of one thing that was borrowed, and the head of that came off; and I am afraid that the same thing often happens with borrowed sermons—the heads come off. Men who read borrowed sermons positively do not know anything about our troubles of mind in preparing for the pulpit, or our joy in preaching with the aid of only brief notes. A dear friend of mine, who reads his own sermons, was talking to me about preaching, and I was telling him how my very soul is moved, and my very heart is stirred within me, when I think of what I shall say to my people, and afterwards when I am delivering my message; but he said that he never felt anything of the kind when he was preaching. He reminded me of the little girl who was crying because her teeth ached, and her grandmother said to her, "Lily, I wonder you are not ashamed to cry about such a small matter." "Well, grandmother," answered the little maid, "it is all very well for you to say that, for, when your teeth ache, you can take them out, but mine are fixed." Some brethren, when the sermon they have selected will not run smoothly, can go to their box, and take out another; but when I have a sermon full of joy, and I myself feel heavy and sad, I am utterly miserable; when I want to beg and persuade men to believe, and my spirit is dull and cold, I feel wretched to the last degree. My teeth ache, and I cannot take them out, for they are my own; as my sermons are my own, and therefore I may expect to find a good deal of trouble, both in the getting of them, and in the using of them.

I remember the answer I received when I once said to my venerable grandfather, "I never have to preach, but that I feel terribly sick, literally sick, I mean, so that I might as well be crossing the Channel," and I asked the dear old man whether he thought I should ever get over that feeling. His answer was, "Your power will be gone if you do." So, my brethren, when it is not so much that you have got a hold of your subject, but that it has got a hold of you, and you feel its grip with a terrible reality yourself, that is the kind of sermon that is most likely to make others feel. If you are not impressed with it yourself, you cannot expect to impress others with it; so mind that your sermons always have something in them, which shall really impress both yourself and the hearers whom you are addressing.

I think also that there should be an impressive delivery of our discourses. The delivery of some preachers is very bad; if your s is so, try and improve it in all possible ways. One young man wanted to learn singing, but he was told by the teacher, "You have only one tone to your voice, and that is outside the scale." So, there are some ministers' voices that have only one tone, and there is no music in that one. Do try, as far as you can, to make the very way in which you speak to minister to the great end you have in view. Preach, for instance, as you would plead if you were standing before a judge, and begging for the life of a friend, or as if you were appealing to the Queen herself on behalf of someone very dear to you. Use such a tone in pleading with sinners as you would use if a gibbet were erected in this room, and you were to be hanged on it unless you could persuade the person in authority to release you. That is the sort of earnestness you need in pleading with men as ambassadors for God. Try and make every sermon such that the most flippant s hall see without any doubt that, if it be an amusement for them to hear you, it is no amusement for you to speak to them, but that you are pleading with them in downright solemn earnest about eternal matters. I have often felt just like this when I have been preaching,—I have known what it is to use up all my ammunition, and then I have, as it were, rammed myself into the great gospel gun, and I have fired myself at my hearers, all my experience of God's goodness, all my consciousness of sin, and all my sense of the power of the gospel; and there are some people upon whom that kind of preaching tells where nothing else would have done, for they see that then you communicate to them not only the gospel, but yourself also. The kind of sermon which is like ly to break the hearer's heart is that which has first broken the preacher's heart, and the sermon which is likely to reach the heart of the hearer is the one which has come straight from the heart of the preacher therefore, dear brethren, always seek to preach so that the people shall be impressed as well as interested and instructed.

Fifthly, I think that we should try *to take out of our sermons everything that is likely to divert the hearer's mind from the object we have in view.*

The best style of preaching in the world, like the best style of dressing, is that which nobody notices. Somebody went to spend the evening with Hannah More, and when he came home his wife asked him, How was Miss More dressed? She must have been dressed very splendidly ." The gentleman answered, "Really she was,—why, dear me, how was she dressed? I did not notice at all how she was dressed; anyway, there was nothing particularly noticeable in her dress, she was herself the object of interest." That is the way that a true lady is dressed, so that we notice her, and not her garments; she is so well dressed that we do not know how she is dressed, and that is the best way of dressing a sermon. Let it never be said of you, as it is sometimes said of certain popular preachers, "He did the thing so majestically, he spoke with such lofty diction, etc., etc., etc."

Never introduce anything into your discourse that would be likely to distract the attention of the hearer from the great object you have in view. If you take the sinner's mind off the main subject,—speaking after the manner of men, there is so much less likelihood of his receiving the impression you desire to convey, and, consequently, the smaller probability of his being converted. I remember once reading what Mr. Finney said in his book on "Revivals." He said that there was a person on the point of being converted, and just then an old woman, with pattens on, came shuffling up the a isle, making a great noise, and that soul was lost! I know what the evangelist meant, though I do not like the form in which the matter was put by him. The noise of the old lady's pattens probably did take off the person's mind from the thing he should have been thinking upon, and it is quite possible that he could not be brought back to exactly the same position again. We are to look to all these little things as if everything depended upon us, at the same time remembering that it is the Holy Spirit alone who can make the work effectual.

Your sermon should not take off the people's attention through its being only very distantly related to the text. There are many hearers still left who believe that there should be some sort of connection between the sermon and the text, and if they begin asking themselves, "How ever did the minister get right over there? What has his talk to do with the text?" —you will have lost their attention, and that wandering habit of yours may be a very destructive one to them; therefore, keep to your texts, brethren. If you do not, you will be like a little boy who went out fishing, and his uncle said to him, "Have you caught many fish, Samuel?" The boy answered, "I have been fishing for three hours, uncle, and I have not caught any fish, but I have lost a lot of worms." I hope you will never have to say, "I did not win any soul s for the Saviour, but I spoiled a lot of precious texts; I confused and con founded many passages of Scripture, but I did no good with them. I was not supremely anxious to learn the mind of the Spirit as revealed in the text so as to get its meaning into my own mind, though it took a deal of squeezing and packing to get my mind into the text." That is not a good thing to do; stick to your texts, brethren, as the cobbler is bidden to stick to his last, and seek to get out of the Scriptures what the Holy Spirit has put into them. Never let your hearers have to ask the question, "What has this sermon to do with the text?" If you do, the people will not be profited, and it may be that they will not be saved.

I would say to you brethren, you of these two Colleges[1], get all the education that you can, drink in everything that your tutors can possibly impart to you. It will take you all your time to get out of them all that is in them; but you should endeavour to learn all that you can, because, believe me, a want of education may hinder the work of soul-winning. That 'orribleomission of the letter "h" from places where it ought to be, that aspiration of the "h" till you exasperate it altogether,—you cannot tell what mischiefs such mistakes may cause. There was a young friend who might have been converted, for she did seem greatly impressed by your discourse; but she was so disgusted by the dreadful way in which you put in "h's" where they ought not to be, or left them out where they ought to be in, that she could not listen to you with any pleasure, and her attention was distracted from the truth by your errors of pronunciation. That letter "h" has done vast mischief, it is "the letter that killeth" in the case of a great many, and all sorts of grammatical blunders may do more harm than you can imagine. You may think, perhaps, that I am speaking of trifling matters that are hardly worthy of consideration; but I am not, for these things may cause most serious results; and as it is easy to learn to speak and write correct English, do try and know all you can of it.

Perhaps someone says, "Well, I know such-and-such a successful brother, and he was not an educated man." That is true; but mark you this, the times are altering. One young woman said to another, "I do not see why we girls need learn so many lessons. The young women before us did not know much, and yet they got married." "Yes," said her companion, " but then, you know, there were no Board Schools in them days; but now the young men will be educated, and it will be a poor look-out for us as ain't." A young man might say, "Such- and-such a minister was ungrammatical, and yet he did well;" but the people of his day were ungrammatical, too, so it did not matter so much; but now, when they have all been to the Board Schools, if they co me and listen to you, it will be a pity if their mind is taken off the solemn things which you wish them to think upon because they cannot help noticing your deficiencies of education. Even if you are not an educated man, God may bless you;

---

[1] This lecture was delivered on a Friday afternoon, when the tutors and students from Harley House came to meet their brethren at the Pastors' College.

but wisdom tells us that we should not let our want of education hinder the gospel from blessing men.

"But," possibly you say, "they must be very hypercritical to find fault like that." But, then, do not hypercritical people need saving just as much as other people? I would not have a hypercritical person who could truthfully say that my preaching so jarred upon his ear, and disturbed his mind, that he could not possibly receive the doctrine which I was trying to set before him. Did you ever hear how it was that Charles Dickens would not become a spiritualist? At a seance, he asked to see the spirit of Lindley Murray. There came in what professed to be the spirit of Lindley Murray, and Dickens asked, "Are you Lindley Murray?" The reply came, " I are." There was no hope of Dickens' conversion to spiritualism after that ungrammatical answer. You may well laugh at the story, but mind that you recollect the moral of it. You can easily see that, by forgetting when to use the nominative or accusative case of a noun or pronoun, or by using the wrong tense of a verb, you might take off the mind of your hearer from what you are trying to bring before him, and so prevent the truth from reaching his heart and conscience. Therefore, divest your sermons as much as ever you can of everything that is at all likely to take away the mind of your hearers from the one object before you. The whole attention and thought of the people must be concentrated on the truth we are setting before them if we are so to preach as to save those who come within sound of our voice.

Sixthly, I believe that *those sermons which are fullest of Christ are the most likely to be blessed to the conversion of the hearers.* Let your sermons be full of Christ, from beginning to end crammed full of the gospel. As for myself, brethren, I cannot preach anything else but Christ and His cross, for I know nothing else, and long ago, like the apostle Paul, I determined not to know anything else save Jesus Christ and Him crucified. People have often asked me, "What is the secret of your success?" I always answer that I have no other secret but this, that I have preached the gospel,— not about the gospel, but the gospel,—the full, free, glorious gospel of the living Christ who is the incarnation of the good news. Preach Jesus Christ, brethren, always and everywhere; and every time you preach be sure to have much of Jesus Christ in the sermon. You remember the story of the old minister who heard a sermon by a young man, and when he was asked by the preacher what he thought of it he was rather slow to answer, but at last he said, "If I must tell you, I did not like it at all; there was no Christ in your sermon." "No," answered the young man, "because I did not see that Christ was in the text." "Oh!" said the old minister, "but do you not know that from every little town and village and tiny hamlet in England there is a road leading to London? Whenever I get hold of a text, I say to myself, 'There is a road from here to Jesus Christ, and I mean to keep on His track till I get to Him.'" "Well," said the young man, "but suppose you are preaching from a text that says nothing about Christ?" "Then I will go over hedge and ditch but what I will get at Him." So must we do, brethren; we must have Christ in all our discourses, whatever else is in or not in them. There ought to be enough of the gospel in every sermon to save a soul. Take care that it is so when you are called to preach before Her Majesty the Queen, and if you have to preach to charwomen or chairmen, still always take care that there is the real gospel in every sermon.

I have heard of a young man asking, when he was going to preach in a certain place, "What kind of church is it? What do the people believe? What is their doctrinal view?" I will tell you how to avoid the necessity of such a question as that; preach Jesus Christ to them, and if that does not suit their doctrinal views then preach Jesus Christ the next Sunday you go; and do the same thing the next Sabbath, and the next, and the next, and never preach anything else. Those who do not like Jesus Christ must have Him preached to them till they do like Him; for they are the very people who need Him most. Recollect that all the tradesmen in the world say that they can sell their goods when there is a demand for them, but our goods create as well as supply the demand. We preach Jesus Christ to those who want him, and we also preach Him to those who do not want Him, and we keep on preaching Christ until we make them feel that they do want Him, and cannot do without Him.

Seventhly, brethren, it is my firm conviction that *those sermons are most likely to convert men that really appeal to their hearts, not those that are fired over their heads, or that are aimed only at their intellects.* I am sorry to say that I know some preachers who will never do much good in the world; they are good men, they have plenty of ability, they can speak well, and they have a good deal of shrewdness; but, somehow or other, there is a very sad omission in their nature, for to anyone who knows them, it is quite evident that they have not any heart. I know one or two men who are as dry as leather. If you were to hang them up on the wall, as you do a piece of seaweed, to tell what kind of weather it is to be, they would be no guide to you, for scarcely any weather would affect them.

But I also know some men who are the very reverse of these brethren. They are not likely to win souls, for they are themselves so flippant, and frivolous, and foolish, there is nothing serious about them, nothing to show that they are living in earnest. I cannot find any trace of a soul in them; they are too shallow to contain one, it could not live in the inch or two of water that is all that they hold, they appear to have been made without any soul, so they cannot do any good in preaching the gospel. You must have souls, brothers, if you are to look after your brothers' souls, depend upon that; as you must have a heart if you are to reach your brother's heart.

Here is another kind of man,—one who cannot weep over sinners,— what is the good of him in the ministry? He never did weep over men in his life: he never agonized before God on their behalf; he never said with Jeremiah, "Oh that my head were waters, and mine eyes a fountain of tears, that I might weep day and night for the slain of the daughter of my people!" I know a brother like this. In a meeting of ministers, after we had been confessing our shortcomings, he said that he was very much ashamed of us all. Well, no doubt, we ought to have been more ashamed of our selves than we were; but he told us that, if we had truly meant what we had said in our confessions to God, we were a disgrace to the ministry; perhaps we were. He said he was not like that; so far as he knew, he never preached a sermon without feeling that it was the best he could preach, and he did not know that he could do any better than he had done. He was a man who always studied just so many hours every day, always prayed exactly so many minutes, always preached a certain length of time, in fact, he was the most regular man I ever knew. When I heard him talk as he had done to us, I asked myself, "What does his ministry show as the result of this perfect way of doing things?" Why, it did not show anything at all that was satisfactory. He has great gifts of dispersion; for, if he goes to a full chapel, he soon empties it; yet he is, I believe, a good man in his way. I could wish that his clock would sometimes stop, or strike in the middle of the half -hour, or that something extraordinary might happen to him, because some goo d might come of it; but he is so regular and orderly, that there is no hope of his doing anything, the fault with him is that he has not any fault. You will notice, brethren, that preachers who have no faults have no excellences either; so try to avoid that flat, dead level, and everything else that makes people less likely to be converted.

Coming back to that matter of the possession of a heart, of which I was speaking, I asked a young girl, who came lately to join the

58

church, "Have you a good heart?" She replied, "Yes, sir." I said, "Have you thought over that question? Have you not an evil heart?" "Oh, yes!" she answered. "Well," I said, "how do your two answers agree?" "Why," responded the girl, "I know that I have a good heart, because God has given me a new heart and a right spirit; and I also know that I have an evil heart, for I often find it fighting against my new heart." She was right, and I had sooner feel that a minister had two hearts than that he had none at all. It must be heart-work with you, brethren, far more than head-work, if you are to win many souls. Amidst all your studies, mind that you never let your spiritual life get dry. There is no necessity that it should, although with many study has had that effect. My dear brethren, the tutors, will bear me witness that there is a very drying influence about Latin, and Greek, and Hebrew. That couplet is true,—

"Hebrew roots, as known to most,
Do flourish best on barren ground."

There is a very drying influence in the classics, and there is a very drying influence in mathematics, and you may get absorbed in any science till your heart is gone. Do not let that be the case with any of you, so that people should have to say of you, "He knows much more than he did when he first came amongst us, but he has not as much spirituality as he used to have." Take care that it never is so. Do not be satisfied with merely polishing up your grates, but stir the fire in your heart, and get your own soul all aflame with love to Christ, or else you will not be likely to be greatly used i n the winning of the souls of others.

Lastly, brethren, I think that *those sermons which have been prayed over are the most likely to convert people.* I mean those discourses that have had much real prayer offered over them, both in the preparation and the delivery, for there is much so-called prayer that is only playing at praying. I rode, some time ago, with a man who professes to work wonderful cures by the acids of a certain wood. After he had told me about his marvelous remedy, I asked him, "What is there in that to effect such cures as you profess to have wrought?" "Oh!" he answered, "it is the way in which I prepare it, much more than the stuff itself ; that is the secret of its curative properties. I rub it as hard as ever I can for a long while, and I have so much vital electricity in me that I put my very life into it." Well, well, he was only a quack, yet we may learn a lesson even from him, for the way to make sermons is to work vital electricity into them, put ting your own life and the very life of God into them by earnest prayer. The difference between a sermon that has been prayed over and one that has been pre pared and preached by a prayerless man is like the difference that Mr. Fergusson suggested in his prayer when he referred to the high priest before and after his anointing. You must anoint your sermons, brethren, and you cannot do it except by much private communion with God. May the Holy Spirit anoint ever y one of you, and richly bless you in winning souls, for our Lord Jesus Christ's sake! Amen.

OBSTACLES TO SOUL-WINNING

I have spoken to you, brethren, at different times, about soul-winning—that most royal employment. May you all become, in this sense, mighty hunters before the Lord, and bring many sinners to the Saviour! I want, at this time, to say a few words upon—

THE OBSTACLES THAT LIE IN OUR PATH AS WE SEEK TO WI N SOULS FOR CHRIST.

They are very many, and I cannot attempt to make a complete catalogue of them; but

the first, and one of the most difficult is, doubtless, *the indifference and lethargy of sinners.* All men are not alike indifferent; in fact, there are some persons who seem to have a sort of religious instinct, which influences them for good, long before they have any real love to spiritual things. But there are districts, especially rural districts, where indifference prevails; and the same state of things exists in various parts of London. It is not infidelity; the people do not care enough about religion even to oppose it. They are not concerned as to what you preach, or where you preach, for they have no interest whatever in the matter. They have no thought of God; they care nothing about Him, or His service, they only use His name in profanity. I have often noticed that any place where there is little business doing is bad for religious effort. Among the negroes of Jamaica, whenever they had not much work, there was little prosperity in the churches. I could indicate districts, not far from here, where business is slack; and there you will find that there is very little good being done. All along the valley of the Thames, there are places where a man might preach his heart out, and kill himself; but there is little or nothing of good being accomplished in those regions, just as there is no active business life there.

Now, whenever you meet with indifference, as you ma y do, my dear brother, in the place where you go to preach,—indifference affecting your own people, and even your own deacons seeming to be tinged with it,—what are you to do? Well, your only hope of overcoming it is, to be doubly in earnest yourself. Keep your own zeal all alive, let it be even vehement, burning, blazing, all-consuming. Stir the people up somehow; and if all your earnestness seems to be in vain, still blaze and burn; and if that has no effect upon your hearers, go elsewhere as the Lord may direct you. This indifference or lethargy, that possesses the minds of some men, is very likely to have an evil influence upon our preaching; but we must strive and struggle against it, and try to wake both ourselves and our hearers up. I would far rather have a man an earnest, intense opposer of the gospel than have him careless and indifferent. You cannot do much with a man if he will not speak abou t religion, or will not come to hear what you have to say concerning the things of God. You might as well have him a downright infidel, like a very leviathan covered with scales of blasphemy, as have him a mere earth-worm wriggling away out of reach.

Another very great obstacle to soul-winning is *unbelief*. You know that it is written of the Lord Jesus when in "His own country that "He did not many mighty works there because of their unbelief." This evil exists in all unregenerate hearts, but in some men it takes a very pronounced form. They do think about religion, but they do not believe in the truth of God which we preach to them. Their opinion is to them more weighty, more worthy of belief, than God's inspired declarations; they will not accept anything that is revealed in the Scriptures. These people are very hard to influence; but I would warn you not to fight them with their own weapons. I do not believe that infidels ever are won by argument; or, if so, it very seldom happens. The argument that convinces men of the reality of religion, is that which they gather from the holiness and earnestness of those who profess to be Christ's followers. As a rule, they barricade their minds against the assaults of reason and if we give our pulpits over to arguing with them, we shall often be doing more harm than good. In all probability, only a very small portion of our audience will understand what we are talking about; and while we are trying to do them good, most likely we shall be teaching infidelity to others who do not know anything about such things, and the first knowledge they eve r have of certain heresies will have come to them from our lips. Possibly our refutation of the error may not have been perfect, and many a young mind may have been tinctured with unbelief through listening to our attempted exposure of it. I believe that you will rout unbelief by your faith rather than by you r reason; by your belief, and your acting up to your conviction of the truth, you will do more good than by any argument, however strong it may be. There is a friend who sits to hear me generally every Sabbath. "What do you think?" he said to me, one day, "you are my only link with better things; but you are an awful man in my estimation, for you have not the slightest sympathy with me." I rep lied, "No, I have not; or, rather, I have not the least sympathy with your unbelief." "That makes me cling to you, for I fear that I shall always remain as I am; but when I see your calm faith, and perceive how God blesses you in exercising it, and know what you accomplish through the power of that faith, I say to myself, 'Jack, you are a fool.'" I said to him, "You are quite right in that verdict; and the sooner you come to my way of thinking, the better, for nobody can be a bigger fool than the man who does not believe in God." One of these days I expect to see him converted; there is a continual battle between us, but I never answer one of his arguments. I said to him once, "If you believe that I am a liar, you are free to think so if you like; but I testify what I do know, and state what I have seen, and tasted, and handled, and felt, and you ought to believe my testimony, for I have no possible object to serve in deceiving you." That man would have beaten me long ago if I had fired at him with the paper pellets of reason. So, I advise you to fight unbelief with belief, falsehood with the truth, and never to cut and pare down the gospel to try to make it fit in with the follies and fancies of men.

A third obstacle in the way of winning souls is that fatal *delay* which men so often make. I do not know whether this evil is not on the whole more widespread and mischievous than the indifference and lethargy and unbelief of which I have spoken. Many a man says to us what Felix said to Paul, "Go thy way for this time; when I have a convenient season, I will call for thee." Such an individual gets into the border country, he seems to be within a few steps of Emmanuel's land, and yet he parries our home-thrusts, and puts us off by saying, "Yes, I will think the matter over, it shall not be long before I decide." There is nothing like pressing men for a speedy decision, and getting the m to settle at once this all- important question. Never mind if they do find fault with your teaching; it is always right to preach what God says, and His word is, "Behold, now is the accepted time; behold, now is the day of salvation."

 This leads me to mention another obstacle to soul-w inning, which is the same thing in another form, viz., *carnal security*. Many men fancy that they are quite safe; they have not really tested the foundation on which they are building, to see that it is sound and firm, but they suppose that all is well. If they are not good Christians, they can at least say that they are rather better than some who are Christians, or who call themselves by that name; and if there is anything lacking in t hem, they can at any time put on the finishing touch, and make themselves fit for God's presence. Thus they have no fear; or, if they do fear at all, they do not live in constant dread of that eternal destruction from the presence of the Lord, and from the glory of His power, which will certainly be their portion unless they repent, and believe in the Lord Jesus Christ. Against these people we ought to thunder day and night. Let us plainly proclaim to them that the unbelieving sinner is "condemned already", and that he is certain to perish everlastingly if he does not trust in Christ. We ought so to preach as to make every sinner tremble in his seat; and if he will not come to the Saviour, he ought at least to have a hard time of it while he stops away from Him. I am afraid that we sometimes preach smooth things, too soothing and agreeable, and that we do not set before men their real danger as we should. If we shun in this respect to declare all the counsel of God, part at least of the responsibility of their ruin will lie at our door.

Another obstacle to soul-winning is despair. The pendulum swings first one way and then the other; and the man who yesterday had no fear, to-day has no hope. There are thousands who have heard the gospel, and yet live in a kind of despair of its power being ever exerted upon the m. Perhaps they have been brought up among people who taught them that the work of salvation was something of God altogether apart from the sinner; and so they say that, if they are to be saved, they will be saved. You know that this teaching contains a great truth, and yet, if it is left by itself, without qualification, it is a horrible falsehood. It is fatalism, not predestination, that makes men talk as if there is nothing whatever for them to do, or that there is nothing they can do. There is no likelihood of anyone being saved while he gives you this as his only hope, "If salvation is for me, it will come to me in due time." You may meet with people who talk thus; and when you have said all you can, they will remain as if they were cased in steel, with no sense of responsibility, because there is no hope awakened in their spirit. Oh, if they would but hope that they might receive mercy by asking for it, and so be led to cast their guilty souls on Christ, what a blessing it would be! Let us preach full and free salvation to all who trust in Jesus, so that we may, if possible, reach these people. If the carnally secure should be tempted to presume, some who are quietly despairing may pluck up heart, and hope, and may venture to come to Christ.

No doubt a great obstacle to soul-winning is the love of sin. "Sinlieth at the door." There are many men who never get saved because of some secret lust; it may be that they are living in fornication. I remember well the case of a man, of whom I thought that he would certainly come to Christ. He was fully aware of the power of the gospel, and seemed to be impressed under the preaching of the Word; but I found out that he had become entangled with a woman who was not his wife, and that he was still living in sin while professing to be seeking the Saviour. When I heard that, I could easily understand how it was that he could not obtain peace; whatever tenderness of hear the may have felt, there was this woman always holding him in the bondage of sin.

There are some men who are guilty of dishonest transactions in business; you will not see them saved all the while they continue to act so. If they will not give up that trickery, they cannot be saved. There are others who are drinking to excess. People who drink, you know, are often very easily affected under our preaching; they have a watery eye, their drinking has made them t-headed, and there is a maudlin kind of sensitiveness in them; but as long as a man clings to "the cup of devils" he will not be likely to come to Christ. With others it is some secret sin, or some hidden lust that is the great difficulty. One says that he cannot help flying into a passion, another declares that he cannot give up getting drunk, while another laments that he cannot find peace, whereas the root of the mischief is that there is a harlot who stands in his way. In all these cases, we have only to keep on preaching the truth, and God will help us to aim the arrow at the joint in the sinner's harness.

Another obstacle is put in our way by *men's self righteousness*. They have not committed any of these sins I have mentioned, they have kept all the commandments from their youth up; what lack the y yet? There is no room for Christ in a full heart; and when a man is clothed from head to foot with his own righteousness, he has no need of the righteousness of Christ; at least, he is not conscious of his need, and if the gospel does not convince him of it, Moses must come with the law, and show him what his true state is. That is the real difficulty in many, many cases; the man does not co me to Christ because he is not conscious that he is lost, he does not ask to be lifted up because he does not know that he is a fallen creature, he does not feel that he has any need of divine mercy or forgiveness, and therefore he does not see k it.

Once more, there are some with whom all we say has no effect because of their *utter worldliness*. This worldliness takes two shapes; in the poor, it is the result of grinding poverty. When a man has scarcely enough bread to eat, and hardly knows how to get clothes to put on, when at home he hears the cries of his little children, and looks into the face of his over-worked wife, we must preach very wonderfully if we are to secure his attention, and make him think about the world to come. "What shall we eat? what shall we drink? and wherewithal shall we be clothed?" are questions that press very heavily upon the poor. To a hungry man, Christ is very lovely when He has a loaf of bread in His hand. Our Lord so appeared when He was breaking the bread and fish for the multitude, for even He did not disdain to feed the hungry; and when we can relieve the wants of the destitute, we may be doing a necessary thing to them, and placing them where they may be capable of listening with profit to the gospel of Christ. The other kind of worldliness comes of having too much of this world, or at least of making too much of this world. The gentleman must be fashionable, his daughters must be dressed in the best style, his sons must learn to dance, and so on. This sort of worldliness has been the great cur se of our Nonconformist churches.

Then there is another kind of man who is from morning to night grinding away at the shop; his one business seems to be to put up the shutters, and take them down again; he will rise early, and sit up late, and eat the bread of carefulness, so as to make money. What can we do for these covetous persons? How can we ever hope to touch the hearts of these m en whose one aim is to be rich, the people who scrape up the halfpennies and farthings? Economy is good, but there is an economy that becomes parsimony, and that parsimony becomes the habit of these miserly folk. Some will even go to chapel because it is the proper and respectable thing, and they hope to gain customers by going. Judas remained unconverted even in the company of the Lord Jesus Christ, and we have some people still among us in whose ears the thirty pieces of silver chink so loudly that the sound of the gospel cannot be heard by them.

I may mention one more obstacle to soul-winning, that is, the obstacle there is with some men through their habits, and resorts, and company. How can we expect a working-man to go home, and sit all the evening in the one room that he has to live in, and sleep in? Perhaps there are two or three children crying, and linen drying, and all sorts of things to produce discomfort. The man comes in, and his wife is scolding, his children are crying, and the linen is drying; what would you do if you were in his place? Suppose you were not Christian men, would you not go somewhere or other? You cannot walk the streets, and you know that there is a cosy room at the public-ho use, with its flashing gaslight, or there is the gin-palace at the corner, where everything is bright and cheerful, and where there are plenty of jolly companions. Well, now, you cannot hope to be the means of saving men while the y go to such places, and while they meet with the company that is found there. All the good that they receive from the hymns they heard on the Sabbath is driven away as they listen to the comic songs in the drink-shop, and all remembrance of the services of the sanctuary is obliterated by the very questionable tales that are told in the bar-parlour. Hence the great mercy of having a place where working-men can come and sit in safety, or of having a Blue Ribbon meeting, a gathering where it may not be all singing, nor all preaching, nor all praying, but where there is something of all these things. Here the man is enabled to get out of the former habits which seemed to hold him fast, and by-and-by he does not go to the public-house at all, but he has two rooms, or perhaps a little cottage, so that his wife can dry the linen in the backyard, and now he finds that the baby does not cry so much as he used to do, probably because his mother has more to give him; and everything gets better and brighter now that the man has forsaken his former resorts. I think a Christian minister is quite justified in using all right and lawful means to wean the people from their evil associations, and it may be well sometimes to do that which seems to be extraordinary if thereby we can by any means win men to the Lord Jesus Christ. That must be our one aim in all that we do; and whatever obstacles may be in our pathway, we must seek the aid of the Holy Spirit that they may be removed, and that thus souls may be saved, and God may be glorified.

HOW TO INDUCE OUR PEOPLE TO WIN SOULS

I have spoken to you at different times, brethren, about the great work of our lives, which is that of winning souls. I have tried to show you various ways in which we win souls, the qualifications both towards God and towards man of those who are likely to be used in winning souls, the kind of sermons that are most likely to win souls, and also the obstacles in the way of soul-winners. Now I should like, this afternoon, to talk to you upon another part of the subject; that is,—

HOW CAN WE INDUCE OUR PEOPLE TO BECOME SOUL-WINNERS?

You are aspiring, each of you, in due time, to become pastors of churches, unless the Lord should call you to be evangelists, or missionaries to the heathen. Well, you commence at first as single sowers of the good seed of the kingdom, and you go forth scattering from your own basket your own handfuls. You desire, however, to become spiritual farmers, and to have a certain acreage which you will not sow entirely yourself, but you will have servants who will aid you in the work. Then, to one you will say, "Go ," and he will go forthwith; or, "Come," and he will come at once; and you will seek to lead them into the art and mystery of seed-sowing, so that, after a while, you may have large numbers of persons round about you doing this good work, and thus a far greater acreage may be brought into cultivation for the great Husbandman. There are some of us who have, by God's grace, been so richly blessed that we have all around us a large number of persons who have been spiritually quickened through our instrumentality, people who have been aroused under our ministry, who have been instructed and strengthened by us, and who are all doing good service for God.

Let me warn you not to look for all this at the first, for it is the work of time. Do not expect to get, in the first year of your pastorate, that result which is the reward of twenty years' continuous toil in one place. Young men sometimes make a very great mistake in the way they talk to t hose who never saw them until about six weeks ago. They cannot speak with the authority of one who has been as a father among his people, having been with them for twenty or thirty years; or if they do, it becomes a sort of foolish affectation on their part, and it is equally foolish to expect the people to be all a t once the same as they might be after they have been trained by a godly minister for a quarter of a century. It is true that you may go to a church where somebody else has faithfully laboured for many years, and long sown the good see d, and you may find your sphere of labour in a most blessed and prosperous state, and happy will you be if you can thus jump into a good man's shoes, and follow the path he has been treading. It is always a good sign when the horses do not know that they have a new driver; and you, my brother, inexperienced as you are, will be a very happy man if that should be your lot; but the probability is that you will go to a place that has been allowed to run almost to ruin, possibly to one that has been altogether neglected.

Perhaps you will try to get the principal deacon to imitate your earnestness; you are at a white heat, and when you find him cold as steel, you will be like a piece of hot iron dipped into a pail of water. He m ay tell you that he recollects others who were at first just as hot as you are, hut they soon cooled down, and he will not be surprised if you do the same. He is a very good man, but then he is old, and you are young, and we cannot put young heads on old shoulders even if we were to attempt to do it. Perhaps next you will resolve to try some of the young people; possibly you can get on better with them; but they do not understand you, they are backward and retiring, and they soon fly off at a tangent. You must not be surprised if this is your experience. Very likely you will have almost everything to do in connection with the work; at all events, expect that it may be so, and then you will not be disappointed if it so turns out. It may be otherwise; but you will be wise if you go into the ministry expecting not to find any very great assistance from the people in the work of soul- winning. Anticipate that you will have to do it yourself and to do it alone; and begin doing it alone, sow the seed, tramp up and down the field, always looking to the Lord of the harvest to bless your labour, and also looking forward to the time when through your efforts, under the divine blessing, instead of a plot of land that is apparently covered with nettles, or full of stones, or weeds, or thorns, or partly trodden down, you shall have a Well-tilled farm in which you may sow the seed to the best advantage, and on which you shall have a little army of fellow-labourers to aid you in the service. Yet all that is the work of time.

I should certainly say to you, do not expect all this at least for some months after you settle down to work. Revivals, if they are genuine, do not always come the moment we whistle for them. Try and whistle for the wind, and see if it will come. The great rain was given in answer to Elijah's prayers; but not even then the first time he prayed, and we must pray again, and again, and again, and at last the cloud will appear, and the showers out of the cloud. Wait a while, work on, plod on, plead on, and in due time the blessing will be given, and you shall find that you have the church after y our own ideal, but it will not come to you all at once. I do not think Mr. John Angell James, of Birmingham, saw much fruit to his ministry for many years. As far as I remember, Carr's Lane Chapel was not the place of any great notoriety before he preached there; but he kept on steadily preaching the gospel, and a t last he drew around him a company of godly people who helped to make him the greatest power for good that Birmingham had at that time. Try to do just the same, and do not expect to see all at once what he and other faithful minister s have only been able to accomplish in many years.

In order to secure this end of gathering around you a band of Christians who will themselves be soul-winners, I should recommend you not to go to work according to any set rule, for what would be right at one time might not be wise at another, and that which would be best for one place would not be so good elsewhere. Sometimes, the very best plan would be to call all the members of the church together, tell them what you would like to see, and plead earnestly with them that each one should become for God a soul-winner. Say to them, "I do not want to be your pastor simply that I may preach to you; but I long to see souls saved, and to see those who are saved seeking to win others for the Lord Jesus Christ. You know how the Pentecostal blessing was given when the whole church met, with one accord in one place, and continued in prayer and supplication, the Holy Spirit was poured out, and thousands were converted. Cannot we get together in like manner, and all of us cry mightily to God for a blessing?" That might succeed in arousing them. Calling them together, and earnestly pleading with them about the matter, pointing out what you wish them specially to do, and to ask of God, may be like setting a light to dry fuel; but, on the other hand, nothing may come of it because of their lack of sympathy in the work of soul-saving. They may say, "It is a very nice meeting, and our pastor expects a good deal of us, and we all wish he may get it," and there it will end so far as they are concerned.

Then, if that should not succeed, God may lead you to begin with one or two. There is usually some "choice young man" in each congregation; and as you notice deeper spirituality in him than in the rest of the members, you might say to him, "Will you come down to my house on such -and-such an evening that we may have a little prayer together?" You can gradually increase the number to two or three, godly young men if possible, or you may begin with some gracious matron, who perhaps lives nearer to God than any of the men, and whose prayers would help you more than theirs. Having secured their sympathy, you might say to them, "Now we will try i f we cannot influence the whole church; we will begin with our fellow-members before we go to the outsiders. Let us try and be ourselves always at the prayer-meetings, to set an example to the rest, and let us also arrange to have gatherings for prayer in our own houses, and seek to get our brethren and sister s to them. You, good sister, can get half-a-dozen sisters together into your house for a little meeting; and you, brother, can say to a few friends, 'Could we not meet together to pray for our pastor?" ' Sometimes, the most effectual way to burn a house is to do it by pouring petroleum down the middle of it, and setting fire to it, as the ladies and gentlemen (!) did in Paris in the days of the Commune; and, sometimes, shortest method is to light it at the four corners. I have never tried either plan; but that is what I think. I like to burn churches rather than houses, because they do not burn down, they burn up, and keep on burning when the fire is of the right sort. When a bush is nothing but a bush, it i s soon consumed when it is set on fire; but when it is a bush that burns on and is not consumed, we may know that God is there. So is it with a church that is f laming with holy zeal. Your work, brethren, is to set your church on fire somehow. You may do it by speaking to the whole of the members, or you may do it by speaking to the few choice spirits, but you must do it somehow. Have a secret society for this sacred purpose, turn yourselves into a band of celestial Fenians whose aim it is to set the whole church on fire. If you do so, the devil will not like it, and you will cause him such disquiet that he will seek the utter breakup of the union, and that is just what we want; we do not desire anything but war to the knife between the church and the world and all its habits and customs. But again I say, all this will take time. I have seen some fellows run so fast at first that they have soon become like broken-winded horses, and truly that is a pitiable sight; so take time, brethren, and do not look for everything you desire to be secured all at once.

I suppose that, in most places, there is a prayer-meeting on Monday night. If you want your people as well as yourself to be soul-winners, try and keep up the prayer meetings all you can. Do not be like certain ministers in the suburbs of London, who say that they cannot get the people out to a prayer-meeting and a lecture, too, so they have one week-night meeting for prayer, at which they give a short address. One lazy man said, the other day, that the week-night address was almost as bad as delivering a sermon, so he has a prayer-meeting and a lecture combined in one, and it is neither a prayer-meeting nor a lecture, it is neither fish, flesh, fowl, nor good red-herring; and soon he will give it up because he says it is no good, and I am sure the people think so, too. And after that, why should he not give up one of the Sunday services? The same reasoning might apply to that as to the week-night meeting. I saw, in an American paper to-day, the following paragraph:—" The well-known fact is again going the rounds that, in Mr. Spurgeon's Church in London, the regular hearers absent themselves one Sunday evening every three months, and the house is given up to strangers. English 'boasting i s excluded' in this matter. Our American Christianity is of so noble a type that hosts of our people give up their pews to strangers every Sunday night in the y ear." I hope it will not be so with your people, brethren, either with respect to the Sabbath services or the prayer-meetings.

If I were you, I would make that prayer-meeting a special feature of my ministry; let it be such a prayer-meeting that there is not the like of it within seven thousand miles. Do not go walking into the prayer-meeting, as so many do, to say anything or nothing that may occur to you at the moment; but do your best to make the meeting interesting to all who are there; and do not hesitate to tell good Mr. Snooks that, God helping you, he shall not pray for five-and-twenty minutes. Earnestly entreat him to cut it short, and if he does not, then stop him. If a man came into my house intending to cut my wife's throat, I would reason with him as to the wrong of it, and then I would effectually prevent him from doing her any harm; and I love the church almost as much as I love my dear wife. So, if a man will p ray long, he may pray long somewhere else, but not at the meeting over which I am presiding. Tell him to finish it up at home if he cannot pray in public for a reasonable length of time. If the people seem dull and heavy, get them to sing Moody and Sankey hymns; and then, when they can sing them all by heart, do not have any more "Moody and Sankey" for a time, but go back to your own hymn-book.

Keep up the prayer-meeting, whatever else flags; it is the great business evening of the week, the best service between the Sabbaths; be you sure to make it so. If you find that your people cannot com e in the evening, then try and have a prayer-meeting when they can come. You might get a good meeting in the country at half-past four in the morning. Why not? You would get more people at five o'clock in the morning than you would at five o'clock at the other end of the day. I believe that a prayer-meeting at six o'clock in the morning among agricultural people would attract many; they would drop in, and just have a few words of prayer, and be glad of the opportunity. Or you might have it at twelve o'clock at night; you would find some people out then whom you could not get at any other time. Try one o'clock, or two o'clock, or three o'clock, or any hour of the day or night, so as somehow or other to get the people out to pray; and if they cannot be induced to come to the meetings, go to their house, and say, "I am going to have a prayer-meeting in your parlour." "Oh, dear! my wife will be in a state." "Oh, no! tell her not to trouble, for we can go into the coach-house, or garden, or anywhere, but we must have a prayer-meeting here." If they will not come to the prayer-meeting, we must go to them; suppose that fifty of us go trudging down the street, and hold a meeting in the open-air; well, there might be many worse things than that. Remember how the women fought the liquor-sellers in America when they prayed them out of the traffic. If we cannot stir the people without doing extraordinary things, in the name of all that is good and great let us do extraordinary things, but somehow we must keep up the prayer-meetings, for they are at the very secret source of power with God and with men.

We must *always be an earnest example ourselves.* A slow-coach minister will not have a lively zealous church, I am sure. A man who is indifferent, or who does his work as if he took it as easily as he could, ought not to—expect to have a people around him who are in earnest about the salvation of souls. I know that you, brethren, desire to have about you a band of Christians who long for the salvation of their friends and neighbours, a set of people who will be always expecting that God will bless the preaching of your sermons, who will watch the countenances of your hearers to see if they are getting impressed, and who will be sorely distressed if there are no conversions, and greatly troubled if souls are not saved. Perhaps they would not complain to you if that were the case, but they would cry to God on your behalf. Possibly, they would also speak to you about the matter. I remember one of my deacons saying to me, as we were going down to the communion, one Sabbath evening, when we had only fourteen to receive into the church, "Governor, this won't pay." We had been accustomed to have forty or fifty every month, and the good man was not satisfied with a smaller number. I agreed with him that we must have more than that in the future if it was possible. I suppose some brethren would have felt annoyed to have had anything like that remark made to them; but I was delighted with what my good deacon said; for it was just what I myself felt.

Then, next, *we want around us Christians who are willing to do all they can to help in the work of winning souls.* There are numbers of people who cannot be reached by the pastor. You must try to get some Christian workers who will "button-hole" people, you know what I mean. It is pretty close work when you hold a friend by a lock of his hair, or by his coat-button. Absalom did not find it easy to get away when he was caught in the oak by the hair of his head. So, try to get at close quarters with sinners ; talk gently to them till you have whispered them into the kingdom of heaven, till you have told into their ears the blessed story that will bring peace and joy to their heart. We want, in the Church of Christ, a band of well-trained sharps hooters, who will pick the people out individually, and be always on the watch for all who come into the place, not annoying them, but making sure that they do not go away without having had a personal warning, a personal invitation, and a personal exhortation to come to Christ. We want to train all our people for this service, so as to make Salvation Armies out of them. Every man, woman, or child who is in our churches should be set to work for the Lo rd. Then they will not relish the fine sermons that the Americans seem to delight in so much; but they will say," Pooh! Flummery! We don't want that kind of thing." What do people who are at work in the harvest-field want with thunder and lightning? They want just to rest a while under a tree, to wipe the sweat from their foreheads, to refresh themselves after their toil, and then to get to work again. Our preaching ought to be like the address of a commander-in-chief to his army, "There are the enemy; do not let me know where they are tomorrow." Something short, something sweet, something that stirs and impresses them, is what our people need.

We are sure to get the blessing we are seeking *when the whole atmosphere in which we are living is favourable to soul-winning.* I remember one of our friends saying to me, one evening," There will be sure to be a blessing to-night, there is such a lot of dew about." May you often know what it is to preach where there is plenty of dew! The Irishman said that it was no use to irrigate while the sun was shining, for he had noticed that, whenever it rained, there were clouds about, so that the sun was hidden. There was a great deal of sense in that observation, more than appears at first sight, as there usually is in Hibernian statements. The shower benefits the plant s because everything is suitable for the rain to come down, the shaded sky, the humidity of the atmosphere, the general feeling of everything is damp all around; but if you were to pour the same quantity of water down while the sun was shining brightly, the leaves would probably be turned yellow, and in the heat they would shrivel and die. Any gardener would tell you that he is always careful to water the flowers in the evening when the sun is off them. This is the reason why irrigation, however well it is done, is not so beneficial as the rain; there must be a favourable influence in the whole atmosphere if the plants and flowers are to derive benefit from the moistening. It is just so in spiritual things. I have often noticed that, when God blesses my ministry to an unusual extent, the people in general are in a praying mood. It is a grand thing to preach in an atmosphere full of the dew of the Spirit. I know what it is to preach with it; and, alas! I know what it is to preach without it. Then is it like Gilboa, when there was no dew nor rain. You may preach, and you may hope that God will bless your message; but it is no use. I hope it will not be so with you, brethren. Perhaps your lot will be cast where some dear brother has long been toiling, and praying, and labouring for the Lord, and you will find all the people just ready for the blessing.

I often feel, when I go out to preach, that there i s no credit due to me, for everything is in my favour. There sit the good folk, with their mouths open, waiting for the blessing; almost everybody there is expecting me to say something good, and because they are all looking for it, it does them good, and when I am gone, they keep on praying for the blessing, and they get it. When a man is put on a horse that runs away with him, he must ride; that is just how it has frequently been with me, the blessing has been given because all the surroundings were favourable. You may often trace the happy results not only to the preacher's discourse, but to all the circumstances connected with its delivery. It was so with Peter's sermon that brought three thousand souls to Christ on the day of Pentecost; there never was a better sermon preached, it was a plain personal message likely to convince people of the sin of their treatment of the Saviour in putting Him to death; but I do not attribute the conversions to the apostle's words alone, for there were clouds about, the whole atmosphere was damp; as my friend said to me, there was "plenty of dew about." Had not the disciples been long continuing in prayer and supplication—for the descent of the Spirit, and had not the Holy Ghost descended upon every one of them as well as upon Peter? In the fulness of time, the Pentecostal blessing was poured out most copiously. Whenever a church gets into the same state as that of the apostles and disciples at that memorable period, the whole heavenly electricity is concentrated at that particular spot. Yet you re member that even Christ Himself could not do many mighty works in some places because of the people's unbelief, and I am sure that all His servants who are thoroughly in earnest are at times hampered in the same way. Some of our brethren who are here have, I fear, a worldly, Christ-less people; s till, I am not sure that they ought to run away from them; I think that, if possible, they should stop, and try to make them more Christ like.

It is true that I have had the other sort of experience, as well as the joyous one I have been describing. I remember preaching, one night, in a place where they had not had a minister for some time. When I reached the chapel, I did not have any kind of welcome; the authorities were to receive pecuniary benefit if nothing else from my visit, but they did not welcome me at all; they said, in fact, that there had been a majority at the church- meeting in favour of inviting me, but the deacons did not approve of it because they did not think I was "sound." There were some brethren and sisters from other churches there; they seemed pleased and profited, but the people who belonged to the place did not get a blessing; they had not expected one, so of course they did not receive it. When the service was over, I went into the vestry, and there stood the two deacons, one on each side of the mantelpiece. I said to them, "Are you the deacons?" "Yes," they answered. "The church does not prosper, does it?" I asked. "No," they replied. "I should not think it would with such deacons," I said. "Did I know anything against them?" they asked. "No," I said," but I did not know anything in their favour." I thought that, if I could not get at them in the mass, I would try what I could do with one or two. I was glad to know that my sermon or my remarks afterwards led to an improvement, and there is one of our brethren there, and doing well to this day. One of the deacons was so irritated by what I said that he left the place, but the other deacon was irritated the right way, so that he remained there, and laboured and prayed until better days came. It is hard when you are rowing against wind and tide, but it is worse even than that if you have a horse on the bank pulling a rope, and dragging your boat the other way. Well, never mind, brethren, if that is your case, but work away all the harder, and pull the horse into the water. Still, remember that when once a favourable atmosphere is created, then the difficulty is to maintain it. You notice that I said, "When the atmosphere is created," and that expression reminds us how little we can do, or rather that we can do nothing without God, for it is He who has to do with atmospheres, He alone can create them and maintain them; therefore, our eyes must be continually lifted up to Him, whence cometh all our help.

It may happen that some of you do preach very earnestly and well, and sermons that are likely to be blessed, and yet you do not see sinners saved. Well, do not leave off preaching; but say to yourself, "I must try to gather around me a number of people who will be all praying with me and for me, and who will talk to their friends about the things of God, and who will so live and labour that the Lord will give a blessed shower of grace because all the surroundings are suitable thereto, and help to make the blessing come. I have heard ministers say that, when they have preached i n the Tabernacle, there has been something in the congregation that has had a wonderfully powerful effect upon them. I think it is because we have good prayer-meetings, because there is an earnest spirit of prayer among the people, and because so many of them are on the watch for souls. There is one brother especially who is always looking after any hearers who have been impressed; I call Him my hunting dog, and he is ever ready to pick up the birds I have shot, and bring them to me. I have known him waylay them one after another, that he might bring them to Jesus; and I rejoice that I have other friends of this kin d. When our brethren, Fullerton and Smith, had been conducting some special service s for a very eminent preacher who is in the habit of using rather long words, he said that the evangelists had the faculty for "the precipitation of decision." He meant that the Lord blessed them in bringing men to decision for Christ. It is a grand thing when a man has the faculty for the precipitation of decision but it is an equally grand thing when he has a number of people around Him who say to each hearer, after every service, "Well, friend, did you enjoy that discourse? Was there something in it for you? Are you saved? Do you know the way of salvation?"

Always have your own Bible ready, and turn to the passages you want to quote to the enquirers. I often noticed that friend of mine, of whom I spoke just now, and he seemed to me to open his Bible at most appropriate passages, he appeared to have them all ready, and handy, so that he would be sure to hit on the right texts. You know the sort of texts I mean, just those that a seeking soul wants:—" The Son of man is come to seek and to save that which was lost." "He that believeth on the Son hath everlasting life." " The blood of Jesus Christ His Son cleanseth us from all sin." "Him that cometh to Me I will in no wise cast out." "Whosoever shall call upon the name of the Lord shall be saved." Well, this brother has a number of such passages printed in bold type, and fastened inside his Bible, so that he can refer to the right one in a moment, and many troubled souls has he thus led to the Saviour. You will not be unwise if you adopt some such method as he has found so exceedingly helpful.

Now lastly, brethren, do not be afraid when you go to a place, and find it in a very bad condition. It is a fine thing for a young man to begin with a real downright bad prospect, for, with the right kind of work, there must come an improvement some time or other. If the chapel is all but empty when you go to it, it cannot well be in a much worse state than that and the probability is that you will be the means of bringing some into the church, and so making matters better. If there is any place where I would choose to labour, it would be just on the borders of the infernal lake, for I really believe that it would bring more glory to God to work among those who are accounted the worst of sinners. If your ministry is blessed to such people as these, they will be likely to cling to you through your whole life; but the very worst sort of people are those who have long been professing Christians, but who are destitute of grace, having a name to live, and yet being dead. Alas! there are people like that among our deacons, and among our church-members, and we cannot get them out; and, as long as they remain, they exert a most baneful influence. It is dreadful to have dead members where every single part of the body should be instinct with divine life; yet in many cases it is so, and we are powerless to cure the evil. We must let the tares grow until the harvest; but the best thing to do, when you cannot root up the tares, is to water the wheat, for there is nothing that will keep back the tares like good strong wheat. I have known ungodly men who have had the place made so hot for them that they have been glad to clear right out of the church. They have said, "The preaching is too strong for us, and these people are too Puritanical and too strict to suit us." What a blessing it is when that is the case! We did not wish to drive them away by preaching the truth; but as they went of their own accord, we certainly do not want them back, and we will leave them where they are, praying the Lord, in the greatness of His grace, to turn them from the error of their ways, and to bring them to Himself, and then we shall be glad to have them back with us to live and labour for the Lord.

HOW TO RAISE THE DEAD

Fellow-labourers in the vineyard of the Lord, let me call your attention to a most instructive miracle wrought by the prophet Elisha, as recorded in the fourth chapter of the Second Book of Kings. The hospitality of the Shunammite woman had been rewarded by the gift of a son; but, alas! all earthly mercies are of uncertain tenure, and after certain days the child fell sick and died.

The distressed but believing mother hastened at once to the man of God; through him God had spoken the promise which fulfilled her heart's desire, and she resolved to plead her case with him, that he might lay it before his Divine Master, and obtain for her an answer of peace. Elis ha's action is recorded in the following verses:—

"Then he said to Gehazi, Gird up thy loins, and take my staff in thine hand, and go thy way: if thou meet any man, salute him not; and if any salute thee, answer him not again: and lay my staff upon the face of the child. And the mother of the child said, As the LORD liveth, and as thy soul liveth, I will not leave thee. And he arose, and followed her. And Gehazi passed on before them, and laid the staff upon the face of the child; but there was neither voice, nor hearing. Wherefore he went again to meet him, and told him, saying, The child is not awaked. And when Elisha was come into the house, behold, the child was dead, and laid upon his bed. He went in therefore, and shut the door upon them twain, and prayed unto the LORD. And he went up, and lay upon the child, and put his mouth upon his month, and his eyes upon his eyes, and his hands upon his hands: and he stretched himself upon the child; and the flesh of the child waxed warm. Then he returned, and walked in the house to and fro; and went up, and stretched himself upon him: and the child sneezed s even times, and the child opened his eyes. And he called Gehazi, and said, Call this Shunammite. So he called her. And when she was come in unto him, he said, Take up thy son. Then she went in, and fell at his feet, and bowed hersel f to the ground, and took up her son, and went out." — 2 Kings 4:29-37.

The position of Elisha in this case is exactly your position, brethren, in relation to your work for Christ. Elisha had to deal with a dead child. It is true that, in his instance, it was natural death; but the

79

death with which you have to come in contact is not the less real death because it is spiritual. The boys and girls in your classes are, as surely as grown-up people, "dead in trespasses and sins." May none of you fail fully to realize the state in which all human beings are naturally found! Unless you have a very clear sense of the utter ruin and spiritual death of your children, you will be incapable of being made a blessing to them. Go to them, I pray you, not as to sleepers whom you can by your own power awaken from their slumber, but as to spiritual corpses who can only be quickened by a power divine. Elisha's great object was not to cleanse the dead body, or embalm it with spices, or wrap it in fine linen, or place it in an appropriate posture, and then leave it still a corpse: he aimed at nothing less than the restoration of the child to life. Beloved teachers, may you never be content with aiming at secondary benefits, or even with realising them; may you strive for the grandest of all ends, the salvation of immortal souls! Your business is not merely to teach the children in you r classes to read the Bible, not barely to inculcate the duties of morality, nor even to instruct them in the mere letter of the gospel, but your high calling is to be the means, in the hands of God, of bringing life from heaven to dead souls. Your teaching on the Lord's-day will have been a failure if your children remain dead in sin. In the case of the secular teacher, the child's fair proficiency in knowledge will prove that the instructor has not lost his pains; but in your case, even though your youthful charge should grow up to be respectable members of society, though they should become regular attendants upon the means of grace, you will not feel that your petitions to heaven have been answered, nor your desires granted to you, nor your highest ends attained, unless something more is done,—unless, in fact, it can be said of your children, "The Lord hath quickened them together with Christ."

Resurrection, then, is our aim! To raise the dead is our mission! We are like Peter at Joppa, or Paul at Troas, we have a young Dorcas or Eutychus to bring to life. How is so strange a work to be achieved? If we yield to unbelief, we shall be staggered by the evident fact that the work to which the Lord has called us is quite beyond our own personal power. we cannot raise the dead. If asked to do so, we might each one of us, like the king of Israel, rend our clothes, and say, "Am I God, to kill and to make alive?" We are, however, no more powerless than Elisha, for he of himself could not restore the Shunammite's son. It is true that we by ourselves cannot bring the de ad hearts of our scholars to palpitate with spiritual life, but a Paul or an Apollos would have been equally as powerless. Need this fact discourage us? Does it not rather direct us to our true power by shutting us out from our own fancied might? I trust we are all of us already aware that the man who lives in the region of faith dwells in the realm of miracles. Faith trades in marvels, and her merchandise is with wonders.

> "Faith, mighty faith, the promise sees,
> And looks to that alone;
> Laughs at impossibilities,
> And cries, 'It shall be done."

Elisha was no common man now that God's Spirit was upon him, calling him to God's work, and aiding him in it. And you, devoted, anxious, prayerful teacher, remain no longer a common being; you have become, in a special manner, the temple of the Holy Ghost, God dwelleth in you, and you by faith have entered upon the career of a wonder-worker. you are sent into the world not to do the things which are possible to man, but those impossibilities which God worketh by His Spirit, by the means of His believing people. You are to work miracles, to do marvels. You are not, therefor e, to look upon the restoration of these dead children, which in God's name you are called to bring about, as being a thing unlikely or difficult when you remember who it is that works by your feeble instrumentality. "Why should it be thought a thing incredible with you that God should raise the dead? " Unbelief will whisper to you, as you mark the wicked giddiness and early obstinacy of your children, "Can these dry bones live?" But your answer must be, "O Lord, Thou knowest" Committing all cases to the almighty hand, it is yours to prophesy to the dry bones and to the heavenly wind, and ere long you, too, shall see in the valley of your vision the signal triumph of life over death. Let us take up at this moment our true position, and let us realise it. We have dead children before us, and our souls yearn to bring them to life. We confess that all quickening must be wrought by the Lord alone, and our humble petition is that, if the Lord will use us in connection with His miracles of grace, He would now show us what He would have us to do.

It would have been well if Elisha had recollected that he was once the servant of Elijah, and had so studied his master's example as to have initiated it. If so, he would not have sent Gehazi with a staff, but have done at once what at last he was constrained to do. In the First Book of Kings, at the seventeenth chapter, you will find the story of Elijah's raisin g a dead child, and you will there see that Elijah, the master, had left a complete example to his servant; and it was not until Elisha followed it in all respects that the miraculous power was manifested. It had been wise, I say, if Elisha had, at the outset, imitated the example of the master whose mantle he wore. With fa r more force may I say to you, my fellow servants, that it will be well for us if, as teachers, we imitate our Master,—if we study the modes and methods of our glorified Master, and learn at His feet the art of winning souls. Just as He came in deepest sympathy into the nearest contact with our wretched humanity, and condescended to stoop to our sorrowful condition, so must we come near to the souls with whom we have to deal, yearn over them with His yearning, and weep over them with His tears, if we would see them raised from the state of sin. Only by imitating the spirit and manner of the Lord Jesus shall we become wise to win souls.

Forgetting this, however, Elisha would fain strike out a course for himself, which would more clearly display his own prophetic dignity. He gave his staff into the hand of Gehazi, his servant, and bade him lay it upon the child, as if he felt that the divine power was so plenteously upon him that it would work in any way, and consequently his own personal presence and efforts might be dispensed with. The Lord's thoughts were not so. I am afraid that very often the truth which we deliver from the pulpit—and doubtless it is much the same in your classes—is a thing which is extraneous and out of ourselves; like a staff which we hold in our hand, but which is not a part of ourselves. We take doctrinal or practical truth as Gehazi did the staff, and we lay it upon the face of the child, but we ourselves do not agonise for its soul. We try this doctrine and that truth, this anecdote and the other illustration, this way of teaching a lesson and that manner of delivering an address; but so long as ever the truth which we, deliver is a matter apart from ourselves, and unconnected with our innermost being, so long it will have no more effect upon a dead soul than Elisha's staff had upon the dead child. Alas! I fear I have frequently preached the gospel in this place, I have been sure that it was my Master's gospel, the true prophetic staff, and yet it has had no result, because I fear I have not preached it with the vehemence and earnestness and heartiness which ought to have gone with it! And will you not make the same confession, that sometimes you have taught the truth,—it was the truth, you know it was,—the very truth which you found in the Bible, and which has at time s been precious to your own soul, and yet no good result has followed from it, because while you taught the truth you did not feel the truth, nor feel for the child to whom the truth was addressed, but were just like Gehazi placing with indifferent hand the prophetic staff upon the face of the child? It was no wonder that you had to say with Gehazi, "The child is not awaked," for the true awakening power found no appropriate medium in your lifeless teaching. We are not sure that Gehazi was convinced that the child was really dead; he spoke as if it were only asleep, and needed waking. God will not bless those teachers who do not grasp in their hearts the really fallen estate of their children. If you think the child is not really depraved, if you indulge foolish notions about the innocence of childhood and the dignity of human nature, it should not surprise you if you remain barren and unfruitful. How can God bless you to work a resurrection when, if He did work it by you, you are incapable of perceiving its glorious nature? If the lad had awaked, it would not have surprised Gehazi; he would have thought that he was only startled from an unusually sound sleep. If God were to bless to the conversion of souls the testimony of those who do not believe in the total depravity of man, they would merely say, "The gospel is very moralising, and exerts a most beneficial influence," but they would never bless and magnify the regenerating grace by which he who sitteth on the throne maketh all things new.

Observe carefully what Elisha did when thus foiled in his first effort. *When we fail at one attempt, we must not therefore give up our work.* If you have been unsuccessful, my dear brother or sister, until now, you must not infer that you are not called to the work, any more than Elisha might have concluded that the child could not be restored. The lesson of your non-success is not—cease the work, but—change the method. It is not the person who is out of place, it is the plan which is unwise. If you have not been able to accomplish what you wished, remember the schoolboy's song,

> "If at first you don't succeed,
> Try, try, try again."

Do not, however, try in the same way unless you are sure that it is the best one. If your first method has been unsuccessful, you must improve upon it. Examine wherein you have failed, and then, by changing your mode, or your spirit, the Lord may prepare you for a degree of usefulness far beyond your expectation. Elisha, instead of being dispirited when he found that the child was not awake, girded up his loins, and hastened with greater vigour to the work before him.

Notice where the dead child was placed: "*And when Elisha was come into the house, behold, the child was dead, and laid upon his bed.*" This was the bed which the hospitality of the Shunammite had prepare d for Elisha, the famous bed which, with the table, the stool, and the candlestick, will never be forgotten in the Church of God. That famous bed had to be use d for a purpose which the good woman little thought of when, out of love to the prophet's God, she prepared it for the prophet's rest. I like to think of the dead child lying on that bed, because it symbolizes the place where our unconverted children must lie if we would have them saved. If we are to be a blessing to them, they must lie in our hearts,—they must be our daily and nightly charge. We must take the cases of our children to our silent couch with us: we must think of them in the watches of the night, and when we cannot sleep because of care, they must share in those midnight anxieties. Our beds must witness to our cries,—" Oh, that Ishmael might live before Thee! Oh, that the d ear boys and girls in my class might become the children of the living God!" Elijah and Elisha both teach us that we must not place the child far from us, out of doors, or down below us in a vault of cold forgetfulness, but, if we would have him raised to life, we must place him in the warmest sympathies of our hearts.

In reading on, we find, *"he went in, therefore, and shut the door upon them twain, and prayed unto the Lord."* Now the prophet is at his work in right earnest, and we have a noble opportunity of learning from him the secret of raising children from the dead. If you turn to the narrative of Elijah, you will find that Elisha adopted the orthodox method of proceeding, the method of his master Elijah. You will read there, "And he said un to her, Give me thy son. And he took him out of her bosom, and carried him up into a loft, where he abode, and laid him upon his own bed. And he cried unto the Lord, and said, O Lord, my God, hast Thou also brought evil upon the woman with whom I sojourn, by slaying her son? And he stretched himself upon the child three times, and cried unto the Lord, and said, O Lord, my God, I pray Thee, let this child's soul come into him again. And the Lord hear d the voice of Elijah, and the soul of the child came into him again, and he revived." The great secret lies, in a large measure, in powerful supplication. "He s hut the door upon them twain, and prayed unto the Lord." The old proverb i s, "Every true pulpit is set up in heaven," by which is meant that the true preacher is much with God. If we do not pray to God for a blessing, if the foundation of the pulpit be not laid in private prayer, our open ministry will not be a success. So it is with you; every real teacher's power must come from on high. If you never enter your closet, and shut to the door, if you never plead at the mercy-seat for your child, how can you expect that God will honour you in its conversion? It is a very excellent method, I think, actually to take the children one by one into your room alone, and pray with them. You will see your children converted when God gives you to individualise their cases, to agonise for them, and to take them one by one, and with the door closed, to pray both with them and for them. There is much more influence in prayer privately offered with one than in prayer publicly uttered in the class,—not more influence with God, of course, but more influence with the child. Such prayer will often be made its own answer; for God may, while you are pouring out your soul, make your prayer to be a hammer to break the heart which mere addresses had never touched. Pray with your children separately, and it will surely be the means of a great blessing. If this cannot be done, at any rate there must be prayer, much prayer, constant prayer, vehement prayer, the kind of prayer which will not take a denial, like Luther's prayer, which he called the bombarding of heaven; that is to say, the planting a cannon at heaven's gates to blow them op en, for after this fashion fervent men prevail in prayer; they will not come from the mercy-seat until they can cry with Luther, "Vici," "I have conquered, I have gained the blessing for which I strove." "The kingdom of heaven suffereth violence, and the violent take it by force." May we offer such violent, God constraining, heaven-compelling prayers, and the Lord will not permit us to seek His face in vain!

After praying, Elisha adopted the means. Prayer and means must go together. Means without prayer—presumption! Prayer without means— hypocrisy! There lay the child, and there stood the venerable man of God! Watch his singular proceeding, he stoops over the corpse, and puts his mouth upon the child's mouth. The cold, dead mouth of the child was touched by the warm, living lips of the prophet, and a vital stream of fresh, hot breath was sent down into the chill, stone-like passages of the dead mouth, and throat, and lungs. Next, the holy man, with loving ardour of hopefulness, placed his eyes upon the child's eyes, and his hands upon the child 's hands; the warm hands of the old man covered the cold palms of the departed child. Then he stretched himself upon the child, and covered him with his whole body, as though he would transfer his own life into the lifeless frame, and would either die with him, or would make him live. We have heard of the chamois hunter acting as guide to a fearful traveller, who, when they came to a very dangerous part of the road, strapped the traveller firmly to himself and said, "Both of us or neither," that is to say, "Both of us shall live, or neither of us; we are one." So did the prophet effect a mysterious union between himself and the lad, and in his own mind it was resolved that he would either be chilled with the child's death, or warm the child with his life. What does this teach us?

The lessons are many and obvious. We see here, as i n a picture, that if we would bring spiritual life to a child, we must most vividly realise that child's state. It is dead, dead. God will have you feel that the child is as dead in trespasses and sins as you once were. God would have you, dear teacher, come into contact with that death by painful, crushing, humbling sympathy. I told you that, in soul-winning, we should observe how our Master worked; now how did He work? When He would raise us from death, what did it behoove Him to do? He must needs die Himself: there was no other way. So is it with you. If you would raise that dead child, you must f eel the chill and horror of that child's death yourself. A dying man is needed to raise dying men. I cannot believe that you will ever pluck a brand from the burning without putting your hand near enough to feel the heat of the fire. You must have, more or less, a distinct sense of the dreadful wrath of God and of the terrors of the judgment to come, or you will lack energy in your work, and so lack one of the essentials of success. I do not think the preacher ever speaks Well upon such topics until he feels them pressing upon him as a personal burden from the Lord. "I did preach in chains," said John Bunyan, "to men in chains." Depend upon it, when the death that is in your children alarms, depresses, and overwhelms you, then it is that God is about to bless you.

Thus realising the child's state, and putting your mouth upon the child's mouth, and your hands upon its hands, you must next strive to adapt yourself as far as possible to the nature, and habits, and temperament of the child. Your mouth must find out the child's words, so that the child may know what you mean; you must see things with a child's eyes; your heart must feel a child's feelings, so as to be his companion and friend; you must be a student of juvenile sin; you must be a sympathiser in juvenile trials; you must, so far as possible, enter into childhood's joys and griefs. you must not fret at the difficulty of this matter, or feel it to be humiliating; for if you count anything to be a hardship, or a condescension, you have no business in the Sunday-school. If anything difficult be required of you, you must do it, and not think it difficult. God will not raise a dead child by you, if you are not willing to become all things to that child, if by any possibility you may win its soul.

The prophet, it is written, "*stretched himself upon the child.*" One would have thought it should be written, "he contracted himself!"

He was a full-grown man, and the other a mere lad. Should it not be "he contracted himself"? No, "he stretched himself;" and, mark you, no stretching is harder than for a man to stretch himself to a child. He is no fool who can talk to children; a simpleton is much mistaken if he thinks that his folly can interest boys and girls. It needs our best wits, our most industrious studies, our most earnest thoughts, our ripest powers, to teach our little ones. You will not quicken the child until you have stretched yourself; and, though it seems a strange thing, yet it is so. The wisest man will need to exercise all his abilities if he would become a successful teacher of the young.

We see, then, in Elisha, a sense of the child's death and an adaptation of himself to his work; but, above all, we see sympathy. While Elisha himself felt the chill of the corpse, his personal warmth was entering into the dead body. This of itself did not raise the child; but God worked through it,—the old man's heat of body passed into the child, and became the medium of quickening. Let every teacher weigh these words of Paul, "But we were gentle among you, even as a nurse cherisheth her children: so, being affectionately desirous of you, we were willing to have imparted unto you, not the gospel of God only, but also our own souls, because ye were dear unto us." The genuine soul-winner knows what this means. For my own part, when the Lord helps me to preach, after I have delivered all my matter, and have fired off my shot so fast that my gun has grown hot, I have often rammed my soul into the gun, and fired my heart at the congregation, and this discharge has, under God, won the victory. God will bless by His Spirit our hearty sympathy with His own truth, and make it do that which the truth alone, coldly spoken, would not accomplish. Here, then, is the secret. You must, dear teacher, impart to the young your own soul; you must feel as if the ruin of that child would be your own ruin. You must feel that, if the child remains under the wrath of God, it is to you as true a grief as if you were under that wrath yourself. You must confess the child's sins before God as if they were your own, and stand as a priest before the Lord pleading on its behalf. The child was covered by Elisha's body, and you must cover your class with your compassion, with the agonizing stretching forth of yourself before the Lord on its behalf. Behold in this miracle the modus operandi of raising the dead; the Holy Spirit remains mysterious in His operations, but the way of the outward means is here clearly revealed.

The result of the prophet's work soon appeared: "the flesh of the child waxed warm." How pleased Elisha must have been; but I do not find that his pleasure and satisfaction caused him to relax his exertions. Never be satisfied, dear friends, with finding your children in a barely hopeful state. Did a girl come to you, and cry, "Teacher, pray for me"? Be glad, for this is a fair token; but look for more. Did you observe tears in a boy's eyes when you were speaking of the love of Christ? Be thankful for it that the flesh is waxing warm, but do not stop there. Can you relax your exertions now? Bethink you, you have not yet gained your end! It is life you want, not warmth alone. What you want, dear teacher, in your beloved charge, is not mere conviction, but conversion; you desire not only impression, but regeneration,—life, life from God, the life of Jesus. This your scholars need, and nothing less must content you.

Again I must bid you watch Elisha. There was now a little pause. *"Then he returned, and walked in the house to and fro."* Notice the restlessness of the man of God; he cannot be easy. The child waxes warm (blessed be God for that, but he does not live yet); so, instead of sitting d own in his chair by the table, the prophet walks to and fro with restless foot, disquieted, groaning, panting, longing, and ill at ease. He could not bear to look upon the disconsolate mother, or to hear her ask, "Is the child restored?" but he continued pacing the house as if his body could not rest because his soul was not satisfied. Imitate this consecrated restlessness. When you see a boy getting somewhat affected, do not sit down, and say, "The child is very hopeful, thank God; I am perfectly satisfied." You will never win the priceless gem of a saved soul in that way; you must feel sad, restless, troubled, if you ever become a parent in the Church. Paul's expression is not to be explained in words, but you must know its meaning in your hearts; "I travail in birth again until Christ be formed in you." Oh, may the Holy Ghost give you such inward travail, such unrest, disquietude, and sacred uneasiness, until you see your hopeful scholars savingly converted!

After a short period of walking to and fro, the prophet again *"went up, and stretched himself upon the child."* What it is well to do once, it is proper to do a second time. What is good twice, is good seven time s. There must be perseverance and patience. You were very earnest last Sabbath; do not be slothful next Sabbath. How easy it is to pull down, on any one day, what we have built up the day before! If by one Sabbath's work God enables me to convince a child that I was in earnest, let me not convince the child next Sunday that I am not in earnest. If my past warmth has made the child's flesh wax warm, God forbid that my future chilliness should make the child's heart cold again! As surely as warmth went from Elisha to the child, so may cold go from you to your class unless you are in an earnest state of mind.

Elisha stretched himself on the bed again, with many a prayer, and many a sigh, and much believing, and at last his desire was granted him: *"The child sneezed seven times, and the child opened his eyes."* Any form of action would indicate life, and content the prophet. The child " sneezed" , some say because he died with a disease of the head, for he said to his father, "My head! my head!" and the sneeze cleared the passages of life which h ad been blocked up. This we do not know. The fresh air entering afresh into the lungs might well compel a sneeze. The sound was nothing very articulate or musical, but it betokened life. This is all we should expect from young children when God gives them spiritual life. Some church-members expect a great deal more, but for my part I am satisfied if the children sneeze,—if they give any true sign of grace, however feeble or indistinct. If the dear child doe s but feel its lost estate, and rest upon the finished work of Jesus, though we only find out the fact by a very indistinct statement, not such as we should accept from a doctor of divinity, or expect from a grown-up person, should we not thank God, and receive the child, and nurse it for the Lord?

Perhaps, if Gehazi had been there, he would not have thought much of this sneezing, because he had never stretched himself up on the child, but Elisha was content with it. Even so, if you and I have really agonised in prayer for souls, we shall be very quick of eye to catch the first sign of grace, and shall be thankful to God if the token be but a sneeze.

Then the child *opened his eyes*, and we will venture to say Elisha thought he had never seen such lovely eyes before. I know not what kind of eyes they were, the hazel or the blue, but this I know, that any eye which God helps you to open will be a beautiful eye to you. I heard a teacher talking the other day about "a fine lad" who had been saved in his class, and another spoke of "a dear girl" in her class who loved the Lord. No doubt of it; it would be a wonder if they were not "fine" and "dear" in the eyes of you who have brought them to Jesus, for to Jesus Christ they are finer and dearer still. Beloved friends, may you often gaze into opened eyes which, but for divine grace owning your teaching, would have been dark with the film of spiritual death! Then will you be favoured indeed.

One word of caution. In this meeting is there a Gehazi? If there be among this host of Sunday-school teachers one who can do no more than carry the staff, I pity him. Ah! my friend, may God in His mercy give you life, for how else can you expect to be the means of quickening others? If Elisha had been a corpse himself; it would have been a hopeless task to expect life to be communicated through placing one corpse upon another. It is vain for that little class of dead souls to gather round another dead soul such as you are. A dead mother, frost-bitten and cold, cannot cherish her little one. What warmth, what comfort, can come to those who shiver before an empty grate? And such are you. May you have a work of grace in your own soul first, and then may the blessed and Eternal Spirit, who alone can quicken souls, make you to be the means of quickening many to the glory of His grace!

Accept, dear friends, my fraternal salutations, and believe that my fervent prayers are with you that you may be blessed, and be made a blessing.

HOW TO WIN SOULS FOR CHRIST

It is a great privilege to have to speak to so noble a band of preachers; I wish that I were more fit for the task. Silver of eloquent speech and gold of deep thought have I none; but such as I have, give I unto you.

Concerning the winning of souls. What is it to win a soul? I hope you believe in the old-fashioned way of saving souls. everything appears to be shaken nowadays, and shifted from the old foundations. It seems that we are to evolve out of men the good that is already in them: much good may you get if you attempt the process! I am afraid that in the process of evolution you will develop devils. I do not know much else that will come out of human nature, for manhood is as full of sin as an egg is full of meat; and the evolution of sin must be everlasting mischief. We all believe that we must go to soul-winning, desiring in God's name to see all things made new. This old creature is dead and corrupt, and must be buried; and the sooner the better. Jesus has come that there may be a passing away of the old things, and a making of all things new. In the process of our work, we endeavour to bless m en by trying to make them temperate; may God bless all work of that sort! But we should think ourselves to have failed if we had produced a world of total abstainers, and had left them all unbelievers. We drive at something more than temperance; for we believe that men must be born again. It is good that even a corpse should be clean, and therefore that the unregenerate should be moral. It would be a great blessing if they were cleansed of the vices which make this city to reek in the nostrils of God and good men. But that is not so much our work as this: that the dead in sin should live, that spiritual life should quicken them, and that Christ should reign where the prince of the power of the air now hath sway. You preach, brethren, with this object, that men may quit their sins, and fly to Christ for pardon, that by His blessed Spirit they may be renovated, and become as much in love with everything that is holy as they are now in love with everything that is sinful. You aim at a radical cure; the axe is la id at the root of the trees; the amendment of the old nature would not content you, but you seek for the imparting, by a divine power, of a new nature, that those who gather round you in the streets may live unto God.

Our object is to turn the world upside down; or, in other words, that where sin abounded grace may much more abound. We are aiming at a miracle: it is well to settle that at the commencement. Some brethren think that they ought to lower their note to the spiritual ability of the hearer; but this is a mistake. According to these brethren, you ought not to exhort a man to repent and believe unless you believe that he can, of himself, repent and believe. My reply is a confession: I command men in the name of Jesus to repent and believe the gospel, though I know they can do nothing of the kind apart from the grace of God; for I am not sent to work according to what my private reason might suggest, but according to the orders of my Lord and Master. Ours is the miraculous method which comes of the endowment of the Spirit of God, who bids His ministers perform wonders in the name of the holy child Jesus. We are sent to say to blind eyes, "See," to deaf ears, "Hear," to dead hearts, "Live," and even to Lazarus rotting in that grave, wherein, by this time, he stinketh,— "Lazarus, come forth." Dare we do this? We shall be wise to begin with the conviction that we are utterly powerless for this unless our Master has sent us, and is with us. But if He that sent us is with us, all things are possible to him that believeth. O preacher, if thou art about to stand up to see what thou canst do, it will be thy wisdom to sit down speedily; but if thou standest up to prove what thine almighty Lord and Master can do through thee, then infinite possibilities lie about thee! There is no bound to what God can accomplish if He works by thy heart and voice. The other Sabbath morning, before I entered the pulpit, when my dear brethren, the deacons and elders of this church, gathered about me for prayer, as they are wont to do, one of them said, "Lord, take him as a man takes a tool in his hand when he gets a firm hold of it, and then uses it to work his own will with it." That is what all workers need; that God may be the Worker by them. You are to be instruments in the hands of God; yourselves, of course, actively putting forth all your faculties and forces which the Lord has lent to you; but still never depending upon your personal power, but resting alone upon that sacred, mysterious, divine energy which worketh in us, and by us, and with us, upon the hearts and minds of men.

Brethren, we have been greatly disappointed, have we not, with some of our converts? We shall always be disappointed with them so far as they are our converts. We shall greatly rejoice over them when they prove to be the Lord's work. When the power of grace works in them, ("Glory!") then it will be, as my brother says, "Glory!" and nothing else but glory; for grace brings glory, but mere oratory will only create sham and shame in the long run. When we are preaching, and we think of a very pretty, flowery passage, a very neat, poetical paragraph, I wish we could be restrained by that fear which acted upon Paul when he said that he would not use the wisdom of words, "lest the cross of Christ should be made of none effect." It is the duty of the gospel preacher, indoors or outdoors, to say, "I can say that very prettily, but then they might notice how I said it; I will, therefore, so say it that they will only observe the intrinsic value of the truth which I would teach them." It is not our way of putting the gospel, nor our method of illustrating it, which wins souls, but the gospel itself does the work in the hands of the Holy Ghost, and to Him we must look for the thorough conversion of men. A miracle is to be wrought by which our hearers shall become the products of that might y power which God wrought in Christ when He raised Him from the dead, and set Him at His own right hand in the heavenly place far above all principality and power; and for this we must look out of ourselves to the living Go d. Must we not? We go in, then, for thorough downright conversion; and therefore we fall back upon the power of the Holy Spirit. If it be a miracle, God must work it, that is clear; it is not to be accomplished by our reasoning, or persuasion, or threatening, it can only come from the Lord.

In what way, since the winning of souls lies here, can we hopefully expect to be endowed with the Spirit of God, and to go for thin His power?' I reply, that a great deal depends upon the condition of the man himself. I am persuaded we have never laid enough stress on the work of God within our own selves in its relation to our service of God. A consecrated man may be charged with the divine energy to the full, so that everybody round about him must perceive it. They cannot tell what it is, nor whence it comes, nor, perhaps, whither it goes; but there is something about that man which is far beyond the common order of things. At another time that same person may be feeble and dull, and be conscious to himself that he is so. Se e! he shakes himself as at other times, but he can do no mighty deed. It is cl ear that Samson himself must be in a right condition, or he can win no victories. If the champion's locks be shorn, the Philistines will laugh at him; if the Lord be gone from a man, he has no power left for useful service. Dear brethren, lo ok carefully to your own condition before God. Take care of the home farm; look well to your own flocks and herds. Unless your walk be close with God, unless you dwell in that clear light which surrounds the throne of God, and which is only known to those who are in fellowship with the Eternal, you will go forth from your chamber, and hasten to your work, but nothing will come of it. The vessel, it is true, is but an earthen one; yet it has its place i n the divine arrangement, but it will not be filled with the divine treasure unless it is a clean vessel, and unless in other respects it is a vessel fit for the Master 's use. Let me show you some ways in which much must depend in soul-winning upon the man himself.

We win some souls to Christ by acting as witnesses. We stand up and testify for the Lord Jesus Christ concerning certain truths. Now, I have never had the great privilege of being bamboozled by a barrister. I have sometimes wondered what I should do if I were put into the witness-box to be examined and cross-examined. I think I should simply stand up, and tell the truth as far as I knew it, and should not make an attempt to display my wit, or my language, or my judgment. If I simply gave straightforward answers to his questions, I should beat any lawyer under heaven. But the difficulty is, that so often when a witness is put into the box, he is more conscious of himself than of what he has to say; therefore, he is soon worried, teased, and bored, and, by losing his temper, he fails to be a good witness for the cause. Now, you men in the open- air are often bamboozled; the devil's barristers are sure to come to you, he has a great number of them constantly retained in his service. The one thing you have to do is to bear witness to the truth. If you enquire in your own mind, "How shall I answer this man cleverly, so as to get a victory over him?" you will not be wise. A witty answer is often a very proper thin g; at the same time, a gracious answer is better. Try to say to yourself: "It does not, after all, matter whether that man proves me to be a fool or not, for I know that already I am content to be thought a fool for Christ's sake, and not to care about my reputation. I have to bear witness to what I know, and by the help of God I will do so right boldly. If the interrupter questions me about other things, I shall tell him that I do not come to bear witness about other matters, but this one thing I do. To one point I will speak, and to no other."

Brethren, the witnessing man, then, must himself be saved, and he should be sure of it. I do not know whether you doubt your own salvation. Perhaps I should recommend you to preach even when that is the case; since, if you are not saved yourself, you yet wish others to be. You do not doubt that you once enjoyed full assurance; and now, if you have sorrow fully to confess, "Alas ! I do not feel the full power of the gospel on my own heart," you can truly add, "Yet I know that it is true, for I have seen it save others, and I know that no other power can save me." Perhaps even that faltering testimony, so truly honest, might bring a tear into your opponent's eye, and make him feel sympathy for you. "I preached," said John Bunyan, " sometimes without hope, like a man in chains to men in chains, and when I heard my own fetters rattle, yet I told others that there was deliverance for them, and I bade them look to the great Deliverer." I would not have stopped Mr. Bunyan in preaching so. At the same time, it is a great thing to be able to declare from your own personal experience that the Lord hath broken the gates of brass, and cut the bars of iron in sunder. Those who hear our witness say, "Are you sure of it?" Sure of it? I am as sure of it as I am sure that I am a living ma n. They call this dogmatism. Never mind about that. A man ought to know what he is preaching about, or else let him sit down. If I had any doubt about the matters I preach from this pulpit, I should be ashamed to remain the pastor of this church; but I preach what I do know, and testify what I have seen. If I am mistaken, I am heartily and intensely mistaken; and I risk my soul and all its eternal interests upon the truth of what I preach. If the gospel which I preach does not save me, I shall never be saved, for what I proclaim to others is my own personal ground of trust. I have no private lifeboat; the ark to which I invite others holds myself and all that I have.

A good witness ought himself to know all that he is going to say; he should feel himself at home in his subject. He is brought up as a witness, say, in a certain case of robbery; he knows what he saw, and has to make a declaration of that only. They begin to question him about a picture in the house, or the colour of a dress which was hanging in the wardrobe. He answers, "You are going beyond my record; I can only witness to that which I saw." What we do know, and what we do not know, would make two very large books, and we may safely ask to be let alone as to the second volume.

Brother, say what you know, and sit down. But be calm and composed while speaking of that with which you have personal acquaintance. You will never properly indulge your emotions in preaching, so as to feel at home with the people, until you are at home with your subject. When you know what you are at, you will have your mind free for earnestness. Unless you open-air preachers know the gospel from beginning to end, and know where you are in preaching it, you cannot preach with due emotion; but when you feel at home with your doctrine, stand up and be as bold, and earnest, and importunate as you please. Face the people feeling that you are going to tell them something worth hearing, about which you are quite sure, which to you is your very life. There are honest hearts in every outdoor assembly, and every indoor assembly, too, that only want to hear honest beliefs, and the y will accept them, and be led to believe in the Lord Jesus Christ.

But you are not only witnesses, you are pleaders for the Lord Jesus Christ. Now, in a pleader, much depends upon the man. It se ems as if the sign and token of Christianity in some preachers was not a tongue of fire, but a block of ice. You would not like to have a barrister stand u p and plead your cause in a cool, deliberate way, never showing the slightest care about whether you were found guilty of murder or acquitted. How could you endure his indifference when you yourself were likely to be hanged? Oh, no! you wish to silence such a false advocate. So, when a man has to speak for Christ, if he is not in earnest, let him go to bed. You smile; but is it not better that he should go to bed than send a whole congregation to sleep without their going to bed? Yes, we must be in downright earnest. If we are to prevail with men, we must love them. There is a genuine love to men that some have, and there is a genuine dislike to men that others have. I know gentlemen, whom I esteem i n a way, who seem to think that the working-classes are a shockingly bad lot, to be kept in check, and governed with vigour. With such views, they will never convert the working- men. To win men, you must feel: "I am one of them. If they are a sad lot, I am one of them; if they are lost sinners, I am one of them; if they need a Saviour, I am one of them." To the very chief of sinners you should preach with this text before you, "Such were some of you." Grace alone makes us to differ, and that grace we preach. Genuine love to God and fervent love to man make up the great qualification for a pleader.

I further believe, although certain persons deny it, that the influence of fear is to be exercised over the minds of men, and that it ought to operate upon the mind of the preacher himself. "Noah, moved with fear, prepared an ark to the saving of his house." There was salvation for this world from perishing in the flood in the fears of Noah; and when a man gets to fear for others, so that his heart cries out, "They will perish, they will perish, they will sink to hell, they will be forever banished from the presence of the Lord," and when this fear oppresses his soul, and weighs him down, and then d rives him to go out and preach with tears, oh, then he will plead with men so as to prevail! Knowing the terror of the Lord, he will persuade men. To know the terror of the Lord is the means of teaching us to persuade, and not to speak harshly. Some have used the terrors of the Lord to terrify; but Paul used them to persuade.

Let us copy him. Say, "We have come out to tell you, men and brethren, that the world is on fire, and you must flee for your lives, and e scape to the mountain, lest ye be consumed." We must give this warning with the full conviction that it is true, or else we shall be but as the boy who in foolishness cried, "Wolf!" Something of the shadow of the last tremendous day must fall upon our spirit to give the accent of conviction to our message of mercy, or we shall miss the pleader's true power. Brethren, we must tell men that there i s pressing need of a Saviour, and show them that we ourselves perceive their need and feel for them, or else we are not likely to turn them to the Saviour.

He that pleads for Christ should himself be moved with the prospect of the judgment-day. When I come in at yonder door at the back of the pulpit, and the sight of that vast crowd bursts upon me, I frequently feel appalled. Think of these thousands of immortal souls gazing through the windows of those wistful eyes, and I am to preach to them all, and be responsible for their blood if I be not faithful to them. I tell you, it makes me feel ready to start back. But then fear is not alone. I am borne up by the hope and be life that God intends to bless these people through the Word which He will enable me to deliver. I believe that everybody in that throng is sent there by God for some purpose, and that I am sent to effect that purpose. I often think to myself, when I am preaching, "Who is being converted now?" It never occurs to me that the Word of the Lord will fail. No, that can never be. I often feel sure that men are being converted, and at all times that God is glorified by the testimony of His truth. You may depend upon it that your hopeful conviction that God's Word cannot return to Him void is a great encouragement to your hearers as well as to yourself. Your enthusiastic confidence that they will be converted may be like the little finger of a mother held out to her babe, to help it to make its way to her. The fire within your hearts may dart a spark into their soul s by which the flame of spiritual life shall be kindled in them. Do let us all learn the art of pleading with the souls of men.

Still, dear open-air preachers, and all of you Christian people here, *we have not only to be witnesses and pleaders, but we have also to be examples.* One of the most successful ways of taking wild ducks is the use of the decoy bird. The decoy duck enters the net itself, and the others follow it. We need to use more, in the Christian Church, the holy art of decoy; that is to say, our example, in ourselves coming to Christ, in ourselves living godly lives in the midst of a perverse generation, our example of joy and sorrow, our example of holy submission to the divine will in the time of trouble, our example in all manner of gracious ways, will be the means of inducing others to enter the way of life. You cannot, of course, stand up in the street, and tell of your example; but there is no street-preacher who is not known better than he thinks. Someone in that crowd may be in the secret of the speaker's private life. I once heard of an out- of-doors preacher, to whom a hearer cried out, "Ah, Jack, you dare not preach like that at your own door!" It so happened, unfortunately, that Mr. John _ had offered to fight one of his neighbours a little while before, and therefore it was not likely that he would have done much preaching very near home. This made the interruption an awkward one. If any man's life at home is unworthy, he should go several miles away before he stands up to preach, and then, when he stands up, he should say nothing. The y know us, brethren; they know far more about us than we imagine, and what they do not know they make up. At the same time, our walk and conversation should be the most powerful part of our ministry. This is what is called being consistent, when lips and life agree.

My time is short; but I must say a word upon another point. I have said that the working of the Holy Spirit depends largely upon the man himself, but I am bound to add that much will also depend upon the kind of people that are round about the preacher. An open-air preacher, who has to go out quite alone, must be in a very unfortunate position. It is extremely helpful to be connected with an earnest living church which will pray for you; and if you cannot find such a church where you labour, the next best thing is to get half-a-dozen brothers or sisters who will back you up, and go out with you, and, especially, will pray with you. Some preachers are so independent that they can do without helpers, but they will be wise if they do not affect solitude. May they not look at the matter in this way: by bringing in half-a-dozen men to go out with me I shall be doing good to these young men, and shall be training them to be workers? If you can associate with yourself half-a-dozen who are not all very young men, but somewhat advanced in their knowledge of divine truth, the association will be greatly to your mutual advantage. I confess to you all that, although God has largely blessed me in His work, yet none of the credit is due to me at all, but to those dear friends at the Tabernacle, and, indeed, all over the world, who make me the special subject of their prayers. A man ought to do well with such a people around him as I have. My dear friend and deacon, Mr. William Olney, once said, "Our minister has hitherto led us forward, and we have followed heartily. Everything has been a success; do you not believe in his leadership?" The people cried, "Yes." Then said my dear friend, "If our pastor has brought us up to a ditch which looks as if it could not be passed, let us fill it up with our bodies, and carry him across." This was grand talk: the ditch was filled, nay, it seemed to fill itself up at once. If you have a true comrade, your strength is more than doubled. What a blessing is a good wife! You women, who would not be in your right place if you began to preach i n the streets, you can make your husband's happy and comfortable when they come home, and that will make them preach all the better! Some of you can even help i n another way if you are prudent and gentle. You can tenderly hint that your spouse was a little out of line in certain small matters, and he may take your hint, and put himself right. A good brother once asked me to give him some instruction, and he pleaded thus:—" The only instructor I have had was m y wife, who had a better schooling than fell to my lot. I used to say, 'We was,' and 'Us did it,' and she quietly hinted that people might laugh at me if I did not attend to grammar." His wife thus became to him a professor of—of English language, and was worth her weight in gold to him, and he knew it. you who have such helpers ought to thank God daily for them.

Next to this, it is a very great assistance to join in brotherly league with some warm-hearted Christian who knows more than we do, and will benefit us by prudent hints. God may bless us for the sake of others when He might not bless us for our own. You have heard, I daresay, the monkish story of the man who had preached, and had won many souls to Christ, and congratulated himself upon it. One night, it was revealed to him that he should have none of the honour of it at the last great day; and he asked the angel in his dream who then would have the credit of it, and the angel rep lied, "That deaf old man who sits on the pulpit stairs, and prays for you, was the means of the blessing." Let us be thankful for that deaf man, or, that old woman, or those poor praying friends who bring down a blessing upon us by their intercessions. God will bless two when He might not bless one. Abraham alone did not get one of the five cities saved, although his prayer was like a ton weight in the scale; but yonder was his nephew Lot, who was about the poorest lot that could be found. He had not more than half-an-ounce of prayer in him; but that tiny fragment turned the scale, and Zoar was preserved. Add then your odd half- ounce to the mightier weight of the pleadings of eminent saints, for they may need it.

Dear brother open-air preachers, I am not trying to instruct you; some of you could far better instruct me; and yet I do not know, for I suspect I must be getting rather old from what I hear. A woman, at the beginning of this year (1887), was trying to get something out of me, and she said, "I remember hearing your dear voice more than forty years ago." I said, "Heard my voice forty years ago! where was that?" She said, "You were preaching at the bottom of Pentonville Hill, near where Mr. Sawday's chapel is." "Well," I said, "was it not more than forty years ago?" "Yes," she said, "I t might be fifty." "Oh," I said, "I suppose I was quite young then?" "Oh, yes!" she said, "you were such a dear young man. That, of course, was a needless assurance; but I do not think she was quite so sure of my dearness when I told her that I never preached at the bottom of Pentonville Hill, and that fifty years ago I was only three years old, and that I thought it shameful for her to suppose that I should give her money for telling falsehoods. However, I shall presume up on the woman's statement to-night, and suppose myself to be that venerable person she described me as being, and I shall make hold to say to you,—Dear brethren, if we are going to win souls, *we must go in for downright labour and hard work.*

And, first, we must work at our preaching. You are not getting distrustful of the use of preaching, are you? (" No.") I hope you do not weary of it, though you certainly sometimes must weary in it. Go on with your preaching. Cobbler, stick to your last; preacher, stick to your preaching. In the great day, when the muster-roll shall be read, of all those who are converted through fine music, and church decoration, and religious exhibitions and entertainments, they will amount to the tenth part of nothing; but it will always please God by the foolishness of preaching to save them that believe. Keep to your preaching; and if you do anything beside, do not let it throw your preaching into the background. In the first place preach, and in the second place preach, and in the third place preach.

Believe in preaching the love of Christ, believe in preaching the atoning sacrifice, believe in preaching the new birth, believe in preaching the whole counsel of God. The old hammer of the gospel will s till break the rock in pieces; the ancient fire of Pentecost will still burn among the multitude. Try nothing new, but go on with preaching, and if we all preach with the Holy Ghost sent down from heaven, the results of preaching will astound us. Why, there is no end after all to the power of the tongue! Look at the power of a bad tongue, what great mischief it can do; and shall not God put more power into a good tongue, if we will but use it aright? Look at the power of fire, a single spark might give a city to the flames; even so, the Spirit of God being with us, we need not calculate how much, or what we can do: there is no calculating the potentialities of a flame,

100

and there is no end to the possibilities of divine truth spoken with the enthusiasm which is born of the Spirit of God. Have great hope yet, brothers, have great hope yet, despite yon shameless midnight streets, despite yon flaming gin-palaces at the corner of every street, despite the wickedness of the rich, despite the ignorance of the poor. Go on; go on; go on; in God's name go on, for if the preaching of the gospel does not save men, nothing will. If the Lord's own way of mercy fails, then hang the skies in mourning, and blot out the sun in everlasting midnight, for there remaineth nothing before our race but the blackness of darkness. Salvation by the sacrifice of Jesus is the ultimatum of God. Rejoice that it cannot fail. Let us believe without reserve, and then go straight ahead with the preaching of the Word.

True-hearted open-air preachers will be sure to join with their preaching very much earnest private talk. What numbers of persons have been converted in this Tabernacle by the personal conversation of certain brothers here, whom I will not further indicate! They are all about this place while I am preaching! I recollect that a brother was speaking to me one Mon day night, and suddenly he vanished before he finished the sentence which he was whispering. I never quite knew what he was going to say; but I speedily saw him in that left-hand gallery, sitting in the pew with a lady unknown to me. After the service, I said to him, "Where did you go?" and he said, "A gleam of sunlight came in at the window, and made me see a face which looked so sad that I hurried upstairs, and took my seat in the pew close to the woman of a sorrowful countenance." "Did you cheer her?" "Oh, yes! she received the Lord Jesus very readily; and just as she did so, I noticed another eager face, and I asked her to wait in the pew till after the service, and I went after the other—a young man." He prayed with both of these, and would not be satisfied until they had given their hearts to the Lord. That is the way to be on the alert. We need a body of sharp-shooters to pick out their men one by one. When we fire great guns from the pulpit, execution is done, but many are missed. We want loving spirits to go round, and deal with individual cases in the singular by pointed personal warnings and encouragements. Every open-air preacher should not only address the hundreds, but he should be ready to pounce upon the ones, and he should have others with him who have the same happy art. How much more good would come of preaching in the streets if every open-air preacher were accompanied by a batch of persons who would drive h is nails home for him by personal conversation!

101

Last Sunday night, my dear brother told us a little story which I shall never forget. He was at Croydon Hospital one night, as one of those appointed to visit it. All the porters had gone home, and it was time to shut up for the night. He was the only person in the hospital, with the exception of the physician, when a boy came running in, saying that there was a railway accident, and someone must go round to the station with a stretcher. The doctor said to my brother, "Will you take one end of the stretcher if I take the other?" "Oh, yes!" was the cheerful reply; and so away went the doctor and the pastor with the stretcher. They brought a sick man back with them. My brother said, "I went often to the hospital during the next week or two, because I felt so much interest in the man whom I had helped to carry." I believe he will always take an interest in that man, because he once felt the weight of him. When you know how to carry a man on your heart, and have felt the burden of his case, you will have his name engraven upon your soul. So you that privately talk to people, you are feeling the weight of souls; and I believe that this is what many regular preachers need to know more of; and then they will preach better.

When preaching and private talk are not available, you have a tract ready, and this is often an effectual method. Some tracts would not convert a beetle: there is not enough in them to interest a fly. Get good striking tracts, or none at all. But a telling, touching gospel tract may often be the seed of eternal life; therefore, do not go out without your tracts.

I suppose, beside giving a tract, if you can, you try and find out where a person lives who frequently hears you, that you may give him a call. What a fine thing is a visit from an open-air preacher! "Why," says the woman, "there is that man come to see you, Bill; that gentleman who preaches at the corner of the street. Shall I tell him to come in?" "Oh, yes! " is the reply; "I have heard him many times; he is a good fellow." Visit as much as you can, for it will be of use to yourselves as well as to the people.

What power there is also in a letter to an individual! Some people still have a kind of superstitious reverence for a letter; and when they get an earnest epistle from one of you reverend gentlemen, they think a great deal of it; and who knows?—a note by post may hit the man your sermon missed. Young people who are not able to preach might do much good if they would write letters to their young friends about their souls; they could speak very plainly with their pens, though they might be diffident in speaking with their tongues. Let us save men by all the means under heaven; let us prevent men going down to hell. We are not half as earnest as we ought to be. Do you not remember the young man, who, when he was dying, said to his brother, "My brother, how could you have been so indifferent to my soul as you have been?" He answered, "I have not been indifferent to your soul, for I have frequently spoken to you about it." "Oh, yes!" he said, "you spoke; but somehow, I think, if you had remembered that I was going down to hell, you would have been more earnest with me; you would have wept over me, and, as my brother, you would not have allowed me to be lost." Let no one say this of you.

But I hear it observed that most fellows, when they grow earnest, do such odd things, and say such strange things. Let them s ay strange things, and let them do strange things, if these come out of genuine earnestness. We do not want pranks and performances which are the mere sham of earnestness; but real white-heat earnestness is the want of the times, and where you see that, it is a pity to be too critical. You must let a great storm rage in its own way. You must let a living heart speak as it can. If you are zealous, and yet cannot speak, your earnestness will invent its own method of working out its purpose. As Hannibal is said to have melted the rocks with vinegar, so earnestness will one way or another dissolve the rocky hearts of men. May the Spirit of God rest upon you, one and all, for Jesus Christ's sake! Amen.

THE COST OF BEING A SOUL-WINNER

I want to say a word to you who are trying to bring souls to Jesus. You long and pray to be useful: do you know what this involves? Are you sure that you do? Prepare yourselves, then, to see and suffer many things with which you would rather be unacquainted. Experiences which would be unnecessary to you personally will become your portion if the Lord uses you for the salvation of others. An ordinary person may rest in his bed all night, but a surgeon will be called up at all hours; a farming-man may take his ease at his fireside, but if he becomes a shepherd he must be out among the lambs, and bear all weathers for them; even so doth Paul say, "Therefore I endure al l things for the elect's sakes, that they may also obtain the salvation which is in Christ Jesus with eternal glory." For this cause we shall be made to undergo experiences which will surprise us.

Some years ago, I was the subject of fearful depression of spirit. Certain troublous events had happened to me; I was also unwell, and my heart sank within me. Out of the depths I was forced to cry un to the Lord. Just before I went away to Mentone for rest, I suffered greatly i n body, but far more in soul, for my spirit was overwhelmed. Under this pressure, I preached a sermon from the words, "My God, My God, why hast Thou forsaken Me?" I was as much qualified to preach from that text as ever I expect to be; indeed, I hope that few of my brethren could have entered so deeply into those heart-breaking words. I felt to the full of my measure the horror of a soul forsaken of God. Now, that was not a desirable experience. I tremble at the bare idea of passing again through that eclipse of soul; I pray that I may never suffer in that fashion again unless the same result should hang upon it.

That night, after sermon, there came into the vestry a man who was as nearly insane as he could be to be out of an asylum. His eyes seemed ready to start from his head, and he said that he should utterly have despaired if he had not heard that discourse, which had made him feel that there was one man alive who understood his feeling, and could describe his experience. I talked with him, and tried to encourage him, and asked him to come again on the Monday night, when I should have a little more time to talk with him. I saw the brother again, and I told him that I thought he was a hopeful patient, and I was glad that the word had been so suited to his case. Apparently, he put aside the comfort which I presented for his acceptance, and yet I had the consciousness upon me that the precious truth which he had heard was at work upon his mind, and that the storm of his soul would soon subside into a deep calm.

Now hear the sequel. Last night, of all the times i n the year, when, strange to say, I was preaching from the words, "The Almighty hath vexed my soul," after the service, in walked this self-same brother who had called on me five years before. This time, he looked as different as noonday from midnight, or as life from death. I said to him, "I am glad to see you, for I have often thought about you, and wondered whether you were brought in to perfect peace." I told you that I went to Mentone, and my patient also wen t into the country, so that we had not met for five years. To my enquiries, this brother replied, "Yes, you said I was a hopeful patient, and I am sure you will be glad to know that I have walked in the sunlight from that day till now. Everything is changed and altered with me." Dear friends, as soon as I saw my poor despairing patient the first time, I blessed God that my fearful experience had prepared me to sympathize with him and guide him; but last night, when I saw him perfectly restored, my heart overflowed with gratitude to God for my former sorrowful feelings. I would go into the deeps a hundred times to cheer a downcast spirit: it is good for me to have been afflicted that I might know how to speak a word in season to one that is weary.

Suppose that, by some painful operation, you could have your right arm made a little longer, I do not suppose you would care to undergo the operation; but if you foresaw that, by undergoing the pain, you would be enabled to reach and save drowning men who else would sink before your eyes, I think you would willingly bear the agony, and pay a heavy fee to the surgeon to be thus qualified for the rescue of your fellows. Reckon, t hen, that to acquire soul-winning power you will have to go through fire and water, through doubt and despair, through mental torment and soul distress. It will not, of course, be the same with you all, nor perhaps with any two of you, but according to the work allotted you, will be your preparation. You must go into the fire if you are to pull others out of it, and you will have to dive in to the floods if you are to draw others out of the water. You cannot work a fire-esc ape without feeling the scorch of the conflagration, nor man a lifeboat without being covered with the waves. If Joseph is to preserve his brethren alive, he must himself go down into Egypt; if Moses is to lead the people through the wilderness, he must first himself spend forty years there with his flock. Pay son truly said, "If anyone asks to be made a successful minister, he knows not what he asks; and it becomes him to consider whether he can drink deeply of Christ's bitter cup and be baptized with His baptism."

I was led to think of this by the prayer which has just been offered by our esteemed brother, Mr. Levinsohn. He is, as you perceive, of the seed of Abraham, and he owed his conversion to a city missionary of his own nation. If that city missionary had not himself been a Jew, he would not have known the heart of the young stranger, nor have won his ear f or the gospel message. Men are usually won to Christ by suitable instruments, and this suitability often lies in the power to sympathize. A key opens a door because it fits the wards of the lock; an earnest address touches the heart because it meets the state of that heart. You and I have to be made into all sorts of shapes to suit all forms of mind and heart; just as Paul says, "And unto the Jews I became as a Jew, that I might gain the Jews; to them that are under the law, as under the law, that I might gain them that are under the law; to them that are without law, as without law (being not without law to God, but under the law to Christ), that I might gain them that are without law. To the weak became I as weak, that I might gain the weak; I am made all things to all men, that I might by all means save some." These processes must be wrought out upon us also. Let us cheerfully bear whatever the Holy Spirit shall work within our spirits that we may thus be the more largely blest to our fellow-men. Come, brethren, and lay your all on the altar! Give yourselves up, you workers, into the Lord's hand. You who have delicacy and refinement, may have to be shocked into the power to benefit the coarse and ignorant. You who are wise and educated, may have to be made fools of, that you may win fools to Jesus; for fools need saving, and many of them will not be saved except by means which men of culture cannot admire.

How finely some people go to work when the thing needed may not be daintiness, but energy! On the other hand, how violent some are when the desired thing is tact and gentleness, and not force ! This has to be learned; we must be trained to it as dogs to follow game. Here is one form of experience— The brother is elegant; he wishes to speak earnestly, but he must be elaborate, too. He has written out a nicely-prepared address, his notes are carefully arranged. Alas! he has left the priceless document at home! What will he do? He is too gracious to give up: he will try to speak. He begins nicely, and gets through firstly. "Fair and softly, good sir." What comes next? See, he is gazing aloft for secondly. What should be said? What can be said? The good man flounders about, but he cannot swim he struggles to land, and as he rises from the flood you can hear him mentally saying, "That's my last attempt." Yet it is not so. He speaks again. He gathers confidence; he grows into an impressive speaker. By such humiliations as these the Lord pre pares him to do his work efficiently. In our beginnings we are too fine to be fit, or too great to be good. We must serve an apprenticeship, and thus learn our trade. A blacklead pencil is of no use at all till it is cut; the fine cedar wood must be cut away; and then the inward metal which marks and writes will have f air play. Brethren, the knife of affliction is sharp, but salutary; you cannot delight in it, but faith may teach you to value it. Are you not willing to pass through every ordeal if by any means you may save some? If this be not your spirit, you had better keep to your farm and to your merchandise, for no man will ever win a soul who is not prepared to suffer everything within the compass of possibility for that soul's sake.

A good deal may have to be suffered through fear, and yet that fear may assist in stirring the soul, and putting it into a fit posture for work; at least, it may drive the heart to prayer, and that alone is a great part of the necessary preparation. A good man thus describes one of his early attempts at visiting, with the view of speaking to individuals upon their spiritual condition:—" I was thinking, on the way to the residence of the party, how I would introduce the subject, and all that I would say. And all the while I was trembling and agitated. Reaching the door, it seemed as if I should sink through the stones; my courage was gone, and, lifting my hand to the knocker, it dropped at my side without touching it. I went partly down the steps from sheer fear; a moment's reflection sent me again to the knocker, and I entered the house. The sentences I uttered and the prayer offered were very broken; but thankful, very thankful I am that my fears and cowardice did not prevail. The 'ice was broken.'" That process of ice-breaking must be gone through, and its result i s highly beneficial.

O poor souls, you that wish to find the Saviour, Jesus has died for you; and now His people live for you! We cannot offer any atoning sacrifice for you; there is no need that we should; but still we would gladly make sacrifices for your soul's sake. Did you not hear what our brother said just now in his prayer,—We would do anything, be anything, give anything, and suffer anything if we might but bring you to Christ? I assure you that many of us feel even so. Will you not care for yourselves? Shall we be earnest about your souls, and will you trifle them away? Be wiser, I beseech you, and may infinite wisdom at once lead you to our dear Saviour's feet. Amen.

THE SOUL-WINNER'S REWARD

On my way to this meeting, I observed upon the notice-board of the police- station a striking placard, offering a large

REWARD

to anyone who can discover and bring to justice the perpetrators of a great crime. No doubt our legislators know that the hope of a huge reward is the only motive which will have power with the comrades of assassins. The common informer earns so much scorn and hate that few can be induced to stand in his place, even when piles of gold are offered. It is a poor business at best.

It is far more pleasant to remember that there is a reward for bringing men to mercy, and that it is of a higher order than the premium for bringing men to justice; it is, moreover, much more within our reach, and that is a practical point worthy of our notice. We cannot all hunt down criminals, but we may all rescue the perishing. God be thanked that assassins and burglars are comparatively few, but sinners who need to be sough t and saved swarm around us in every place. Here is scope for you all; and none need think himself shut out from the rewards which love bestows on all who do her service.

At the mention of the word REWARD, some will prick up their ears, and mutter "legality." Yet the reward we speak of is not of debt, but of grace; and it is enjoyed, not with the proud conceit of merit, but with the grateful delight of humility.

Other friends will whisper, "Is not this a low and mercenary motive?" We reply that it is as mercenary as the spirit of Moses, who "had respect unto the recompense of the reward." In this matter, all depends upon what the reward is; and if that happens to be the joy of doing good, the comfort of having glorified God, and the bliss of pleasing the Lord Jesus,—then the aspiration to be allowed to endeavour to save our fellow-men from going down into the pit is in itself a grace from the Lord; and if we did not succeed in it, yet the Lord would say of it, as He did of David's intent to build a temple, "It was well that it was in thine heart." Even if the souls we seek should all persist in unbelief if they all despise and reject and

109

ridicule us, yet still it will be a divine work to have at least made the attempt. If there comes no rain out of the cloud, yet it has screened off the fierce heat of the sun; all is not lost even if the greater design be not accomplished. What if we only learn how to join the Saviour in His tears, and cry, "How often would I have gathered you, but ye would not!" It is sublimity itself to be allowed to stand on the same platform with Jesus, and weep with Him. We are the better for such sorrows, if no others are.

But, thank God, our labours are not in vain in the Lord. I believe that the most of you, who have really tried, in the power of the Holy Spirit, by Scriptural teaching and by prayer, to bring others to Jesus, have been successful. I may be speaking to a few who have not succeeded; if so, I would recommend them to look steadily over their motive, their spirit, their work, and their prayer, and then begin again. Perhaps they may get to work more wisely, more believingly, more humbly, and more in the power of the Holy Spirit. They must act as farmers do who, after a poor harvest, plough again in hope. They ought not to he dispirited, but they ought to be aroused. We should be anxious to find out the reason of failure, if there be any, and we should be ready to learn from all our fellow-labourers; but we must steadfastly set our faces, if by any means we may save some, resolving that whatever happens we will leave no stone unturned to effect the salvation of those around us. How can we bear to go out of the world without sheaves to bear with us rejoicingly? I believe that the most of us who are now assembled to pray have been successful beyond our expectations. God has blessed us, not beyond our de sires, but yet beyond our hopes.

I have often been surprised at the mercy of God to myself. Poor sermons of mine, that I could cry over when I get home, have led scores to the cross; and, more wonderful still, words that I have spoken in ordinary conversation, mere chance sentences, as men call them, have nevertheless been as winged arrows from God, and have pierced men's hearts, and laid t hem wounded at Jesus' feet. I have often lifted up my hands in astonishment, and said, "How can God bless such a feeble instrumentality?" This is the feeling of most who addict themselves to the blessed craft of fishing for men, and the desire of such success furnishes as pure a motive as could move an angel's heart, as pure, indeed, as that which swayed the Saviour when, for the joy that was set before Him, He endured the cross, despising the shame. "Doth Job serve God for nought?" said Satan. If he could have answered the question in the affirmative, if it could have been proved that the perfect and upright man found no reward in his holy living, then Satan would have caviled at the justice of God, and urged men to renounce a service so unprofitable. Verily there is a reward to the righteous, and in the lofty pursuits of grace there are recompenses of infinite value. When we endeavour to lead men to God, we pursue a business far more profitable than the pearl-fisher's diving or the diamond-hunter's searching. No pursuit of mortal men is to be compared with that of soul-winning. I know what I say when I bid you think of it as men think of entering the cabinet of the nation, or occupying a throne; it is a royal business, and they are true kings who follow it successfully.

The harvest of godly service is not yet: "we do with patience wait for it;" but we have earnests of our wage, refreshing pledges of that which is laid up in heaven for us. Partly, this reward lies in the work itself. Men go hunting and shooting for mere love of the sport; surely, in an infinitely higher sphere, we may hunt for men's souls for the pleasing indulgence of our benevolence. To some of us, it would be an unendurable misery to see men sink to hell, and to be making no effort for their salvation. It is a ward to us to have a vent for our inward fires. It is woe and weariness to us to be shut up from those sacred activities which aim at plucking fire-brands from the flame. We are in deep sympathy with our fellows, and feel that, in a measure, their sin is our sin, their peril our peril.

> If another lose the way,
> My feet also go astray;
> If another downward go,
> In my heart is also woe.

It is therefore a relief to set forth the gospel, that we may save ourselves from that sympathetic misery which echoes in our hearts the crash of soul-ruin.

Soul-winning is a service which brings great benefit to the individual who consecrates himself to it. The man who has watched for a soul, prayed for it, laid his plans for it, spoken with much trembling, and endeavoured to make an impression, has been educating himself by the effort. Having been disappointed, he has cried to God more earnestly, has tried again, has looked up the promise to meet the case of the convicted one, has turned to that point of the divine character which seems most likely to encourage trembling faith,—he has in every step been benefiting himself. When he has gone over the old, old story of the cross to the weeping penitent, and has at last gripped the hand of one who could say,—" I do believe, I will believe, that Jesus died for me;" I say, he has had a reward in the process through which his own mind has gone.

It has reminded him of his own lost estate; it has shown him the struggles that the Spirit had in bringing him to repentance; it has reminded him of that precious moment when he first looked to Jesus; and it has strengthened him in his firm confidence that Christ will save men. When we see Jesus save another, and see that marvellous transfiguration which passesover the face of the saved one, our own faith is greatly confirmed. Sceptics and modern-thought men have little to do with converts: those who labour for conversions believe in conversions; those who behold the processes of regeneration see a miracle wrought, and are certain that "this is the finger of God." It is the most blessed exercise for a soul, it is the divinest ennobling of the heart, to spend yourself in seeking to bring another to the dear Redeemer's fee t. If it ended there, you might thank God that ever He called you to a service so comforting, so strengthening, so elevating, so confirming, as that of converting others from their evil ways.

Another precious recompense is found in *the gratitude and affection of those you bring to Christ*. This is a choice boon,—the blessedness of joying i n another's joy, the bliss of hearing that you have led a soul to Jesus. Measure the sweetness of this recompense by the bitterness of its opposite. Men of God have brought many to Jesus, and all things have gone well in the church till declining years or changing fashions have thrown the good man into the shade, and then the minister's own spiritual children have been eager to turn him out of doors. The unkindest cut of all has come from those who owed their souls to him. His heart was broken while he has sighed, "I could have borne it, had not the persons that I brought to the Saviour have turned against me." The pang is not unknown to me. I can never forget a certain household, in which the Lord gave me the great joy to bring four employers and several persons engaged by them to Jesus' feet. Snatched from the utmost carelessness of worldliness, these who had previously known nothing of the grace of God were joyful confessors of the faith. After a while, they imbibed certain o pinions differing from ours, and from that moment some of them had nothing but hard words for me and my preaching. I had done my best to teach them all the truth I knew, and if they had found out more than I had discovered, they might at least have remembered where they learned the elements of the faith. It is years ago now, and I have never said as much as this before; but I feel the wound much. I only mention these sharp pricks to show how very sweet it is to have those about you whom you have brought to the Saviour.

A mother feels great delight in her children, for a n intense love comes with natural relationships; but there is a still deeper love connected with spiritual kinship, a love which lasts through life, and will continue in eternity, for even in heaven each servant of the Lord shall say, "Here am I, and the children whom Thou hast given me." They neither marry nor are given in marriage in the city of our God, but fatherhood and brotherhood in Christ shall still survive. Those sweet and blessed bonds which grace has formed continue forever, and spiritual relationships are rather developed than dissolved by translation to the better land. If you are eager for real joy, such as you may think over and sleep upon, I am persuaded that no joy of growing wealthy, no joy of increasing knowledge, no joy of influence over your fellow-creatures, no joy of any othersort, can ever be compared with the rapture of saving a soul from death, and helping to restore our lost brethren to our great Father's house. Talk of ten thousand pounds reward! It is nothing at all, one might easily spend that amount; but one cannot exhaust the unutterable delights which come from the gratitude of souls converted from the error of their ways.

But the richest reward lies in *pleasing God, and causing the Redeemer to see of the travail of His soul.* That Jesus should have His reward, is worthy of the Eternal Father; but it is marvellous that we should be employed by the Father to give to Christ the purchase of His agonies. This is a wonder of wonders! O my soul, this is an honour too great for thee! A bliss too deep for words! Listen, dear friends, and answer me. What would you give to cause a thrill of pleasure in the heart of the Well-beloved? Recollect the grief you cost Him, and the pangs that shot through Him that He might deliver you from your sin and its consequences; do you not long to make Him glad? When you bring others to His feet, you give Him joy, and no small joy either. Is not that a wonderful text,—" There is joy in the presence of the angels of God over one sinner that repenteth"? What does that mean? Does it mean that the angels have joy? We generally read it so, but it is not the intent of the verse. It says, "There is joy in the presence of the angels of God," —that is, joy in the heart of God, around whose throne the angels stand. It is a joy which angels delight to behold,—what is it? Is the blessed God capable of greater joy than His own boundless happiness? Wondrous language this! The in finite bliss of God is more eminently displayed, if it cannot be increased. Can we be the

113

instruments of this? Can we do anything which will make the Eve r-blessed glad? Yes, for we are told that the great Father rejoices above measure when His prodigal son that was dead is alive again, and the lost one is found.

If I could say this as I ought to say it, it would make every Christian cry out, "Then I will labour to bring souls to the Saviour;" and it would make those of us who have brought many to Jesus instant, in season and out of season, to bring more to Him. It is a great pleasure to be doing a kindness to an earthly friend, but to be doing something distinctly for Jesus, something which will be of all things in the world most pleasing to Him, is a great delight! It is a good work to build a meeting-house, and give it outright to the cause of God, if it is done with a right and proper motive; but one living stone, built upon the sure foundation by our instrumentality, will give the Master more pleasure than if we erected a vast pile of natural stones, which might only cumber the ground. Then go, dear friends, and seek to bring your children and your neighbours, your friends and your kinsfolk, to the Saviour's feet, for nothing will give him so much pleasure as to see them turn unto Him and live. By your love to Jesus, I beseech you, become fishers of men.

THE SOUL-WINNER'S LIFE AND WORK

"The fruit of the righteous is a tree of life; and he that winneth souls is wise."

Proverbs 11:30.

It seems to me that there is a higher joy in looking at a body of believers than that which arises from merely regarding them as saved. Not but what there is a great joy in salvation, a joy worthy to stir the angelic harps. Think of the Saviour's agony in the ransom of every one of His redeemed, think of the work of the Holy Spirit in every renewed heart, think of the love of the Father as resting upon every one of the regenerate: I could not, if I took up my parable for a month, set forth all the mass of joy that is to be seen in a multitude of believers if we only look at what God has done for them, and promised to them, and will fulfill in them. But there is yet a wider field of thought, and my mind has been traversing it all this day,— the thought of the capacities of service contained in a numerous band of believers, the possibilities of blessing others which lie within the bosoms of regenerate persons. We must not think so much of what we already are as to forget what the Lord m ay accomplish by us for others. Here are the coals of fire, but who shall describe the conflagration which they may cause?

We ought to regard the Christian Church, not as a luxurious hostelry where Christian gentlemen may each one dwell at his ease in his own inn, but as a barracks in which soldiers are gathered together to be drilled and trained for war. We should regard the Christian Church, not as an association for mutual admiration and comfort, but as an army with banners, marching to the fray, to achieve victories for Christ, to storm the strongholds of the foe, and to add province after province to the Redeemer's kingdom. We may view converted persons gathered into church-membership as so much wheat in the granary. God be thanked that it is there, and that so far the harvest has rewarded the sower; but far more soul-inspiring is the view when we regard those believers as each one likely to be made a living centre for the extension of the kingdom of

115

Jesus, for then we see them sowing the fertile v alleys of our land, and promising ere long to bring forth some thirty, some forty, some fifty, and some a hundredfold. The capacities of life are enormous, one becomes a thousand in a marvellously brief space. Within a short time, a few grains of wheat would suffice to seed the whole world, and a few true saints might suffice for the conversion of all nations. Only take that which comes of one ear, store it well, sow it all, again store it next year, and then sow it all again, and the multiplication almost exceeds the power of computation. Oh, that every Christian were thus year by year the Lord's seed corn! If all the wheat in the world had perished except a single grain, it would not take many years to replenish all the earth, and sow her fields and plains; but in a far shorter time, in the power of the Holy Spirit, one Paul or one Peter would have evangelised all lands. View yourselves as grains of wheat predestinated to seed the world. That man lives grandly who is as earnest as if the very existence of Christianity depended upon himself, and is determined that to al l men within his reach shall be made known the unsearchable riches of Christ.

If we whom Christ is pleased to use as His seed corn were only all scattered and sown as we ought to be, and were all to sprout and bring forth the green blade and the corn in the ear, what a harvest there would be! Again would it be fulfilled, "There shall be an handful of corn in the earth upon the top of the mountains;" —a very bad position for it,— "the fruit thereof shall shake like Lebanon: and they of the city shall flourish like grass of the earth." May God grant us to feel some degree of the Holy Spirit's quickening power while we talk together, not so much about what God has done for us as about what God may do by us, and how far we may put ourselves into a right position to be used by Him.

There are two things in the text, and these are found laid out with much distinctness in its two sentences. The first is, the life of the believer is, or ought to be, full of soul-blessing. "The fruit of the righteous is a tree of life." In the second place, the pursuit of the believer ought always to be soul -winning. The second is much the same as the first, only the first head sets forth our unconscious influence, and the second our efforts which we put forth with the avowed object of winning souls for Christ.

Let us begin at the beginning, because the second cannot be carried out without the first: without fulness of life within there cannot be an overflow of life to others. It is of no use for any of you to try to be soul-winners if you are not bearing fruit in your own lives. How can you serve the Lord with your lips if you do not serve Him with your lives? How can you preach His gospel with your tongues, when with hands, feet, and hearts you are preaching the devil's gospel, and setting up antichrist by your practical unholiness? We must first have life and bear personal fruit to the divine glory, and then out of our example will spring the conversion of others. Let us go to the fountain-head, and see how the believer's own life is essential to his being useful to others.

I. THE LIFE OF THE BELIEVER IS FULL OF SOUL-BLESSIN G.

This fact we shall consider by means of a few observations growing out of the text; and, first, let us remark that the believer's outward life comes as a matter of fruit from him. This is important to notice. "The fruit of the righteous" —that is to say, his life—is not a thing fastened upon him, but it grows out of him. It is not a garment which he puts off and on, but it is inseparable from himself. The sincere man's religion is the man himself, and not a cloak for his concealment. True godliness is the natural outgrowth of a renewed nature, not the forced growth of pious hothouse excitement. Is it not natural for a vine to bear clusters of grapes? natural for a palm tree to bear dates? Certainly, as natural as it is for the apples of Sodom to be found on the trees of Sodom, and for noxious plants to produce poisonous berries. When God gives a new nature to His people, the life which comes out of that new nature springs spontaneously from it. The man who has a religion which is not part and parcel of himself will by-and-by discover that it is worse than useless to him. The man who wears his piety like a mask at a carnival, so that, when he gets home, he changes from a saint to a savage, from an angel to a devil, from John to Judas, from a benefactor to a bully,—such a man, I say, knows very well what formalism and hypocrisy can do for him, but he has no vestige of true religion. Fig trees do not bear figs on certain days, and thorns at other times; but they are true to their nature at all seasons.

Those who think that godliness is a matter of vestment, and has an intimate relation with blue, and scarlet, and fine linen, are consistent if they keep their religion to the proper time for the wearing of their sacred pomposities; but he who has discovered what Christianity is knows that it is much more a life than an act, a form, or a profession. Much as I love the creed of Christendom, I am ready to say that true Christianity is far more a life than a creed. It is

117

a creed, and it has its ceremonies, but it is mainly a life; it is a divine spark of heaven's own flame which falls into the human bosom and burn s within, consuming much that lies hidden in the soul, and then at last, as a heavenly life, flaming forth, so as to be seen and felt by those around. Under the indwelling power of the Holy Spirit, a regenerate person becomes like that bush in Horeb, which was all aglow with Deity. The God within him makes him shine so that the place around him is holy ground, and those who look at him feel the power of his hallowed life.

Dear brethren, we must take care that our religion is more and more a matter of outgrowth from our souls. Many professors are hedged about with, "You must not do this, or that," and are driven onward with, "You must do this, and you must do that." But there is a doctrine, too often perverted, which is, nevertheless, a blessed truth, and ought to dwell i n your hearts. "Ye are not under the law, but under grace:" hence you do not obey the will of God because you hope to earn heaven thereby, or dream of escaping from divine wrath by your own doings, but because there is a life in you which seeks after that which is holy, pure, right, and true, and cannot endure that which is evil. You are careful to maintain good works, not from either leg al hopes or legal fears, but because there is a holy thing within you, born of G od, which seeks, according to its nature, to do that which is pleasing to God. Look to it more and more that your religion is real, true, natural, vital,—not artificial, constrained, superficial, a thing of times, days, places, a fungus produced by excitement, a fermentation generated by meetings and stirred by oratory. We all need a religion which can live either in a wilderness or in a crowd; a religion which will show itself in every walk of life, and in every company. Give me the godliness which is seen at home, especially around the fireside, for it is never more beautiful than there; that is seen in the battle and tussle of ordinary business among scoffers and gainsayers as well as among Christian men. Show me the faith which can defy the lynx eyes of the world, and walk fearlessly where all scowl with the fierce eyes of hate, as well as where there are observers to sympathize, and friends to judge leniently. May you be filled with the life of the Spirit, and your whole conduct and conversation be the natural and blessed outgrowth of that Spirit's indwelling!

Note, next, that *the fruit which comes from a Christian is fruit worthy of his character*: "The fruit of the righteous is a tree of life." Each tree bears its own fruit, and is known by it. The righteous man bears righteous fruit; and do not let us be at all deceived, brethren,

118

or fall into any error about this, "he that doeth righteousness is righteous," and "he that doeth not righteousness is not of God, neither he that loveth not his brother." We are pre pared, I hope, to die for the doctrine of justification by faith, and to assert before all adversaries that salvation is not of works; but we also confess that we are justified by a faith which produces works, and if any man has a faith which does not produce good works, it is the faith of devils. Saving faith appropriates the finished work of the Lord Jesus, and so saves by itself alone, for we are justified by faith without works; but the faith which is without works cannot bring salvation to any man. We are saved by faith without works, but not by a faith that is without works, for the real faith that saves the soul works by love and purifies the character. If you can cheat across the counter, your hope of heaven is a cheat, too; though you can pray as prettily as anybody, and practice acts of outward piety as well as any other hypocrite, you are deceived if you expect to be right at last. If as a servant you are lazy, lying, and loitering, or if as a master you are hard, tyrannical, and unchristianlike towards your men,—y our fruit shows that you are a tree of Satan's own orchard, and bear apples which will suit his tooth. If you can practise tricks of trade, and if you can li e,—and how many do lie every day about their neighbours or about their goods!—you may talk as you like about being justified by faith, but all liars will have their portion in the lake that burneth with fire and brimstone, and amongst the biggest liars you will be, for you are guilty of the lie of saying, "I am a Christian," whereas you are not. A false profession is one of the worst of lies, since it brings the utmost dishonour upon Christ and His people. The fruit of the righteous is righteousness: the fig tree will not bring forth thorns, neither shall we gather grapes from thistles. The tree is known by its fruit, and if we cannot judge men's hearts, and must not try to do so, we can judge their lives; and I pray God we may all be ready to judge our own lives, and see if we are bringing forth righteous fruit, for if not, we are not righteous men.

Let it, however, never be forgotten that the fruit of the righteous, though it comes from him naturally, for his new-born nature yields the sweet fruit of obedience, yet it is always the result of grace, and the gift of G od. No truth ought to be remembered more than this, "From Me is thy fruit found." We can bring forth no fruit except as we abide in Christ. The righteous shall flourish as a branch, and only as a branch. How does a branch flourish? By its connection with the stem, and the consequent inflowing of the sap; and so, though the righteous man's righteous actions are his own, yet they are always produced by the grace which is imparted to him, and he never da res to take any credit for them, but he sings, "Not unto us, O Lord, not unto us, but unto Thy name give praise." If he fails, he blames himself; if he succeeds, he glorifies God. Imitate his example. Lay every fault, every weakness, every infirmity at your own door; and if you fall in any respect short of perfection, —and I am sure you do,—take all that to yourself, and do not excuse yourself; but if there be any virtue, any praise, any true desire, any real prayer, anything that is good, ascribe it all to the Spirit of God. Remember, the righteous man would not be righteous unless God had made him righteous, and the fruit of righteousness would never come from him unless the divine sap within him had produced that acceptable fruit. To God alone be all honour and glory.

The main lesson of the passage is that this outburst of life from the Christian, this consequence of life within him, this fruit of his soul becomes a blessing to others. Like a tree, it yields shade and sustenance to all around. It is a tree of life, an expression which I cannot fully work out as I would wish, for there is a world of instruction compressed into the illustration. That which to the believer himself is fruit becomes to others a tree: it is a singular metaphor, but by no means a lame one. From the child of God there falls the fruit of holy living, even as an acorn drops from the oak; this holy living becomes influential and produces the best results in others, even as the acorn becomes itself an oak, and lends its shade to the birds of the air. The Christian's holiness becomes a tree of life. I suppose it means a living tree, a tree calculated to give life and sustain it in others. A fruit becomes a tree! A tree of life! Wonderful result this! Christ in the Christian produces a character which becomes a tree of life. The outward character is the fruit of the inner life; t his outer life itself grows from a fruit into a tree, and as a tree it bears fruit in others to the praise and glory of God. Dear brothers and sisters, I know some of God' s saints who live very near to Him, and they are evidently a tree of life, for their very shadow is comforting, cooling, and refreshing to many weary souls. I have known the young, the tried, the downcast, go to them, sit beneath their shade, and pour out the tale of their troubles, and they have felt it a rich blessing to receive their sympathy, to be told of the faithfulness of the Lord, and to be guided in the way of wisdom. There are a few good men in this world whom to know is to be rich. Such men are libraries of gospel truth; but they are better than books, for the truth in them is written on living pages. Their character is a true and living tree; it is not a mere post of the dead wood of doctrine, bearing an inscription, and rotting while it does so, but it is a vital, organized, fruit-producing thing, a plant of the Lord's right-hand planting.

Not only do some saints give comfort to others, but they also yield them spiritual nourishment. Well-trained Christians become nursing fathers and nursing mothers, strengthening the weak, and binding up the wounds of the broken-hearted. So, too, the strong, bold, generous deeds of large-hearted Christians are of great service to their fellow-Christians, and tend to raise them to a higher level. You feel refreshed by observing how they act; their patience in suffering, their courage in danger, their holy faith in God, their happy faces under trial,—all these nerve you for your own conflicts. In a thousand ways, the sanctified believer's example acts in a healing and comforting way to his brethren, and assists in raising them above anxiety and unbelief. Even as the leaves of the tree of life are for the healing of the nations, so the words and deeds of saints are medicine for a thousand maladies.

And then what fruit, sweet to the taste of the godly, instructed believers bear! We can never trust in men as we trust in the Lord, but the Lord can cause the members to bless us in their measure, even as their Head is ever ready to do. Jesus alone is the Tree of Life, but He makes some of His servants to be instrumentally to us little trees of life, by whom He gives us fruit of the same sort that He bears Himself, for He puts it there, and it is Himself in His saints causing them to bring forth golden apples, with which our souls are gladdened. May we every one of us be made like our Lord, and m ay His fruit be found upon our boughs!

We have put into the tomb many of the saints who have fallen asleep, and among them there were some of whom I will not at this moment speak particularly, whose lives as I look back upon them are still a tree of life to me. I pray God that I may be like them. Many of you knew them, and if you will only recall their holy, devoted lives, the influence the y have left behind will still be a tree of life to you. They being dead yet speak; hear ye their eloquent exhortations! Even in their ashes live their wonted fires; kindle your souls at their warmth. Their noble examples are the endowments of the church, her children are ennobled and enriched as they remember their walk of faith and labour of love. Beloved, may we every one of us be true benedictions to the churches in whose gardens we are planted! "Oh!" say sone, "I am afraid I am not much like a tree, for I feel so weak and insignificant." If you have faith as a grain of mustard seed, you have the commencement of the tree beneath whose branches the birds of the air will yet find a lodging. The very birds that would have eaten the tiny seed come and find lodgment in the tree which grows out of it; and people who despise and mock at you, now that you are a young beginner, will one of these days, if God blesses you, be glad to borrow comfort from your example and experience.

But one other thought on this point. Remember that the completeness and development of the holy life will be seen above. There is a city of which it is written, "In the midst of the street of it, and on either side of the river, was there the tree of life." The tree of life is a heavenly plant, and so the fruit of the Christian is a thing of heaven; though not transplanted to the glory land, it is getting fit for its final abode. What is holiness but heaven on earth? What is living unto God but the essence of heaven? What are uprightness, integrity, Christ-likeness? Have not these even more to do with heaven than harps and palms and streets of purest gold? Holiness, purity, loveliness of character,— these make a heaven within a man's own bosom; and even if there were no place called heaven, that heart would have a heavenly happiness which is set free from sin, and made like the Lord Jesus. See, t hen, dear brethren, what an important thing it is for us to be indeed righteous before God, for then the outcome of that righteousness shall be fruit which will be a tree of life to others, and a tree of life in heaven above, world without end. O blessed Spirit, make it so, and Thou shalt have all the praise!

II. This brings us to our second head. THE PURSUIT OF THE BELIEVER SHOULD BE SOUL-WINNING. For "he that winneth souls is wise. The two things are put together—the life first, the effort next: what God hath joined together, let no man put asunder.

It is implied in our text that *there are souls which need winning.* Ah, me! all souls of men are lost by nature, You might walk through the streets of London, and say, with sighs and tears, of the masses of men you meet upon those crowded pavements, "Lost, lost, lost!" Wherever Christ is not trusted, and the Spirit has not created a new heart, and the soul has not come to the great Father, there is a lost soul. But here is the mercy —these lost souls can be won. They are not hopelessly lost; not yet has God determined that they shall forever abide as they are. It is not yet said, "He that is filthy, let him be filthy still;" but they are in the land of hope where mercy may reach them, for they are spoken of as capable of being won. They may yet be delivered, but the phrase hints that it will need all our efforts: "He that *winneth souls.*"

What do we mean by that word win? We use it in love-making. We speak of the bridegroom who wins his bride; and sometimes there is a large expense of love, many a pleading word, and many a wooing ac t, ere yet the valued heart is all the suitor's own. I use this explanation because in some respects it is the very best, for souls will have to be won for Christ in this fashion, that they may be espoused unto Him. We must make love to the sinner for Christ; that is how hearts are to be won for Him. Jesus is the Bridegroom, and we must speak for Him, and tell of His beauty, as Abraham's servant, when he went to seek a wife for Isaac, acted as a wooer in his stead. Have you never read the story? Then turn to it when you get home, and see how he talked about his master, what possessions he had, and how Isaac was to be heir of it all, and so on, and then he finished his address by urging Rebecca to go with him. The question was put home to her, "Wilt thou go with this man?" So the minister's business is to commend his Master and his Master's riches, and the n to say to souls, "Will you be wedded to Christ?" He who can succeed in this very delicate business is a wise man.

We also use the term in a military fashion. We speak of winning a city, a castle, or a battle. We do not win victories by going to sleep. Believe me, castles are not captured by men who are only half a wake. To win a battle, needs the best skill, the greatest endurance, and the utmost courage. To storm fortresses, which are regarded as almost impregnable, men need to burn the midnight oil, and study well the arts of attack; an d, when the time comes for the assault, not a soldier must be a laggard, but all force of artillery and manhood must be brought to bear on the point assailed. To carry man's heart by main force of grace, to capture it, to break down the bars of brass and dash the gates of iron in pieces, requires the exercise of a skill which only Christ can give. To bring up the big battering-rams, and shake every stone in the sinner's conscience, to make his heart rock and reel within him for fear of the wrath to come,—in a word, to assail a soul with all the artillery of the gospel, needs a wise man, and one fully aroused to his work. To hold up the white flag of mercy, and, if that be despised, to use the battering-ram of threatening until a breach is made, and then, with the sword of the Spirit in his hand, to capture the city, to tear down the black flag of sin, and run up the banner of the cross, needs all the force the choicest preacher can command, and a great deal more. Those whose souls are as cold as the Arctic regions, and whose energy is reduced to the vanishing point, are not likely to take the city of Mansoul for Prince Emmanuel. If you think you are going to win souls, you must throw your soul into your work, just as a warrior must throw his soul into a battle, or victory will not be yours.

We use the words "to win" in reference to making a fortune, and we all know that the man who becomes a millionaire has to rise up early, and sit up late, and eat the bread of carefulness, and it takes a deal of toiling and saving, and I know not what besides, to amass immense wealth. We have to go in for winning souls with the same ardour and concentration of our faculties as old Astor of New York went in to build up that fortune of so many millions which he has now left behind him. It is, indeed, a race, and you know that, in a race, nobody wins unless he strains every muscle and sinew. "They that run in a race run all, but one receiveth the prize;" and that one is generally he who had more strength than the rest; certainly, whether he had more strength or not, he put out all he had, and we shall not win souls unless we imitate him in this.

Solomon in the text declares that, "He that winneth souls is wise," and such a declaration is all the more valuable as coming from so wise a man. Let me show you why a soul-winner is wise. First, he must be taught of God before he will attempt it. The man who does not know that, whereas he was once blind, now he sees, had better think of his own blindness before he attempts to lead his friends in the right way. If not saved yourself, you cannot be the means of saving others. He that winneth souls must be wise unto salvation first for himself.

That being taken for granted, he is a wise man to select such a pursuit. Young man, are you choosing an object worthy to be the great aim of your life? I do hope you will judge wisely, and select a noble ambition. If God has given you great gifts, I hope they will not be wasted on any low, sordid, or selfish design. Suppose I am now addressing one who has great talents, and has an opportunity of being what he likes, of going into Parliament, and helping to pass great measures, or of going into business, and making himself a man of importance; I hope he will weigh the claims of Jesus and immortal souls as well as other claims. Shall I addict myself to study? Shall I surrender myself to business? Shall I travel? Shall I spend my time in pleasure? Shall I become the principal fox-hunter of the county? Shall I lay out my time in promoting political and social reforms? Think them all over; but if you are a Christian man, my dear friend, nothing will equal in enjoyment, in usefulness, in honour, and in lasting recompense the giving yourself up to the winning of souls. Oh, it is grand hunting, I can tell you, and beats all the fox-hunting in the world in excitement and exhilaration! Have I not sometimes g one with a cry over hedge and ditch after some poor sinner, and kept well up with him in every twist and turn he took, till I have overtaken him by God's gr ace, and been in at the death, and rejoiced exceedingly when I have seen him captured by my Master? Our Lord Jesus calls His ministers fishermen, and no other fishermen have such labour, such sorrow, and such delight as we have. what a happy thing it is that you may win souls for Jesus, and may do this though you abide in your secular callings! Some of you would never win souls in pulpits; it would be a great pity if you tried, but you can win souls in the workshop, and in the laundry, in the nursery, and in the drawing-room. Our hunting grounds are everywhere: by the wayside, by the fireside, in the corner, and in the crowd. Among the common people Jesus is our theme, and among the great ones we have no other. You will be wise, my brother, if for you the one absorbing desire is that you may turn the ungodly from the error of their ways. For you there will be a crown glittering with many stars, which you shall cast at Jesus' feet in the day of His appearing.

Further, it is not only wise to make this your aim, but you will have to be very wise if you succeed in it because the souls to be won are so different in their constitutions, feelings, and conditions, and you will have to adapt yourselves to them all. The trappers of North America have to find out the habits of the animals they wish to catch, and so you will have to learn how to deal with each class of cases. Some are very depressed, you will have to comfort them. Perhaps you will comfort them too much, and make them unbelieving; and, therefore, possibly, instead of comforting them, you will need sometimes to administer a sharp word to cure the sulkiness into which they have fallen. Another person may be frivolous, and if you put on a serious face you will frighten your bird away; you will have to be cheerful, and drop a word of admonition as if by accident. Some people, again, will not let you speak to them, but will talk to you; you must know the art of putting a word in edgeways. You will have to be very wise, and become all thing s to all men, and your success will prove your wisdom. Theories of dealing with souls may look very wise, but they often prove to be useless when actually tried: he who by God's grace accomplishes the work is a wise man, though perhaps he knows no theory whatever. This work will need all your wit, and far more, and you will have to cry to the great Winner of souls above to give you of His Holy Spirit.

But, mark you, he that wins souls is wise, because he is engaged in a business which makes men wiser as thy proceed with it. You will bungle at first, and very likely drive sinners off from Christ by your attempts to draw them to Him. I have tried to move some souls with all my might with a certain passage of Scripture, but they have taken it in an opposite light to what it was intended, and have started off in the wrong direction. It is very difficult to know how to act with bewildered enquirers. If you want some people to go forward, you must pull them backwards; if you want them to go to the right, you must insist upon their going to the left, and then they go to the right directly. You must be ready for these follies of poor human nature. I knew a poor aged Christian woman who had been a child of God fifty years, but she was in a state of melancholy and distress, from which nobody could arouse her. I called several times, and endeavoured to cheer her up, but generally when I left she was worse than before. So, the next time I called to see her, I did not say anything to her about Christ or religion. She soon introduced t hose topics herself, and then I remarked that I was not going to talk to her about such holy things, for she did not know anything about them, for she was not a believer in Christ, and had been, no doubt, a hypocrite for many years. She could not stand that, and asserted, in self-defence, that the Lord above knew her better than I did, and He was her witness that she did love the Lord Jesus Christ. She scarcely forgave herself afterwards for that admission, but she could never talk to me quite so despairingly any more. True lovers of men's souls l earn the art of dealing with them, and the Holy Spirit makes them expert soul-surgeons for Jesus. It is not because a man has more abilities, nor altogether because he has more grace, but the Lord makes him to love the souls of men intensely, and this imparts a secret skill, since, for the most part, the way to get sinners to Christ is to love them to Christ.

Beloved brethren, I will say, once more, he who really wins souls for Jesus, however he wins them, is a wise man. Some of you are slow to admit this. You say,—" Well, So-and-so, I daresay, has been very useful, but he is very rough." What does his roughness matter if he wins souls? "A h!" says another, "but I am not built up under him." Why do you go to hear him to get built up? If the Lord has sent him to pull down, let him pull down, and Do you go elsewhere for edification; but do not grumble at a man who does one work because he cannot do another. We are also too apt to pit one minister against another, and say, "You should hear my minister." Perhaps we should, but it would be better for you to hear the man who edifies you, and let others go where they also are instructed. "He that winneth souls is wise." I do not ask you how he did it. He sang the gospel, and you did not like it; but if he won souls, he was wise. Soul- winners have all their own ways; and if they do but win souls, they are wise. I will tell you what is not wise, and will not be thought so at the last, namely, to go about the churches, doing nothing yourself, and railing at all the Lord's useful servants.

Here is a dear brother on his dying bed, he has the sweet thought that the Lord enabled him to bring many souls to Jesus, and the expectation when he comes to the gates that many spirits will come to meet him. They will throng the ascent to the New Jerusalem, and welcome the ma n who brought them to Jesus. They are immortal monuments to his labours. He is wise. Here is another who has spent all his time in interpreting the prophecies, so that everything he read of in the newspapers he could see in Daniel or the Revelation. He is wise, so some say, but I had rather spend my time in winning souls. I would sooner bring one sinner to Jesus Christ than unpick all the mysteries of the divine Word, for salvation is the thing we are to live for. I would to God that I understood all mysteries, yet chief of all would I proclaim the mystery of soul-saving by faith in the blood of the Lamb. It is com paratively a small matter for a minister to have been a staunch upholder of orthodoxy all his days, and to have spent himself in keeping up the hedges of his church; soul-winning is the main concern. It is a very good thing to contend earnestly for the faith once delivered to the saints; but I do not think I should like to say in my last account, "Lord, I have lived to fight the Romanists and the State Church, and to put down the various erroneous sects, but I never led a sinner to the cross." No, we will fight the good fight of faith, but the winning of souls is the greater matter, and he who attends to it is wise. Another brother has preached the truth, but he did so polish up his sermons that the gospel was hidden. Never a sermon was fit to preach, he thought, until he had written it out a dozen times to see whether every sentence would be according to the canons of Cicero and Quintillian, and then he went and delivered the gospel as a grand oration. Is that wise? Well, it takes a wise man to be a thorough orator; but it is better not to be an orator if fine speech prevents your being understood. Let eloquence be flung to the dogs rather than souls be lost. What we want is to win souls, and they are not to be won by flowery speeches. We must have the winning of souls at heart, and be red hot with zeal for their salvation; and then, however much we blunder, according to the critics, we shall be numbered among those whom the Lord calls wise.

Now, Christian men and women, I want you to take this matter up practically, and to determine that you will try this very night to win a soul. Try the one next to you in the seat if you cannot think of anybody else. Try on the way home; try with your own children. Have I not told you of what happened one Sunday evening? In my sermon I said, "Now, you mothers, have you ever prayed with each of your children, one by one, and urged them to lay hold on Christ? Perhaps dear Jane is now in bed, and you have never yet pleaded with her about eternal things. Go home to-night, wake he r up, and say, 'Jane, I am sorry I have never told you about the Saviour personally, and prayed with you, but I mean to do it now.' Wake her up, and put your arms round her neck, and pour out your heart to God with her." Well, there was a good sister here who had a daughter named Jane. What do you think? She came on Monday to bring her daughter Jane to see me in the vestry, for when she woke her up, and began, "I have not spoken to you about Jesus," or something to that effect, "Oh, dear mother!" said Jane, "I have loved the Saviour these six months, and wondered you had not spoken to me about Him;" and then there was great kissing and rejoicing. Perhaps you may find that to be the case with a dear child at home; and, if you do not, so much the more reason why you should begin at once to speak. Did you never win a soul for Jesus? You shall have a crown in heaven, but no jewels in it. You will go to heaven childless; and you know how it was in the old times, how the women dreaded lest they should be childless. Let it be so with Christian people; let them dread being spiritually childless. We must hear the cries of those whom God has given to be born unto Himself by our means. We must hear them, or else cry out in anguish, "Give me converts, or I die." Young men, and old men, and sisters of all ages, if you love the Lord, get a passion for souls. Do you not see them? They are going down to hell by thousands; as often as the hand upon the dial completes its circuit, hell devours multitudes, some of them ignorant of Christ, and others willfully rejecting Him. The world lies in darkness: this great city still pines for the light your own friends and kinsfolk are unsaved, and they may be dead ere this week is over. Oh, if you have any humanity, let alone Christianity, if you have found the remedy, tell the diseased about it! If you have found life, proclaim it to the dead; if you have found liberty, publish it to the captives; if you have found Christ, tell of Him to others. My brethren in the College, let this be your choice work while studying, and let it be the one object of you r lives when you go forth from us. Do not be content when you get a congregation, but labour to win souls; and as you do this, God will bless you. As f or us, we hope during the rest of our lives to follow Him who is The Soul-Winner, and to put ourselves in His hands who maketh us soul-winners, so that our life may not be a long folly, but may be proved by results to have been directed by wisdom.

O you souls not won to Jesus, remember that faith i n Christ saves you! Trust in Him. May you be led to trust in Him, for His name's sake! Amen.

SOUL-WINNING EXPLAINED

"He that winneth souls is wise."

Proverbs 11:30.

The text does not say, "He that winneth sovereigns is wise," though no doubt he thinks himself wise, and perhaps, in a certain grovelling sense, in these days of competition, he must be so; but such wisdom is of the earth, and ends with the earth; and there is another world where the currencies of Europe will not be accepted, nor their past possession be any sign of wealth or wisdom. Solomon, in the text before us, awards no crown for wisdom to crafty statesmen, or even to the ablest of rulers; he issues no diplomas even to philosophers, poets, or men of wit; he crowns with laurel only those who win souls. He does not declare that he who preaches is necessarily wise; and alas! there are multitudes who preach, and gain much applause and eminence, who win no souls, and who shall find it go hard with them at the last, because in all probability they have run and the Master has never sent them. Solomon doe s not say that he who talks about winning souls is wise, since to lay down rules for others is a very simple thing, but to carry them out one's self is far more difficult. He who actually, really, and truly turns men from the error of their ways to God, and so is made the means of saving them from going down to hell, is a wise man; and that is true of him whatever his style of soul-winning may be. He may be a Paul, deeply logical, profound in doctrine, able to command all candid judgments; and if he thus wins souls, he is wise. He may be an Apollos, grandly rhetorical, whose lofty genius soars into the very heaven of eloquence; and if he wins souls in that way, he is wise, but not otherwise. or he may be a Cephas, rough and rugged, using uncouth metaphor and stern declamation; but, if he wins souls, he is no less wise than his polished brother or his argumentative friend, but not else. The great wisdom of soul-winners, according to the text, is proven only by their actual success in really winning soul s. To their own Master they are accountable for the ways in which they go to work, not to us. Do not let us be comparing and contrasting this minister and that. Who art thou that judgest another man's servants? Wisdom is justified in all her children. Only children wrangle about incidental methods: men look at sublime results. Do these workers of many sorts and divers manners win souls? Then they are wise; and you who criticise them, being yourselves unfruitful, cannot be wise, even though you affect to be their judges. God proclaims soul-winners to be wise, dispute it who dare. This degree from the College of Heaven may surely stand them in good stead, let their fellow-mortals say what they will of them.

"He that winneth souls is wise," and this can be se en very clearly. He must be a wise man in even ordinary respects who can by grace achieve so divine a marvel. Great soul-winners never have been fools. A man whom God qualifies to win souls could probably do anything else which providence might allot him. Take Martin Luther, for instance. Why, sirs, the ma n was not only fit to work a Reformation, but he could have ruled a nation or have commanded an army! Think of Whitefield, and remember that the thundering eloquence which stirred all England was not associated with a weak judgment, or an absence of brain- power; the man was a master-orator, and if he had addicted himself to commerce, would have taken a chief place amongst the merchants, or had he been a politician, amid admiring senates would have commanded the listening ear. He that winneth souls is usually a man who could have done anything else if God had called him to it. I know the Lord uses what means He wills, but He always uses means suitable to the end; and if you tell me that David slew Goliath with a sling, I answer—it was the best weapon in the world to reach so tall a giant, and the very fittest weapon that David could have used, for he had been skilled in it from his youth up. There is always an adaptation in the instruments which God uses to produce the ordained result; and though the glory is not to them, nor the excellence in them, but all is to be ascribed to God, yet is there a fitness and preparedness which God seeth, even if we do not. It is assuredly true that soul-winners are by no means idiots or simpletons, but such as God maketh wise for Himself, though vain-glorious wise-acres may dub them fools.

"He that winneth souls is wise," because he has selected a wise object. I think it was Michael Angelo who once carved certain magnificent statues in snow. They are gone; the material readily compacted by the frost as readily melted in the heat. Far wiser was he when he fashioned the enduring marble, and produced works which will last all down the age s. But even marble itself is consumed and fretted by the tooth of time; and he i s wise who selects for his raw material immortal souls, whose existence shall outlast the stars. If God shall bless us to the winning of souls, our work shall remain when the wood, and hay, and stubble of earth's art and science shall have gone to the dust from which they sprang. In heaven itself, the soul-winner, blessed of God, shall have memorials of his work preserved for ever in the galleries of the skies. He has selected a wise object, for what can be wiser than to glorify God, and what, next to that, can be wiser than in the highest sense to bless our fellow-men; to snatch a soul from the gulf that yawns, to lift it up to the heaven that glorifies; to deliver an immortal from the thraldom of Satan, and to bring him into the liberty of Christ? What more excellent than this? I say, that such an aim would commend itself to all right minds, and that angels themselves may envy us poor sons of men that we are permitted to make this our life-object, to win souls for Jesus Christ. Wisdom herself assents to the excellence of the design.

To accomplish such a work, a man must he wise, for to win a soul requires infinite wisdom. God Himself wins not souls without wisdom, for the eternal plan of salvation was dictated by an infallible judgment, and in every line of it infinite skill is apparent. Christ, God's great Soul-Winner, is "the wisdom of God" as well as "the power of God." There is as much wisdom to be seen in the new creation as in the old. In a sinner saved, there is as much of God to be beheld as in a universe rising out of nothing; and we, then, who are to be workers together with God, proceeding side by side with Him to the great work of soul-winning, must be wise, too. It is a work which filled the Saviour's heart, a work which moved the mind of the Eternal Jehovah or ever the earth was. It is no child's play, nor a thing to be achieved while we are half asleep, nor to be attempted without deep consideration, nor to be carried on without gracious help from the only-wise God, our Saviour. The pursuit is wise.

Mark ye well, my brethren, that he who is successful in soul-winning, will prove to have been a wise man in the judgment of those who see the end as well as the beginning. Even if I were utterly selfish, and had no care for anything but my own happiness, I would choose, if I might, under God, to be a soul-winner, for never did I know perfect, overflowing, unutterable happiness of the purest and most ennobling order, till I first heard of one who had sought and found a Saviour through my means. I recollect the thrill of joy which went through me! No young mother ever rejoiced so much over her first-born child, no warrior was so exultant over a hard-won victory. Oh! the joy of knowing that a sinner once at enmity has been reconciled to God, by the Holy Spirit, through the words spoken by our feeble lips. Since then, by grace given to me, the thought of which prostrates me in self-abasement, I have seen and heard of, not hundreds only, but even thousands of sinners turned from the error of their ways by the testimony of God in me. Let afflictions come, let trials be multiplied as God willeth, still this joy preponderates above all others, the joy that we are unto God a sweet savour of Christ in every place, and that as often as we preach the Word, hearts are unlocked, bosoms heave with a new life, eyes weep for sin, and their tears are wiped away as they see the great Substitute for sin, and live.

Beyond all controversy, it is a joy worth worlds to win souls, and, thank God, it is a joy that does not cease with this mort al life. It must be no small bliss to hear, as one wings his flight up to the eternal throne, the wings of others fluttering at one's side towards the same glory, and turning round and questioning them, to hear them say, "We are entering with you through the gates of pearl, you brought us to the Saviour," and to be welcomed to the skies by those who call us father in God,—father in better bonds than those of earth, father through grace and sire for immortality. It will be bliss beyond compare, to meet in yon eternal seats with those begotten of us in Christ Jesus, for whom we travailed in birth, till Christ was formed in them the hope of glory. This is to have many heavens,—a heaven in every one won for Christ, according to the Master's promise, "they that turn many to righteous ness shall shine as the stars for ever and ever."

I have said enough, brethren, I trust, to make some of you desire to occupy the position of soul-winners: but before I further address myself to my text, I should like to remind you that the honour does not belong to ministers only; they may take their full share of it, but it belong s to every one of you who have devoted yourselves to Christ: such honour have all the saints. Every man here, every woman here, every child here, whose heart is right with God, may be a soul-winner. There is no man placed by God's providence where he cannot do some good. There is not a glowworm under a hedge but gives a needed light; and there is not a laboring man, a suffering woman, a servant-girl, a chimney- sweeper, or a crossing-sweeper, but has some opportunities for serving God; and what I have said of soul-winners, belongs not to the learned doctor of divinity, or to the eloquent preacher alone, but to you all who are in Christ Jesus. You can each of you, if grace enables you, be thus wise, and win the happiness of turning souls to Christ through the Holy Spirit.

I am about to dwell upon my text in this way—He that winneth souls is wise; "I shall, first, make that fact stand out a little clearer *by explaining the metaphor used in the text—winning souls*; and then, secondly, *by giving you some lessons in the matter of soul-winning*, through which I trust the conviction will be forced upon each believing mind that the work needs the highest wisdom.

I. First, LET US CONSIDER THE METAPHOR USED IN THE TEXT: "He that winneth souls is wise."

We use the word "win" in many ways.It is sometimes found in very bad company, in those games of chance, juggling tricks and sleight-of-hand, or thimble-rigging (to use a plain word), by which sharpers are so fond of winning. I am sorry to say that much of legerdemain and trickery are to be met with in the religious world. Why, there are those who pretend to save souls by curious tricks, intricate manoeuvres, and dexterous posture-making! A basin of water, half-a-dozen drops, certain syllables—heigh, presto —the infant is made a child of God, a member of Christ, and an inheritor of the kingdom of heaven! This aqueous regeneration surpasses my belief; it is a t rick which I do not understand: the initiated only can perform the beautiful piece of magic, which excels anything ever attempted by the Wizard of the North. There is a way, too, of winning souls by laying hands upon heads, only the elbows of the aforesaid hands must be encased in lawn, and then the machinery acts, and there is grace conferred by blessed fingers! I must confess I do not understand the occult science, but at this I need not wonder, for the profession of saving souls by such juggling can only be carried out by certain favoured persons who have received apostolical succession direct from Judas Iscariot. This episcopal confirmation, when men pretend that it confers grace, is an infamous piece of juggling. The whole thing is an abomination. Only to think that, in this nineteenth century, there should be men who preach lip salvation by sacraments, and salvation by themselves, forsooth! Why, sirs, it is surely too late in the day to come to us with this drivel! Priestcraft, let us hope, is an anachronism, and the sacramental theory out of date. These things might have done for those who could not read, and in the days when books were scarce; but ever since the day when the glorious Luther was helped by God to proclaim with thunder-claps the emancipating truth, "By grace are ye saved through faith; and that not of yourselves: it is the gift of God," there has been too much light for these Popish owls. Let them go back to their ivy-mantled towers, and complain to the moon of those who spoiled of old their kingdom of darkness. Let shaven crowns go to Bedlam, and scarlet hats to the scarlet harlot, but let not Englishmen yield them respect. Modern Tractarianism is a bastard Popery, too mean, too shifty, too double-dealing to delude men of honest minds. If we win souls, it shall be by other arts than Jesuits and shavelings can teach us. Trust not in any man who pretends to priesthood. Priests are liars by trade, and deceivers by profession. We cannot save souls in their theatrical way, and Do not want to do so, for we know that with such jugglery as that, Satan will hold the best hand, and laugh at priests as he turns the cards against them at the last.

How do we win souls, then? Why, the word "win" has a better meaning far. It is used in warfare. Warriors win cities and provinces. Now, to win a soul, is a much more difficult thing than to win a city. Observe the earnest soul-winner at his work; how cautiously he seeks his great Captain 's directions to know when to hang out the white flag to invite the heart to surrender to the sweet love of a dying Saviour; when, at the proper time, to hang out the black flag of threatening, showing that, if grace be not received, judgment will surely follow; and when to unfurl, with dread reluctance, the red flag of the terrors of God against stubborn, impenitent souls. The soul-winner has to sit down before a soul as a great captain before a walled town; to draw his lines of circumvallation, to cast up his entrenchments, and fix his batteries. He must not advance too fast, or he may overdo the fighting; he must not move too slowly, or he may seem not to be in earnest, and may do mischief. Then he must know which gate to attack—how to plant his guns at Ear-g ate, and how to discharge them; how, sometimes, to keep the batteries going, day and night, with red-hot shot, if perhaps he may make a breach in the walls; at other times, to lie by and cease firing, and then, on a sudden, to open all the batteries with terrific violence, if peradventure he may take the soul by surprise, or cast in a truth when it was not expected, to burst like a shell in the soul, and do damage to the dominions of sin. The Christian soldier must know how to advance by little and little,—to sap that prejudice, to undermine that old enmity, to blow into the air that lust, and at the last, to storm the citadel. it is his to throw the scaling ladder up, and to have his ears gladdened as he hears a clicking on the wall of the heart, telling that the scaling ladder has grasped and has gained firm hold; and then, with his sabre between his teeth, to climb up, spring on the man, slay his unbelief in the name of God, capture the city, run up the blood-red flag of the cross of Christ, and say, "The heart is won, won for Christ at last." This needs a warrior well-trained, a master in his art. After many days attack, many weeks of waiting, many an hour of storming by prayer and battering by entreaty, to carry the Malakoff of depravity, this is the work, this i s the difficulty. It takes no fool to do this. God's grace must make a man wise thus to capture Mansoul, to lead its captivity captive, and open wide the heart's gates that the Prince Immanuel may come in. This is winning a soul.

The word "win" was commonly used among the ancients, to signify winning in the wrestling match. When the Greek sought to win the laurel, or the ivy crown, he was compelled a long time before to put himself through a course of training; and when he came forth at last stripped for the encounter, he had no sooner exercised himself in the first few efforts than you saw how every muscle and every nerve had been developed in him. He had a stern opponent, and he knew it, and therefore left none of his energy unused. While the wrestling was going on, you could see the man's eye, how he watched every motion, every feint of his antagonist, and how his hand, his foot, and his whole body were thrown into the encounter. He feared to meet with a fall: he hoped to give one to his foe. Now, a true soul-winner has often to co me to close quarters with the devil within men. He has to struggle with their prejudice, with their love of sin, with their unbelief, with their pride, and then again, all of a sudden, to grapple with their despair; at one moment he strives with their self-righteousness, at the next moment with their unbelief in God. Ten thousand arts are used to prevent the soul-winner from being conqueror in the encounter; but if God has sent him, he will never renounce his hold of the soul he seek s till he has given a throw to the power of sin, and won another soul for Christ.

Besides that, there is another meaning to the word "win" upon which I cannot expatiate here. We use the word, you know, in a softer sense than these which have been mentioned, when we come to deal with hearts. There are secret and mysterious ways by which those who love win the object of their affection, which are wise in their fitness to the purpose. I cannot tell you how the lover wins his fond one, but experience has probably taught you. The weapon of this warfare is not always the same, yet where that victory is won the wisdom of the means becomes clear to every eye. The weapon of love is sometimes a look, or a t word whispered and eagerly listened to; sometimes it is a tear; but this I know, that we have, most of us in our turn, cast around another heart a chain which that other would not care to break, and which has linked us twain in a blessed captivity which has cheered our life. Yes, and that is very nearly the way in which we have to save souls. That illustration is nearer the mark than any of the others. Love is the true way of soul-winning, for when I spoke of storming the walls, and when I spoke of wrestling, those were but metaphors, but this is near the fact. We win by love. We win hearts for Jesus by love, by sympathy with their sorrow, by anxiety lest they should perish, by pleading with God for them with all our hearts that they should not be left to die unsaved, by pleading with them for God that, for their own sake, they would seek mercy and find grace. Yes, sirs, there is a spiritual wooing and winning of hearts for the Lord Jesus; and if you would learn the way, you must ask God to give you a tender heart and a sympathising soul. I believe that much of the secret of soul-winning lies in having bowels of compassion, in having spirits that can be touched with the feeling of hum an infirmities. Carve a preacher out of granite, and even if you give him a n angel's tongue, he will convert nobody. Put him into the most fashionable pulpit, make his elocution faultless, and his matter profoundly orthodox, but so long as he bears within his bosom a hard heart he can never win a soul. Soul-saving requires a heart that beats hard against the ribs. It requires a soul full of the milk of human kindness; this is the sine qua non of success. This is the chief natural qualification for a soul-winner, which, under God, and blessed of Him, will accomplish wonders.

I have not looked at the Hebrew of the text, but I find-and you who have marginal references to your Bibles will find—that it is, "He that taketh souls is wise," which word refers to fishing, or to bird-catching. Every Sunday, when I leave my house, as I come along, I cannot help seeing men, with their cages and their captive birds, trying all around the common, and in the fields, to catch poor little warblers. They understand the method of alluring and entrapping their victims. Soul-winners might learn much from t hem. We must have our lures for souls, adapted to attract, to fascinate, to grasp. We must go forth with our bird-lime, our decoys, our nets, our baits, so that we may but catch the souls of men. Their enemy is a fowler possessed of the basest and most astounding cunning; we must outwit him with the guile of honesty, the craft of grace. But the art is to be learned only by divine teaching, and herein we must be wise and willing to learn.

The man who takes fish must also have some art in him. Washington Irving, I think it is, tells us of some three gentlemen who had read in Izaak Walton all about the delights of fishing. So they must needs enter upon the same amusement, and accordingly they became disciples of the gentle art. They went into New York, and bought the best rods and lines that could be purchased, and they found out the exact fly for the particular day or month, so that the fish might bite at once, and as it were fly into the basket with alacrity. They fished, and fished, and fished the live-long day; but the basket was empty. They were getting disgusted with a sport that had no sport in it, when a ragged boy came down from the hills, without shoes or stockings, and humiliated them to the last degree. He had a bit of a bough pulled off a tree, and a piece of string, and a bent pin; he put a worm on it, threw it in, and out came a fish directly, as if it were a needle drawn to a magnet. In again went the line, and out came another fish, and so on, till his basket was quite full. They asked him how he did it. Ah! he said, he could not tell them that, but it was easy enough when you had the way of it.

Much the same is it in fishing for men. Some preachers who have silk lines and fine rods, preach very eloquently and exceedingly gracefully, but they never win souls. I know not how it is, but another man comes, with very simple language, but with a warm heart, and, straightway, men are converted to God. Surely there must be a sympathy between the minister and the souls he would win. God gives to those whom He makes soul-winners a natural love to their work, and a spiritual fitness for it. There is a sympathy between those who are to be blessed and those who are to be the means of blessing, and very much by this sympathy, under God, souls are taken but it is as clear as noonday that, to be a fisher of men a man must be wise. "He that winneth souls is wise."

II. And now, brethren and sisters, you who are engaged in the Lord's work from week to week, and who seek to win men's souls to Christ, I am, in the second place, to illustrate this by telling you of SOME OF THE WAYS BY WHICH SOULS ARE TO BE WON.

The preacher himself wins souls best, I believe, when he believes in the reality of his work,—when he believes in instantaneous conversions. How can he expect God to do what he does not believe God will do? He succeeds best who expects conversion every time he preaches. According to his faith so shall it be done unto him. To be content without conversions, is the surest way never to have them; to drive with a single aim entirely a t the saving of souls, is the surest method of usefulness. If we sigh and cry till men are saved, saved they will be.

He will succeed best, who keeps closest to soul-saving truth. Now, all truth is not soul-saving, though all truth may be edifying. He that keeps to the simple story of the cross, tells men over and over again that whosoever believeth in Christ is not condemned, that to be saved, nothing is wanted but a simple trust in the crucified Redeemer; he whose ministry is much made up of the glorious story of the cross, the sufferings of the dying Lam b, the mercy of God, the willingness of the great Father to receive returning prodigals; he who cries, in fact, from day to day, "Behold the Lamb of God, which taketh away the sin of the world," he is likely to be a soulwinner, especially if he adds to this much prayer for souls, much anxious desire that men may be brought to Jesus) and then in his private life seeks as much as in his public ministry to be telling out to others of the love of the dear Saviour of men.

But I am not talking to ministers, but to you who sit in the pew, and therefore to you let me turn myself more directly. Brothers and sisters, you have different gifts. I hope you use them all. Perhaps some of you, though members of the church, think you have none; but every believer has his gift, and his portion of work. What can you do to win souls?

Let me recommend to those who think they can do nothing, *the bringing of others to hear the Word.* That is a duty much neglected. I can hardly ask you to bring anybody here, but many of you attend other places which are not perhaps half filled. Fill them. Do not grumble at the small congregation, but make it larger. Take somebody with you to the very next sermon, and at once the congregation will be increased. Go up with the prayer that your minister's sermon may be blessed, and if you cannot yourselves preach, yet, by bringing others under the sound of the Word, you may be doing what is next best. This is a very common-place and simple remark, but let me press it upon you, for it is of great practical value. Many churches and chapels, which are almost empty, might soon have large audiences if those who profit by the Word would tell others about the blessing they have received, and induce them to attend the same ministry. Especially in this London of ours, w here so many will not go up to the house of God, persuade your neighbours to co me forth to the place of worship; look after them, make them feel that it is a wrong thing to stop at home on the Sunday from morning till night. I do not say, upbraid them, that does little good; but I do say, entice them, persuade them. Let them have your tickets for the Tabernacle, for instance, sometimes, or stand in the aisles yourself, and let them have your seat. Get them under the Word, and who knoweth what may be the result? Oh, what a blessing it would be to you if you heard that what you could not do,—for you could scarcely speak for Christ,— was done by your pastor, by the power of the Holy Spirit, through your inducing one to come within gunshot of the gospel!

Next to that, soul-winners, try after sermon to talk to strangers. The preacher may have missed the mark, but you need not miss it; or the preacher may have struck the mark, and you can help to make the impression deeper by a kind word. I recollect several persons joining the church who traced their conversion to the ministry in the Surrey Music Hall - but who said it was not that alone, but another agency co-operating therewith. They were fresh from the country, and some good man,—I knew him well,—think he is in heaven now,—met them at the gate, spoke to them, said he hoped they had enjoyed what they had heard, heard their answer, asked them if they were coming in the evening, said he would be glad if they would drop into his house to tea; they did, and he had a word with them about the Master. The next Sunday it was the same, and at last, those whom the sermons had not much impressed, were brought to hear with other ears, till by-and-by, through the good old man's persuasive words, and the good Lord's gracious work, they were converted to God. There is a fine hunting-ground here, and indeed in every large congregation, for you who really want to do good. How many come into this house every morning and evening with no thought about receiving Christ! Oh, if you would all help me, you who love the Master, if you would all help me by speaking to your neighbours who sit near to you, ho w much might be accomplished! Never let anybody say, "I came to the Tabernacle three months, and nobody spoke to me;" but do, by a sweet familiarity, which ought always to be allowable in the house of God, seek with your whole heart to impress upon your friends the truth which I can only put into the ear, but which God may help you to put into the heart.

Further, let me commend to you, dear friends, the art of button-holing acquaintances and relatives. If you cannot preach to a hundred, preach to one. Get a hold of the man alone, and in love, quietly and prayerfully, talk to him. "One!" say you. Well, is not one enough? I know you r ambition, young man; you want to preach here, to these thousands; be con tent, and begin with the ones. Your Master was not ashamed to sit on the well, and preach to one; and when He had finished His sermon, He had really done good to the whole city of Sychar, for that one woman became a missionary to her friends. Timidity often prevents our being useful in this direction, but we must not give way to it; it must not be tolerated that Christ should be unknown through our silence, and sinners unwarned through our negligence. We must school and train ourselves to deal personally with the unconverted. We must not excuse ourselves, but force ourselves to the irksome task till it becomes easy. This is one of the most honourable modes of soul-winning; and if it require s more than ordinary zeal and courage, so much the more reason for our resolving to master it. Beloved, we must win souls, we cannot live and see men damned; we must have them brought to Jesus. Oh! then, be up and doing, and le t none around you die unwarned, unwept, uncared-for. A tract is a useful thing, but a living word is better. Your eye, and face, and voice will all help. Do not be so cowardly as to give a piece of paper where your own speech would be so much better. I charge you, attend to this, for Jesus' sake.

Some of you could write letters for your Lord and Master. To far-off friends, a few loving lines may be most influential for good. Be like the men of Issachar, who handled the pen. Paper and ink arenever better used than in soul- winning. Much has been done by this method. Could not you do it? Will you not try? Some of you, at any rate, if you could not speak or write much, could live much. That is a fine way of preaching, that of preaching with your feet,—I mean preaching by your life, and conduct, and conversation. That loving wife, who weeps in secret over an infidel husband, but is always so kind to him; that dear child, whose heart is broken by his father's blasphemy, but is so much more obedient than he used to be before conversion; that servant, at whom the master swears, but whom he could trust with his purse, and the gold uncounted in it; that man in trade, who is sneered at as a Presbyterian, but who, nevertheless, is straight as a line, and would not be compelled to do a dirty action, no, not for all the mint; these are the men and women who preach the best sermons; these are your practical preachers. Give us your holy living, and with your holy living as the leverage, we will move the world. Under God's blessing, we will find tongues if we can, but we greatly need the lives of our people to illustrate what our tongues have to say. The gospel is something like an illustrated paper. The preacher's words are the letterpress, but the pictures are the living men and women who form our churches; and as when people take up such a newspaper, they very often do not read the letterpress, but they always look at the pictures, so in a church, outsiders may not come to hear the preacher, but they always consider, observe, and criticise the lives of the members. If you would be soul-winners, then, dear brethren and sisters, see that you live the gospel. I have no greater joy than this, that my children walk in the truth.

One thing more, *the soul-winner must be a master of the art of prayer*. You cannot bring souls to God if you go not to God yourself. You must get your battle-axe, and your weapons of war, from the armoury of sacred communion with Christ. If you are much alone with Jesus, you will catch His Spirit; you will be fired with the flame that burned in His breast, and consumed His life. You will weep with the tears that fell upon Jerusalem when He saw it perishing; and if you cannot speak so eloquently as He did, ye t shall there be about what you say somewhat of the same power which in Him thrilled the hearts and awoke the consciences of men. My dear hearers, specially you members of the church, I am always so anxious lest any of you should begin to lie upon your oars, and take things easy in the matters of God's kingdom. There are some of you—I bless you, and I bless God at the remembrance of you,—who are in season, and out of season, in earnest for winning souls, and you are the truly wise; but I fear there are others whose hands are s lack, who are satisfied to let me preach, but do not themselves preach; who take these seats, and occupy these pews, and hope the cause goes well, but that is all they do. Oh, do let me see you all in earnest! A great host of nearly five thousand members, what ought we not to do if we are all alive, and all in earnest? But such a host, without the spirit of enthusiasm, becomes a mere mob, an unwieldy mass, out of which mischief grows, and no good results arise. If you were all firebrands for Christ, you might set the nation on a blaze. If you were all wells of living water, how many thirsty souls might drink and be refreshed!

Beloved, there is one question I will ask, and I have done, and that is, Are your own souls won? You cannot win others else. Are you yourselves saved? My hearers, every one of you, under that gallery there, and you behind here, are you yourselves saved? What if this night you should have to answer that question to another and greater than I am? What if the bony finger of the last great orator should be uplifted instead of mine? what if his unconquerable eloquence should turn those bones to stone, and glaze those eyes, and make the blood chill in your veins? Could you hope, in your last extremity, that you were saved? If not saved, how will you ever be? When will you be saved if not now? Will any time be better than now? The way to be saved is simply to trust in what the Son of man did when He became man, and suffered punishment for all those who trust Him. For all His people, Christ was a Substitute. His people are those who trust Him. If you trust Him, He was punished for your sins; and you cannot be punished for them, for God cannot punish sin twice, first in Christ, and then in you. If you trust Jesus, who now liveth at the right hand of God, you are this moment pardoned, and you shall for eve r be saved. Oh, that you would trust Him now! Perhaps it may be now or never with you. May it be now, even now, and then, trusting in Jesus, dear friends, you will have no need to hesitate when the question is asked, "Are you saved?," for you can answer, "'Ay, that I am, for it is written, 'He that believeth in Him is not condemned.'" Trust Him, then, trust Him now; and then God help you to be a soul-winner, and you shall be wise, and God shall be glorified!

SOUL-SAVING OUR ONE BUSINESS

"I am made all things to all men, that I might by all means save some."

I Corinthians 9:22

It is a grand thing to see a man thoroughly possessed with one master-passion. Such a man is sure to be strong, and if the master-principle be excellent, he is sure to be excellent, too. The man of one object is a man indeed. Lives with many aims are like water trickling through innumerable streams, none of which are wide enough or deep enough to float the merest cockleshell of a boat; but a life with one object is like a mighty river flowing between its banks, bearing to the ocean a multitude of ships, and spreading fertility on either side. Give me a man not only with a great object in his soul, but thoroughly possessed by it, his powers all concentrated, and himself on fire with vehement zeal for his supreme object, and you have put before me one of the greatest sources of power which the world can produce. Give me a man en grossed with holy love as to his heart, and filled with some masterly celestial thought as to his brain, and such a man will be known wherever his lot may be cast, and I venture to prophesy that his name will be remembered long after the place of his sepulchre shall be forgotten.

Such a man was Paul. I am not about to set him upon a pedestal, that you may look at him and wonder, much less that you may kneel down and worship him as a saint. I mention Paul, because what he was we ought every one of us to be; and though we cannot share in his office, not being apostles; though we cannot share in his talents or in his inspiration, yet we ought to be possessed by the same spirit which actuated him, and let me also add we ought to be possessed by it in the same degree. Do you demur to that? I ask you what there was in Paul, by the grace of God, which may not be in you, and what had Jesus done for Paul more than for you? He was divinely changed; and so have you been if you have passed from darkness into marvellous light. He had much forgiven; and so have you also been freely pardoned. He was redeemed by the blood of the Son of God; and so have you been,—at least, so you profess to have been.

He was filled with the Spirit of God; and so are you, if you are truly such as your Christian profession makes you out to be. Owing, then, your salvation to Christ, being debtors to the precious blood of Jesus, and being quickened by the Holy Spirit, I ask you why there should not be the same fruit from the same sowing? Why not the same effect from the same cause? Do not tell me that the apostle was an exception, and cannot be set up as a rule or model for commoner folk, for I shall have to tell you that we must be such as Paul was if we hope to be where Paul is. Paul did not think that he had attained, neither that he was already perfect. Shall we think him to be so—so think him to be so as to regard him as inimitable, and so be content to fall short of what he was? Nay, verily, but let it be our incessant prayer, as believers in Christ, that we may be followers of him so far as he followed Christ, and wherein he failed to set his feet in his Lord's footprints may we even outstrip him, and be more zealous, more devoted to Christ than even the apostle of the Gentiles was. Oh, that the Holy Spirit would bring us to be like our Lord Jesus Himself!

At this time, I shall have to speak to you upon *Paul's great object in life*; he tells us it was, to "save some" ; we will then look into Paul's heart, and show you a few of the *great reasons which made him think it so import ant that some at least should be saved*; then, thirdly, we will indicate certain of the means which the apostle used to that end; and all with this view, that you, my dear hearers, may seek to "save some" that you may seek this because of potent reasons which you cannot withstand, and that you ma y seek it with wise methods such as shall in the end succeed.

I. First, then, brethren, WHAT WAS PAUL'S GREAT OBJ ECT IN HIS DAILY LIFE AND MINISTRY? He says it was, *to save some*.

There are ministers of Christ present at this hour, together with City missionaries, Bible-women, Sunday-school teachers, and other workers in my Master's vineyard, and I make bold to enquire of each one of them,—Is this your object in all your Christian service? Do you above all things aim at saving souls? I am afraid that some have forgotten this gr and object but, dear friends, anything short of this is unworthy to be the great end of a Christian's life. I fear there are some who preach with the view of amusing men; and as long as people can be gathered in crowds, and their ears can be tickled, and they can retire pleased with what they have heard, the orator is content, and folds his hands, and goes back self-satisfied. But Paul did not lay himself out to please the public, and collect the crowd. If he did not save them, he felt that it was of no avail to interest them. Unless the truth had pierced their hearts, affected their lives, and made new men of them, Paul would have gone home crying, "Who hath believed our report, and to whom is the arm of the Lord revealed?"

It seems to be the opinion of a large party in the present day that the object of Christian effort should be to educate men. I grant you that education is in itself an exceedingly valuable thing, so valuable that I am sure the whole Christian Church rejoices greatly that at last we have a national system of education, which only needs to be carefully carried out and every child in this land will have the keys of knowledge in his hand. Whatever other price others may set upon ignorance, we are promoters of knowledge, and the more it can be spread the better shall we be pleased. But if the Church of God thinks that it is sent into the world merely to train the mental faculties, it has made a very serious mistake, for the object of Christianity is not to educate men for their secular callings, or even to train them in the politer arts, or the more elegant professions, or to enable them to enjoy the beauties of nature or the charms of poetry. Jesus Christ came not into the world for an y of these things, but He came to seek and to save that which was lost; and on the same errand has He sent His Church, and she is a traitor to the Master who sent her if she is beguiled by the beauties of taste and art to forget that to preach Christ and Him crucified is the only object for which she exists among the sons of men. The business of the Church is salvation. The minister i s to use all means to save some; he is no minister of Christ if this be not the one desire of his heart. Missionaries sink far below their level when they are content to civilize; their first object is to save. The same is true of the Sunday-school teacher, and of all other workers among children; if they have merely t aught the child to read, to repeat hymns, and so forth, they have not yet touched their true vocation. We must have the children saved. At this nail we must drive, and the hammer must come down upon this head always,—that we might by all means save some, for we have done nothing unless some are saved.

Paul does not even say that he tried to moralize men. The best promoter of morality is the gospel. When a man is saved, he becomes moral; he becomes more, he becomes holy. But to aim first at morality is altogether to miss the mark; and if we did attain it,— as we shall not,—yet we should not have attained that for which we were sent into the world. Dr. Chalmers' experience is a very valuable one to those who think that the Christian ministry ought to preach up mere morality, for he says that in his first parish he preached morality, and saw no good whatever arising out of his exhortations. But, as soon as he began to preach Christ crucified, then there was a buzz, and a stir, and much opposition, but grace prevailed. He who wishes for perfumes must grow the flowers; he who desires to promote morality must have men saved. He who wants motion in a corpse should first seek life for it, and he who desires to see a rightly ordered life should first desire an inward renewal by the Holy Spirit. We are not to be satisfied when we have taught men their duties towards their neighbours, or even their duties towards God; this would suffice for Moses, but not for Christ. The law came by Moses, but grace and truth came by Jesus Christ. We teach men what they ought to be, but we do far more; by the power of the gospel, applied by the Holy Ghost, we make them what they ought to be by the power of God's Spirit. We put not before the blind the things that they ought to see, but we open their eyes in the name of Jesus. We tell not the captive how free he ought to be, but we open the door, and take away his fetters. We are not content to tell men what they must be, but we show them how this character can be obtained, and how Jesus Christ freely presents all that is essential to eternal life to all those who come and put their trust in Him.

Now observe, brethren, if I, or you, or any of us, or all of us, shall have spent our lives merely in amusing men, or educating men, or moralizing men, when we shall come to give in our account at the last great day, we shall be in a very sorry condition, and we shall have but a very sorry record to render; for of what avail will it be to a man to be educated when he comes to be damned? Of what service will it be to him to have been amused when the trumpet sounds, and heaven and earth are shaking, and the pit opens wide her jaws of fire, and swallows up the soul unsaved? Of what avail even to have moralized a man if still he is on the left hand of the Judge, and if s till, "Depart, ye cursed," shall be his portion? Blood-red with the murder of men's souls will be the skirts of professing Christians, unless the drift, and end, and aim of all their work has been to "save some." Oh! I beseech you, especially you, dear friends, who are working in Sunday and Ragged Schools, and elsewhere, do not think that you have done anything unless the children's souls are saved. Settle it that this is the top and bottom of the business, and throw your whole strength, in the name of Christ, and by the power of the Eternal Spirit, into this object—if by any means you may save some, and bring some to Jesus that the y may be delivered from the wrath to come.

What did Paul mean by saying that he desired to save some? What is it to be saved? Paul meant by that nothing less than that some should be born again; for no man is saved until he is made a new creature in Christ Jesus. The old nature cannot be saved; it is dead and corrupt; the best thing that can be done with it is to let it be crucified, and buried in the sepulchre of Christ. There must be a new nature implanted in us by the power of the Holy Ghost, or we cannot be saved. We must be as much new creations as if we had never been; we must come a second time as fresh from the hand of the eternal God as if we had been to-day moulded by divine wisdom as Adam was in Paradise. The great Teacher's words are, "The wind bloweth where it listeth, and thou hearest the sound thereof, but canst not tell whence it cometh, and whither it goeth: so is every one that is born of the Spirit." "Except a ma n be born again (from above), he cannot see the kingdom of God." This, then, Paul meant, that men must be new creatures in Christ Jesus, that we may never rest till we see such a change wrought upon them. This must be the object of our t eaching, and of our praying, indeed, the object of our lives, that "some" may be regenerated.

He meant, beside that, *that some might be cleansed from their past iniquity through the merit of the atoning sacrifice of the son of God.* No man can be saved from his sin except by the atonement. Under the Jewish law it was written, "Cursed is every one that continueth not in all things that are written in the book of the law to do them." That curse has never been reversed, and the only way to escape from it is this: Jesus Christ was made a curse for us, as it is written, "Cursed is every one that hangeth on a tree." Now, he who believes in Jesus, who puts his hand upon the head of Jesus of Nazareth, the Scapegoat of His people, has lost his sins. His faith is sure evidence that his iniquities were of old laid upon the head of the great Substitute. The Lord Jesus Christ was punished in our room, and we are no longer obnoxious to the wrath of God. Behold, the sin-atoning sacrifice is slain, and offered on the altar, and the Lord has accepted it, and is so well pleased that he has declared that whosoever believeth in Jesus is fully and eternally forgiven. Now, we long to see men thus forgiven. We pine to bring the prodigal's head into the Father's bosom, the wandering sheep to the good Shepherd's shoulder, the lost piece of money into the Owner's hands; and until this is done, nothing is done, I mean, brethren, nothing spiritually, nothing eternally, nothing that is worthy of the agony of a Christian's life, nothing that can be looked upon as deserving of an immortal spirit's spending all its fires upon it. O

Lord, our soul yearns to see Jesus rewarded by the salvation of the blood-bought! Aid us by Thine effectual grace to lead souls to Him.

Once more, when the apostle wished that he might save some, he meant that, being regenerated, and being pardoned, they might also be purified and made holy, for a man is not saved while he lives in sin. Let a man say what he will, he cannot be saved from sin whilst he is the slave of it. How is a drunkard saved from drunkenness whilst he still riots as before? How can you say that the swearer is saved from blasphemy while he is still profane? Words must be used in their true meaning. Now, the great object of the Christian's work should be that some might be saved from their sins, purified, and made white, and made examples of integrity, chastity, honesty, and righteousness, as the fruit of the Spirit of God; and where this is not the case, we have laboured in vain, and spent our strength for nought.

Now, I do protest before you all that I have in this house of prayer never sought anything but the conversion of souls, and I call heaven and earth to witness, and your consciences, too, that I have never laboured for anything except this, the bringing of you to Christ, that I might present you at last unto God "accepted in the Beloved." I have not sought to gratify depraved appetites either by novelty of doctrine or ceremonial, but I have kept to the simplicity of the gospel. I have kept back no part of the price of God's Word from you, but I have endeavoured to give you the whole counsel of G od. I have sought out no fineries of speech, but have spoken plainly, and right straight at your hearts and consciences; and if you be not saved, I mourn and l ament before God that up to this day, though I have preached hundreds of times to you, yet I have preached in vain. If you have not closed in with Christ, if you have not been washed in the fountain filled with blood, you are waste piece soil from which no harvest has yet come.

You tell me, perhaps, that you have been kept from a great many sins, that you have learned a great many truths by coming here. So far, so good; but could I afford to live for this, merely to teach you certain truths, or keep you back from open sins? How could this content me if I knew all the while that you were still unsaved, and must, therefore, after death, be cast into the flames of hell? Nay, beloved, before the Lord, I count nothing to be worthy of your pastor's life, and soul, and energy, but the winning of you to Christ. Nothing but your salvation can ever make me feel that my he art's desire is granted. I ask every worker here to see to this, that he never turns aside from shooting at this target, and at the centre of this target, too, namely, that he may win souls for Christ, and see them born to God, and washed in the fountain filled with blood. Let the workers' hearts ache, and yearn, and their voices cry till their throats are hoarse; but let them judge that they have accomplished nothing whatever until, at least, in some cases, men are really saved. As the fisherman longs to take the fish in his net, as the hunter pants to bear home h is spoil, as the mother pines to clasp her lost child to her bosom, so do we faint f or the salvation of souls; and we must have them, or we are ready to die. Save the m, O Lord, save them for Christ's sake.

But now we must leave that point for another.

II. THE APOSTLE HAD GREAT REASONS FOR ELECTING SUCH AN OBJECT IN LIFE.

Were he here, I think he would tell you that his reasons were something of this kind. To save souls! If they be not saved, how is God dishonoured! Did you ever think over the amount of dishonour that is done to the Lord our God in London in any one hour of the day? Take, if you will, this prayer-hour, when we are gathered here ostensibly to pray. If the thoughts of this great assembly could all be read, how many of them would be dishonouring to the Most High! But outside of every house of prayer, outside of every place of worship of every kind, think of the thousands, and tens of thousands, the hundreds of thousands, who have all this day neglected the very semblance of the worship of the God who has made them, and who keeps them in being! Think of how many times the door of the gin-palace has swung on its hinges during this holy hour, how many times God's name has been blasphemed at the drinking-bar! There are worse things than these, if worse can be, but I shall not lift the veil. Transfer your thoughts to an hour or so later, when the veil of darkness has descended. Shame will not permit us even to think of how God's name is dishonoured in the persons of those whose first fat her was made after the image of God, but who pollute themselves to be the slaves of Satan and the prey of bestial lusts! Alas! alas! for this city, it is full of abominations, of which the apostle said, "It is a shame even to speak of those things which are done of them in secret."

Christian men and women, nothing but the gospel can sweep away the social evil. Vices are like vipers, and only the voice of Jesus can drive them out of the land. The gospel is the great besom with which to cleanse the filthiness of this city, and nothing else will avail. Will

150

you not, for God's sake, whose name is every day profaned, seek to save some? If you will enlarge your thoughts, and take in all the great cities of the Continent; ay, further still, take all the idolaters of China and Hindostan, the worshippers of the false prophet and antichrist, what a mass of provocation have we here! What a smoke in Jehovah's nose must this false worship be! How He must often put His hand to the hilt of His sword as though He would say, "Ah! I will ease Me of Mine adversaries." But He bears it patiently. Let us not become indifferent to His longsuffering, but day and night let us cry unto him, and daily let us labour for Him, if by any means we may save some for His glory 's sake.

Think, dear friends, also, of the extreme misery of this our human race. It would be a very dreadful thing if you could get any idea of the aggregate of the misery of London at the present moment in the hospitals and workhouses. Now, I would not say half a word against poverty, wherever it comes it is a bitter ill but you will mark as you notice carefully that, while a few are poor because of unavoidable circumstances, a very large mass of the poverty of London is the sheer and clear result of wastefulness, want of for ethought, idleness, and, worst of all, of drunkenness. Ah, that drunkenness! That is the master-evil. If drink could but be got rid of; we might be sure of conquering the very devil himself. The drunkenness created by the infernal liquor-dens which plague-spot the whole of this huge city is appalling. No, I did not speak in haste, or let slip a hasty word; many of the drink-houses are nothing less than infernal: in some respects they are worse, for hell has its uses as the divine protest against sin, but as for the gin-palace, there is nothing to be said in its favour. The vices of the age cause three-fourths of all the poverty. If you could look at the homes,— the wretched homes where women will tremble at the sound of their husband's foot as he comes home, where little children will crouch down with fear upon their little heap of straw because the human brute who calls himself "a man" will come reeling home from the place where he has been indulging his appetites,—if you could look at such a sight, and remember that it will be seen ten thousand times over to-night, I think you would say, "God help us by all means to save some!" Since the great axe to lay at the root of the deadly upas tree is the gospel of Christ, may God help us to hold that axe there, and to work constantly with it till the huge trunk of the poison tree begins to rock to and fro, and we get it down, and London is saved, and the world is saved from the wretchedness and the misery which now drip from every bough!

Again, dear friends, the Christian has other reason s for seeking to save some; and chiefly because of the terrible future of impenitent souls. That veil which hangs before me is not penetrated by every glance but he who has his eye touched with heavenly eye-salve sees through it, and what does he see? Myriads upon myriads of spirits in dread procession passing from their bodies, and passing— whither? Unsaved, unregenerate, unwashed in precious blood, we see them go up to the solemn bar whence in silence the sentence comes forth, and they are banished from the presence of G od, banished to horrors which are not to be described nor even to be imagined. This alone is enough to cause us distress day and night. This decision of destiny has about it a terrible solemnity. But the resurrection trumpet sounds. Those spirits come forth from their prison-house. I see them returning to earth, rising from the pit to the bodies in which they lived: and now I see them stand— multitudes, multitudes, multitudes, multitudes—in the Valley of Decision. and He comes, sitting on a great white throne, with the crown upon His head, and the books before Him; and there they stand as prisoners at the bar. My vision now perceives them— how they tremble! How they quiver, like aspen leave sin the gale! Whither can they flee? Rocks cannot hide them, mountains will not open their bowels to conceal them! What shall become of them? The dread angel takes the sickle, reaps them as the reaper cuts up the tares for the oven; and as he gathers them, he casts them down where despair shall be their everlasting torment. Woe is me, my heart sinks as I see their doom, and hear the terrible cries of their too-late awaking. Save some, O Christians! By all means, save some. By yonder flames, and outer darkness, and the weeping, and the wailing, and the gnashing of teeth, seek to save some! Let this, as in the case of the apostle, be your great, your ruling object in life, that by all means you may save some.

For, oh! if they be saved, observe the contrast. Their spirits mount to heaven, and after the resurrection their bodies ascend also, and there they praise redeeming love. No fingers more nimble on the harp- strings than theirs! No notes more sweet than theirs, as they sing, "Unto Him that loved us, and washed us from our sins in His own blood, and hath made us kings and priests unto God and His Father; to Him be glory and dominion for ever and ever." What bliss to see the once-rebellious brought home to God, and heirs of wrath made possessors of heaven! All this is involved in salvation. Oh, that myriads may come to this blessed state! "Save some" —oh! save some, at least. Seek that some may be there in glory. Behold your Master. He is y our pattern. He left heaven to save some. He went to the cross, to the grave, to "save some" : this was the great object of His life, to lay down His life for His sheep. He loved His Church, and gave Himself for her, that He might redeem her unto Himself. Imitate your Master. Learn His self-denial and His blessed consecration, if by any means you may save some.

My soul yearneth that I personally may "save some" , but broader is my desire than that. I would have every one of you, my beloved friends, associated here in church-fellowship, to become spiritual parents of children for God. Oh, that every one of you might "save some" ! Yes, my venerable brethren, you are not too old for service. Yes, my young friends, ye young men and maidens, ye are not too young to be recruits in the King's service. If the kingdom is ever to come to our Lord,—and come it will,—it never will come through a few ministers, missionaries, or evangelists preaching the gospel. It must come through every one of you preaching it,—in the shop and by the fireside, when walking abroad and when sitting in the chamber. You must all of you be always endeavouring to "save some." I would enlist you all afresh to-night, and bind anew the King's colours upon you. I would that you would fall in love with my Master over anew, and enter a second time upon the love of your espousals. There is a hymn of Cowper's which we sometimes sing ,—

"Oh, for a closer walk with God!"

May we get to have a closer walk with Him; and if we do so, we shall also feel a more vehement desire to magnify Christ in the salvation of sinners.

I would like to press the enquiry upon you who are saved,—How many others have you brought to Christ? You cannot do it by yourself, I know; but I mean, how many has the Spirit of God brought by you? How many, did I say? Is it quite certain that you have led any to Jesus? Can you not recollect one? I pity you, then! The Lord said to Jeremiah, concerning Coniah, "Write ye this man childless." That was considered to be a fearful curse. Shall I write you childless, my beloved friends? Your children are not saved, your wife is not saved, and you are spiritually childless. Can you bear this thought? I pray you, wake from your slumbering, and ask the Master to make you useful. "I wish the saints cared for us sinners," said a young man. "They do care for you," answered one, "they care very much for you." "Why don't they show it, then?" said he, "I have often wished to have a talk about good things, but my friend, who is a member of the church, never broaches the subject, and seems to study how to keep clear of it when I am with him." Do not let them say so. Do tell them about Christ and things divine and make this y our resolve, every one of you, that if men perish they shall not perish for w ant of your prayers, nor for want of your earnest and loving instructions. God give you grace, each one of you, to resolve by all means to save some, and then to carry out your resolution!

III. But my time is almost gone, and therefore I have to mention, in the last place, THE GREAT METHODS WHICH THE APOSTLE USED.

How did he who so longed to "save some" set about i t? Why, first of all, by simply preaching the gospel of Christ. He did not attempt to create a sensation by startling statements, neither did he preach erroneous doctrine in order to obtain the assent of the multitude. I fear that some evangelists preach what in their own minds they must know to be untrue. They keep back certain doctrines, not because they are untrue, but because they do not give scope enough for their ravings, and they make loose statements because they hope to reach more minds. However earnest a man may be for the salvation of sinners, I do not believe that he has the right to make any statement which his sober judgment will not justify. I think I have heard of things said and done at revival meetings which were not according to sound doctrine, but which were always excused by "the excitement of the occasion." I hold that I have no right to state false doctrine, even if I knew it would save a soul. The supposition is, of course, absurd; but it makes you see what I mean. My business is to bring to bear upon men, not falsehood, but truth; and I shall not be excused if; under any pretence, I palm a lie upon the people. Rest assured that, to keep back any part of the gospel, is not the right, nor the true method for saving men. Tell the sinner all the doctrines. If you hold Calvinistic doctrine, as I hope you do, do not stutter about it, nor stammer over it, but speak it out. De pend upon it, many revivals have been evanescent because a full-orbed gospel wa s not proclaimed. Give the people every truth, every truth baptized in holy fi re, and each truth will have its own useful effect upon the mind.

But the great truth is the cross, the truth that "G od so loved the world, that He gave His only begotten Son, that whosoever believeth in Him should not perish, but have everlasting life." Brother, keep to that. That is the bell for you to ring. Ring it, man! Ring it! Keep on ringing it. Sound forth that note upon your silver trumpet, or if you are only a ram's horn, sound it forth, and the walls of Jericho will come down. Alas, for the fineries of our "cultured" modern divines! I hear them crying out, and denouncing my old-fashioned advice. This talking about Christ crucified is said to be archaic, conventional, and antique, and not at all suitable to the refinement of this wonderful age. It is astonishing how learned we have all grown lately. We are getting so very wise, I am afraid we shall ripen into fools before long, even if we have not arrived at it already. People want "thinking" nowadays, so it is said; and the working-men will go where science is deified, and profound "thought" is enshrined. I have noticed that, as a general rule, wherever the new "thinking " drives out the old gospel, there are more spiders than people, but where there is the simple preaching of Jesus Christ, the place is crowded to the doors. Nothing else will crowd a meeting-house, after all, for any length of time, but the preaching of Christ crucified. But as to this matter, whether it be popular or unpopular, our mind is made up, and our foot is put down. Question we have none as to our own course. If it be foolish to preach up atonement by blood, we will be fools; and if it be madness to stick to the old truth, just as Paul delivered it, in all its simplicity, without any refinement, or improvement, we mean to stick to it, even if we be pilloried as being incapable of progressing with the age, for we are persuaded that this "foolishness of preaching" is a divine ordinance, and that the cross of Christ, which stumbles so many, and is ridiculed by so many more, is still the power of God and the wisdom of G od. Yes, just the old- fashioned truth—if thou believest, thou shalt be saved,—that will we stick to, and may God send His blessing upon it according to His own eternal purpose! We do not expect this preaching to be popular, but we know that God will justify it ere long. Meanwhile, we are not staggered because—

> The truths we love a sightless world blasphemes
> As childish dotage, and delirious dreams;
> The danger they discern not they deny;
> Laugh at their only remedy, and die."

Next to this, *Paul used much prayer*. The gospel alone will not be blessed; we must pray over our preaching. A great painter was asked what he mixed his colours with, and he replied that he mixed them with brains. 'Twas well for a painter, but if anyone should ask a preacher what he mixes truth with, he ought to be able to answer—with prayer, much prayer: When a poor man was breaking granite by the roadside, he was down on his knees while he gave his blows, and a minister passing by said, "Ah, my friend, here you are at your hard work; your work is just like mine; you have to break stones, and so do I." "Yes," said the man, "and if you manage to break stony hearts, you will have to do it as I do, down on your knees." The man was right, no one can use the gospel hammer well except he is much on his knees, but the gospel hammer soon splits flinty hearts when a man knows how to p ray. Prevail with God, and you will prevail with men. Straight from the closet to the pulpit let us come, with the anointing oil of God's Spirit fresh upon us. What we receive in secrecy we are cheerfully to dispense in public. Let us never venture to speak for God to men, until we have spoken for men to God. Yes, dear hearers, if you want a blessing on your Sunday-school teaching, or any other form of Christian labour, mix it up with fervent intercession.

And then observe one other thing. Paul went to his work always with an intense sympathy for those he dealt with, a sympathy which made him adapt himself to each ease. If he talked to a Jew, he did not begin at once blurting out that he was the apostle of the Gentiles, but he said he was a Jew, as Jew he was. He raised no questions about nationalities or ceremonies. He wanted to tell the Jew of Him of whom Isaiah said, "He is despised and rejected of men, a Man of sorrows, and acquainted with grief," in order that he might believe in Jesus and so be saved. If he met a Gentile, the apostle of the Gentiles never showed any of the squeamishness which might have been expected to cling to him on account of his Jewish education. He ate as the Gentile ate, and drank as he did, sat with him, and talked with him; was, as it were, a Gentile with him; never raising any question about circumcision or uncircumcision, but solely wishing to tell him of Christ, who came into the world to save both Jew and Gentile, and to make them one. If Paul met with a Scythian, he spoke to him in the Barbarian tongue, and not in classic Greek. If he met a Greek, he spoke to him as he did at the Areopagus, with language that was fitted for the polished Athenian. He was all things to all men, that he might by all means save some.

So let it be with you, Christian people; your one business in life is to lead men to believe in Jesus Christ by the power of the Holy Spirit, and every other thing should be made subservient to this one object ; if you can but get them saved, everything else will come right in due time. Mr. Hudson Taylor, a dear man of God, who has laboured much in Inland China, finds it helpful to dress as a Chinaman, and wear a pigtail. He always mingle s with the people, and as far as possible lives as they do. This seems to me to be a truly wise policy. I can understand that we shall win upon a congregation of Chinese by becoming as Chinese as possible; and if this be the case, we are bound to be Chinese to the Chinese to save the Chinese. It would not be amiss to become a Zulu to save the Zulus, though we must mind that we do it in another sense than Colenso did. If we can put ourselves on a level with those whose good we seek, we shall be more likely to effect our purpose than if we remain aliens and foreigners, and then talk of love and unity. To sink myself to save others is the idea of the apostle. To throw overboard all peculiarities, and yield a thousand indifferent points, in order to bring men to Jesus, is our wisdom if we would extend our Master's kingdom. Never may any whim or conventionality of ours keep a soul from considering the gospel,—that were horrible indeed. Better far to be personally inconvenienced by compliance with things indifferent, than to retard a sinner's coming by quarrelling about trifles.

If Jesus Christ were here to-day, I am sure he would not put on any of those gaudy rags in which the Puseyite delights himself. I cannot imagine our Lord Jesus Christ dressed out in that style. Why, the apostle tells our women that they are to dress themselves modestly, and I do not think Christ would have His ministers set an example of tomfoolery: but yet eve n in dress something may be done on the principle of our text. When Jesus Chris t was here, what did He wear? To put it in plain English, He wore a smock f rock. He wore the common dress of his countrymen, a garment woven from the t op throughout, without seam; and I think he would have His ministers wear that costume which is most like the dress which their hearers wear in common, and so even in dress associate with their hearers, and be one among them. He would have you teachers, if you want to save your children, talk to them like children, and make yourselves children if you can. You who want to get at young peoples' hearts must try to be young. You who wish to visit the sic k must sympathise with them in their sickness. Get to speak as you would like to be spoken to if you were sick. Come down to those who cannot come up to you. You cannot pull people out of the water without stooping down and getting hold of them. If you have to deal with bad characters, you must come down to them, not in their sin, but in their roughness and in their style of language, so as to get a hold of them. I pray God that we may learn the sacred art of soul - winning by adaptation. They called Mr. Whitefield's chapel at Moorfields, "The Soul-trap." Whitefield was delighted, and said he hoped it always would be a soul-trap. Oh, that all our places of worship were soul-traps, and every Christian a fisher of men, each one doing his best, as the fisherman does, by every art and artifice, to catch those he fishes for! Well may we use all means to win so great a prize as a spirit destined for eternal weal or woe. The diver plunges deep to find pearls, and we may accept any labour or hazard to win a soul. Rouse yourselves, my brethren, for this God-like work, and may the Lord bless you in it!

INSTRUCTION IN SOUL-WINNING

"And he saith unto them, Follow Me, and I will make you fishers of men."

Matthew 4:19

Hen Christ calls us by His grace, we ought not only to remember what we are, but we ought also to think of what He can make us. It is "Follow Me, and I will make you." We should repent of what we have been, but rejoice in what we may be. It is not, "Follow Me, because of what you are already." It is not, "Follow Me, because you may make something of yours elves;" but, "Follow Me, because of what I will make you." Verily, I might say of each one of us as soon as we are converted, "It doth not yet appear what we shall be." It did not seem a likely thing that lowly fishermen would develop into apostles, that men so handy with the net would be quite as much at hom e in preaching sermons and in instructing converts. One would have said, " How can these things be? You cannot make founders of churches out of peasant Galilee." That is exactly what Christ did; and when we are brought lo w in the sight of God by a sense of our own unworthiness, we may feel encouraged to follow Jesus because of what He can make us. What said the woman of a sorrowful spirit when she lifted up her song? "He raiseth up the poo r out of the dust, and lifteth up the beggar from the dunghill, to set them among princes." We cannot tell what God may make of us in the new creation, since it would have been quite impossible to have foretold what He made of chaos i n the old creation. Who could have imagined all the beautiful things that came forth from darkness and disorder by that one fiat, "Let there be light"? and who can tell what lovely displays of everything that is divinely fair may yet appear in a man's formerly dark life, when God's grace has said to him, "Let there be light"? O you who see in yourselves at present nothing that is desirable, come you and follow Christ for the sake of what He can make out of you! Do you not hear His sweet voice calling to you, and saying, "Follow Me, and I will make you fishers of men"?

Note, next, that we are not made all that we shall be, nor all that we ought to desire to be, when we are ourselves fished for and caught.

159

This is what the grace of God does for us at first; but it is not all. We are like the fishes, making sin to be our element, as they live in the sea; and the good Lord comes, and with the gospel net He takes us, and He delivers us from the life and love of sin. But He has not wrought for us all that He can do, n or all that we should wish Him to do, when He has done this; for it is another and a higher miracle to make us who were fish to become fishers,—to make the saved ones saviours,— to make the convert into a converter,—the receiver of the gospel into an imparter of that same gospel to other people. I think I may say to every person whom I am addressing,—If you are yourself saved, the work is but half done until you are employed to bring others to Christ. you are as yet but half formed in the image of your Lord. You have not attained to the full development of the Christ-life in you unless you have commenced in some feeble way to tell others of the grace of God; and I trust that you will find no rest to the sole of your foot till you have been the means of leading many to that blessed Saviour who is your confidence and your hope. His word is, "Follow Me, not merely that you may be saved, nor even that you may be sanctified; but, 'Follow Me, and I will make you fishers of men.'" Be following Christ with that intent and aim; and fear that you are not perfectly following Him unlessin some degree He is making use of you to be fishers of men. The fact is, that every one of us must take to the business of a man-catcher. If Christ has caught us, we must catch others. If we have been apprehended of Him, we must be His constables, to apprehend rebels for Him. Let us ask Him to give us grace to go a-fishing, and so to cast our nets that we may take a great multitude of fishes. Oh, that the Holy Ghost may raise up from among us some master-fishers, who shall sail their boats in many a sea, and surround great shoal fish!

My teaching at this time will be very simple, but I hope it will be eminently practical; for my longing is that not one of you that love the Lord may be backward in His service. What says the Song of Solomon concerning certain sheep that come up from the washing? It says, "Every one bareth twins, and there is not one barren among them." May that be so with all the members of this church, and all the Christian people who hear or read this sermon! The fact is, the day is very dark. The heavens are lowering with heavy thunder-clouds. Men little dream of what tempests may soon shake this city, and the whole social fabric of this land, even to a general breaking up of society. So dark may the night become that the stars may seem to fall like blighted fruit from the tree. The times are evil. Now, if never before, every glow-worm must show its spark. You with the tiniest farthing candle must take it from under the bushel, and set it on a candlestick. There is need of you all. Lot was a poor creature. He was a very, very wretched kind of believer; but still, he might have been a great blessing to Sodom had he but pleaded for it as he should have done. And poor, poor Christians, as I fear many are, one begins to value every truly converted soul in these evil days, and to pray that each one may glorify the Lord. I pray that every righteous man, vexed as he is with the conversation of the wicked, may be more importunate in prayer than he has ever been, and return unto his God, and get more spiritual life, that he may be a blessing to the perishing people around him. I address you, therefore, at this time first of all upon this thought. Oh, that the Spirit of God may make each one of you feel his personal responsibility!

Here is for believers in Christ, in order to their usefulness, something for them to do: "Follow Me." But, secondly, here is something to be done by their great Lord and Master: "Follow Me, and I will make you fishers of men." you will not of yourselves grow into fishers, but that is what Jesus will do for you if you will but follow Him. And then, lastly, here is a good illustration, used according to our great Master's wont; for scarcely without a parable did He speak unto the people. He presents us with an illustration of what Christian men should be—fishers of men. We may get some useful hints out of it, and I pray the Holy Spirit to bless them to us.

I. First, then, I will take it for granted that every believer here wants to be useful. If he does not, I take leave to question whether he can be a true believer in Christ. Well, then, if you want to be really useful, here is SOMETHING FOR YOU TO DO TO THAT END: "Follow Me, and I will make you fishers of men."

What is the way to become an efficient preacher? "Young man," says one, "go to college." "Young man," says Christ, "follow Me, and I will make you a fisher of men." How is a person to be useful? "Attend a training-class," says one. Quite right; but there is a surer answer than that,—Follow Jesus, and He will make you fishers of men. The great training school for Christian workers has Christ at its head and He is at its head, not only as a Tutor, but as a Leader: we are not only to learn of Him in study, but to follow Him in action. "Follow Me, and I will make you fishers of men." The direction is very distinct and plain, and I believe that it is exclusive, so that no man can become a fisherman by any other process. This process may appear to be very simple; but assuredly it is most efficient. The Lord Jesus Christ, who knew all about fishing for men, was Himself the Dictator of the rule, "Follow Me, if you want to be fishers of men. If you would be useful, keep in My track."

I understand this, first, in this sense: be separate unto Christ. These men were to leave their pursuits they were to leave their companions; they were, in fact, to quit the world, that their one business might be, in their Master's name, to be fishers of men. We are not called to leave our daily business, or to quit our families. That might be rather running away from the fishery than working at it in God's name but we are called most distinctly to come out from among the ungodly, and to be separate, and not to touch the unclean thing. We cannot be fishers of men if we remain among men in the same element with them. Fish will not be fishers. The sinner will not convert the sinner. The ungodly man will not convert the ungodly man; and, what is more to the point, the worldly Christian will not convert the world. If you are of the world, no doubt the world will love its own; but you cannot save the world. If you are dark, and belong to the kingdom of darkness, you cannot remove the dark ness. If you march with the armies of the wicked one, you cannot defeat the m. I believe that one reason why the Church of God at this present moment has so little influence over the world is because the world has so much influence over the Church. Nowadays, we hear Nonconformists pleading that they may do this, and they may do that,—things which their Puritan forefathers would rather have died at the stake than have tolerated. They plead that they may live like worldlings, and my sad answer to them, when they crave for this liberty, i s, "Do it if you dare. It may not do you much hurt, for you are so bad already. Your cravings show how rotten your hearts are. If you have a hungering after such dog's meat, go, dogs, and eat the garbage! Worldly amusements are fit foo d for mere pretenders and hypocrites. If you were God's children, you would loathe the very thought of the world's evil joys, and your question would not be, 'How far may we be like the world?' but your one cry would be, 'How far can we get away from the world? How much can we come out from it?' Your temptation would be rather to become sternly severe, and ultra-Puritanical in your separation from sin, in such a time as this, than to ask, 'How can I make myself like other men, and act as they do?" '

Brethren, the use of the Church in the world is that it should be like salt in the midst of putrefaction; but if the salt has lost its savour, what is the good of it? If it were possible for salt itself to putrefy, it could but be an increase and a heightening of the general putridity. The worst day the world ever saw was when the sons of God were joined with the daughters of men. Then came the flood; for the only barrier against a flood of vengeance on this world is the separation of the saint from the sinner. Your duty as a Christian is to stand fast in your own place, and to stand out for God, hating even the garment spotted by the flesh, resolving like one of old that, let others do as they will, as for you and your house, you will serve the Lord.

Come, ye children of God, you must stand with your Lord outside the camp. Jesus calls you to-day, and says, "Follow Me." Was Jesus found at the theatre? Did He frequent the sports of the race-course? Was Jesus seen, think you, in any of the amusements of the Herodian court? Not He. He was "holy, harmless, undefiled, and separate from sinners." In one sense, no one mixed with sinners so completely as He did when, like a physician, He went among them healing His patients; but, in another sense, there was a gulf fixed between the men of the world and the Saviour, which He never essayed to cross, and which they could not cross to defile Him.

The first lesson which the Church has to learn is this: Follow Jesus into the separated state, and He will make you fishers of me n. Unless you take up your cross, and protest against an ungodly world, you cannot hope that the holy Jesus will make you fishers of men.

A second meaning of our text is very obviously this : abide with Christ, and then you will be made fishers of men. These disciples whom Christ called were to come and live with Him. They were every day to be associated with Him. They were to hear Him teach publicly the everlasting gospel, and in addition they were to receive choice explanations in private of the Word which He had spoken. They were to be His body-servants and His familiar friends. They were to see His miracles and hear His prayers; and, better still, they were to be with Himself, and become one with Him in His holy labour. It was given to them to sit at the table with Him, and even to have their feet washed by Him. Many of them fulfilled that word, "Where thou dwellest, I will dwell:" they were with Him in His afflictions and persecutions. They witnessed His secret agonies, they saw His many tears, they marked the passion and the compassion of His soul, and thus, after their measure, they caught his spirit, and so they learned to be fishers of men.

At Jesus' feet we must learn the art and mystery of soul-winning: to live with Christ is the best education for usefulness. it is a great boon to any man to be associated with a Christian minister whose heart is on fire. The best training for a young man is that which the Vaudois pastors w ere wont to give, when each old man had a young man with him who walked with him whenever he went up the mountainside to preach, and lived in the house with him, and marked his prayers, and saw his daily piety. This was a fine course of instruction, was it not? But it will not compare with that of the apostles who lived with Jesus Himself, and were His daily companions. Matchless was the training of the twelve. No wonder that they became what they were with such a heavenly Tutor to saturate them with His own spirit. His bodily presence is not now among us; but His spiritual power is perhaps more fully known to us than it was to the apostles in those two or three years of the Lord's corporeal presence. There be some of us to whom He is intimately near. We know more about Him than we do about our dearest earthly friend. We have never been able quite to read our friend's heart in all its twistings and windings, but we know the heart of the Well-beloved. We have leaned our head upon His bosom, and have enjoyed fellowship with Him such as we could not have with any of our own kith and kin. This is the surest method of learning how to do good. Live with Jesus, follow Jesus, and He will make you fishers of men. See how He does the work, and so learn how to do it yourself. A Christian man should be bound apprentice to Jesus to learn the trade of a Saviour. We can never save men by offering a redemption, for we have none top resent; but we can learn how to save men by warning them to flee from the wrath to come, and setting before them the one great effectual remedy. See how Jesus saves, and you will learn how the thing is done: there is no learning it anyhow else. Live in fellowship with Christ, and there shall be about you an air and a manner as of one who has been made in heart and mind apt to teach, and wise to win souls.

A third meaning, however, must be given to this "Follow Me," and it is this: "Obey Me, and then you shall know what to do to save men." We must not talk about our fellowship with Christ, or our being separated from the world unto Him, unless we make Him our Master and Lord in everything. Some public teachers are not true at all points to their convictions; how can they look for a blessing? A Christian man, anxious to be useful, ought to be very particular as to every point of obedience to his Master. I have no doubt whatever that God blesses our churches even when they are very faulty, for His mercy endureth forever. When there is a measure of error in the teaching, and a measure of mistake in the practice, He may still vouchsafe to use the ministry, for He is very gracious; but a large measure of blessing must necessarily be withheld from all teaching which is knowingly or glaringly faulty. God can set His seal upon the truth that is in it, but He cannot set His seal upon the error that is in it. Out of mistakes about Christian ordinances and other things, especially errors in heart and spirit, there may come evils which we never looked for. Such evils may even now be telling upon the present age, and m ay work worse mischief upon future generations.

If we desire, as fishers of men, to be largely used of God, we must copy our Lord Jesus in everything, and obey Him in every poi nt. Failure in obedience may lead to failure in success. Each one of us, if he would wish to see his child saved, or his Sunday-school class blessed, or his congregation converted, must take care that, bearing the vessels of the Lord, he is himself clean. Anything we do that grieves the Spirit of God must take away from us some part of our power for good. The Lord is very gracious and pitiful; but yet He is a jealous God. He is sometimes sternly jealous towards His people who are living in neglect of known duty, or in associations which are not clean in His sight. He will wither their work, weaken their strength, and humble them until at last they each one say, "My Lord, I will take Thy way after all. I will do what Thou biddest me to do, for else Thou wilt not accept me. " The Lord said to His disciples, "Go ye into all the world, and preach the gospel to every creature: he that believeth and is baptized shall be saved;" and He promised them that signs should follow, and so they did follow, and so they will. But we must get back to apostolic practice and to apostolic teaching; we must lay aside the commandments of men and the whimseys of our own bra ins, and we must do what Christ tells us, as Christ tells us, and because Christ tells us. Definitely and distinctly, we must take the place of servants; and if we will not do that, we cannot expect our Lord to work with us and by us. Let us be determined that, as true as the needle is to the pole, so true will we be, as far as our light goes, to the command of our Lord and Master. Jesus says, "Follow Me, and I will make you fishers of men." By this teaching He seems to say, "Go beyond Me, or fall back away from Me, and you may cast the net; but it shall be night with you, and that night you shall take nothing. When you shall do as I bid you, you shall cast your net on the right side of the ship, and you shall find."

Again, I think that there is a great lesson in my text to those who preach their own thoughts instead of preaching the thought Christ. These disciples were to follow Christ that they might listen to Him, hear what He had to say, drink in His teaching, and then go and teach what He had taught them. Their Lord said, "What I tell you in darkness, that speak ye in light: and what ye hear in the ear, that preach ye upon the housetops." If they will be faithful reporters of Christ's message, He will make them "fishers of men." But you know the boastful method, nowadays, is this: "I am not going to preach this old, old gospel, this musty Puritan doctrine. I will sit down in my study, and burn the midnight oil, and invent a new theory; then I will come out with my brand-new thought, and blaze away with it." Many are not following Christ, but following themselves, and of them the Lord may well say, "Thou shalt see whose word shall stand, Mine or theirs:" Others are wickedly prudent, and judge that certain truths which are evidently God's Word, had better be kept back. You must not be rough, but must prophesy smooth things. To talk about the punishment of sin, to speak of eternal punishment, why, these are unfashionable doctrines. It may be that they are taught in the Word of God, but they do not suit the genius of the age; we must pare them down! Brothers in Christ, I will have no share in this. Will you? O my soul, come not thou into their secret! Certain things not taught in the Bible our enlightened age has discovered. Evolution may be clean contrary to the teaching of Genesis, but that does not matter. We are not going to be believers of Scripture, but original thinkers. This is the vainglorious ambition of the period.

Mark you, in proportion as the modern theology is p reached, the vice of this generation increases. To a great degree, I attribute the looseness of the age to the laxity of the doctrine preached by its teachers. From the pulpit they have taught the people that sin is a trifle. From the pulpit these traitors to God and to His Christ have taught the people that there is no hell to be feared. A little, little hell, perhaps, there may be; but just punishment for sin is made nothing of. The precious atoning sacrifice of Christ has been derided and misrepresented by those who were pledged to preach it. They have given the people the name of the gospel, but the gospel itself has evaporated in their hands. From hundreds of pulpits the gospel is as clean gone as the dodo from its old haunts; and still the preachers take the position and name of Christ' s ministers. Well, and what comes of it? Why, their congregations grow thinner and thinner and so it must be. Jesus says, "Follow Me, and I will make you fishers of men;" but if you go in your own way, with your own net, you will make nothing of it, and the Lord promises you no help in it. The Lord's directions make Himself our Leader and Example. It is, "Follow Me, follow Me. Preach My gospel. Preach what I preached. Teach what I taught, and keep to that." with that blessed servility which becomes one whose ambition it is to be a copyist, and never to be an original, copy Christ even in jots and tittles. Do this, and He will make you fishers of men; but if you do not do this, you shall fish in vain.

I close this head of my discourse by saying that we shall not be fishers of men unless we follow Christ in one other respect; and that is, by endeavouring, in all points, to imitate His holiness. Holiness is the most real power that can be possessed by men or women. We may preach orthodoxy, but we must also live orthodoxy. God forbid that we should preach anything else; but it will be all in vain, unless there is a life at the back of the testimony. An unholy preacher may even render truth contemptible. In proportion as an y of us draw back from a living and zealous sanctification, we shall draw back from the place of power. Our power lies in this word, "Follow Me." Be Jesus- like. In all things endeavour to think, and speak, and act as Jesus did, and He will make you fishers of men. This will require self-denial. We must daily take up the cross. This may require willingness to give up our reputation,—readiness to be thought fools, idiots, and the like, as men are apt to call those who are keeping close to their Master. There must be the cheerful resigning of everything that looks like honour and personal glory, in order that we may be wholly Christ's, and glorify His name. We must live His life, and be ready to die His death, if need be. O brothers, sisters, if we do this, and follow Jesus, putting our feet into the footprints of His pierced feet, He will make us fishers of men! If it should so please Him that we should even die without having gathered many souls to the cross, we shall speak from our graves. In some way or other, the Lord will make a holy life to be an influential life. It is not possible that a life which can be described as a following of Christ should be an unsuccessful one in the sight of the Most High. "Follow Me," and there is an "I will" such as God can never draw back from: "Follow Me, and I will make you fishers of men."

Thus much on the first point. There is something for us to do: we are graciously called to follow Jesus. Holy Spirit, lea d us to do it!

II. But, secondly, and briefly, there is SOMETHING FOR THE LORD TO DO. When His dear servants are following Him, He says, "I will make you fishers of men," and be it never forgotten that it is He that makes us follow Him; so that, if the following of Him be the step to being made a fisher of men, yet this He gives us. 'Tis all of His Spirit. I have talked about catching His spirit, and abiding in Him, and obeying Him, and hearkening to Him, and copying Him;

but none of these things are we capable of apart from His working them all in us. "From Me is thy fruit found," is a text which we must not for a moment forget. So, then, if we do follow Him, it is He that makes us follow Him; and so He makes us fishers of men.

But, further, if we follow Christ, He will make us fishers of men by all our experience. I am sure that the man who is really consecrated to bless others will be helped in this by all that he feels, especially by his afflictions. I often feel very grateful to God that I have undergone fearful depression of spirits. I know the borders of despair, and the horrible brink of that gulf of darkness into which my feet have almost gone; but hundreds of times I have been able to give a helpful grip to brethren and sisters who have come into that same condition, which grip I could never have given if I had not known their deep despondency. So I believe that the darkest and most dreadful experience of a child of God will help him to be a fisher of men if he will but follow Christ. Keep close to your Lord, and He will make every step a blessing to you. If God in providence should make you rich, He will fit you to speak to t hose ignorant and wicked rich who so much abound in this city, and so often are the cause of its worst sin. And if the Lord is pleased to let you be poor, you can go down and talk to those wicked and ignorant poor people who so often are the cause of sin in this city, and so greatly need the gospel. The winds of providence will waft you where you can fish for men. The wheels of providence are full of eyes, and all those eyes will look this way to help us to be winners of souls. You will often be surprised to find how God has been in a house that you visit: before you get there, His hand has been at work in its chambers. when you wish to speak to some particular individual, God's providence has been dealing with that individual to make him ready for just that word which you could say, but which nobody else but you could say. Oh, be you following Christ, and you will find that He will, by every experience through which you are passing, make you fishers of men!

Further than that, if you will follow Him, He will make you fishers of men by distinct monitions in your heart. There are many monitions from God's Spirit which are not noticed by Christians when the y are in a callous condition; but when the heart is right with God, and living in communion with God, we feel a sacred sensitiveness, so that we do not need the Lord to shout, but His faintest whisper is heard. Nay, he need not even whisper. He will guide us with His eye. Oh, how many mulish Christians there are, who must be held in with bit and bridle, and receive a cut of the whip every now and then! But the Christian who follows his Lord shall be tenderly guided. I do not say that the Spirit of God will say to you, "Go near, and join thyself to this chariot," or that you will hear a word in your ear; but yet in your soul, as distinctly as the Spirit said to Philip, "Go near, and join thyself to this chariot," you shall hear the Lord's will. As soon as you see an individual, the thought shall cross your mind, "Go and speak to that person." Every opportunity of usefulness shall be a call to you. If you are ready, the door shall open before you, and you shall hear a voice behind you saying, "This is the way; walk ye in it." If you have the grace to run in the right way, you shall never be long without an intimation as to what the right way is. That right way shall lead you to river or sea, where you can cast your net, and be a fisher of men.

Then, too, I believe that the Lord meant by this that He would give His followers the Holy Ghost. They were to follow Him, and then, when they had seen Him ascend into the holy place of the Most High, they were to tarry at Jerusalem for a little while, and the Spirit would come upon them, and clothe them with a mysterious power. This Word was spoken to Peter and Andrew; and you know how it was fulfilled to Peter. What a host of fish he brought to land the first time he cast the net in the power of the Holy Ghost! "Follow Me, and I will make you fishers of men."

Brethren, we have no conception of what God could Do by this company of believers gathered in the Tabernacle to-night. If now we were to be filled with the Holy Ghost, there are enough of us to evangelize London. There are enough here to be the means of the salvation of the world. God saveth not by many nor by few. Let us seek to be made a benediction to our fellow-creatures; and if we seek it, let us hear this directing voice, "Follow Me, and I will make you fishers of men." You men and women that sit before me, you are by the shore of a great sea of human life swarming with the souls of men. You live in the midst of millions; but if you will follow Jesus, and be faithful to Him, and true to Him, and do what He bids you, He will make you fishers of men. Do not say, "Who shall save this city?" The weakest shall be strong enough. Gideon's barley cake shall smite the tent, and make it lie along the ground. Samson, with the jawbone, taken up from the earth where it was lying bleaching in the sun, shall smite the Philistines. Fear not, neither be dismayed. Let your responsibilities drive you closer to your Master. Let horror of prevailing sin make you look into His dear face who long ago wept over Jerusalem, and now weeps over London. Clasp Him, and never let go your hold. By the strong and mighty impulses of the divine life within you, quickened and brought to maturity by the

169

Spirit of God, learn this lesson from your Lord's own mouth: "Follow Me, and I will make you fishers of men." You are not fit for it, but He will make you fit. You cannot do it of yourselves, but He will make you do it. You do not know how to spread nets and draw shoals of fish to shore, but He will teach you. Only follow Him, and He will make you fishers of men.

I wish that I could somehow say this as with a voice of thunder, that the whole Church of God might hear it. I wish I could w rite it in stars athwart the sky, "Jesus saith, Follow Me, and I will make you fishers of men." If you forget the precept, the promise shall never be yours. If you follow some other track, or imitate some other leader, you shall fish in vain. God grant us to believe fully that Jesus can do great things in us, and then do great things by us for the good of our fellows!

III. The last point you might work out in full for yourselves in your private meditations with much profit. We have here A FIGURE FULL OF INSTRUCTION. I will give you but two or three thoughts which you can use. "I will make you fishers of men." You have been fishers of fish: if you follow Me, I will make you *fishers of men*.

A fisher is a person who is *very dependent, and needs to be trustful*. He cannot see the fish. One who fishes in the sea must go and cast in the net, as it were, at a peradventure. Fishing is an act of faith. I have often seen, in the Mediterranean, men go with their boats, and enclose acres of sea with vast nets; and yet, when they have drawn the net to shore, the y have not had as much result as I could put in my hand. A few wretched silvery nothings have made up the whole take. Yet they have gone again, and cast the great net several times a day, hopefully expecting something to come of it. Nobody is so dependent upon God as the minister of God. Oh, this fishing from the Tabernacle pulpit! What a work of faith! I cannot tell that a soul will be brought to God by it. I cannot judge whether my sermon will be suitable to the persons who are here, except that I do believe that God will guide me in the casting of the net. I expect Him to work salvation, and I depend upon Him for it. I love this complete dependence, and if I could be offered a certain amount of preaching power, which should be entirely at my own disposal, and by which I could save sinners, I would beg the Lord not to let me have it, for it is far more delightful to be entirely dependent upon Him at all times. It is good to be a fool when Christ is made unto you wisdom. It is a blessed thing to be weak if Christ becomes more fully your strength. Go to work, you who would be fishers of men, and yet feel

170

your insufficiency. You that have no strength, attempt this divine work. Your Master's strength will be seen when your own has all gone. A fisherman is a dependent person, he must look up for success every time he puts the net down; but still he is a trustful person, and therefore he casts in the net joyfully.

A fisherman who gets his living by it is a diligent and persevering man. The fishers are up at dawn. At day-break, our fishermen off the Dogger-bank are fishing, and they continue fishing till late in the afternoon. As long as hands can work, men will fish. May the Lord Jesus make us hard-working, persevering, unwearied fishers of men! "In the morning sow thy seed, and in the evening withhold not thine hand; for thou knowest not whether shall prosper, either this or that."

The fisherman in his own craft is intelligent and watchful. It looks very easy, I dare say, to be a fisherman, but you would find that it was no child's play if you were to take a real part in it. There i s an art in it, from the mending of the net right on to the pulling it to shore. How diligent the fisherman is to prevent the fish leaping out of the net! I heard a great noise one night in the sea, as if some huge drum were being beaten by a giant; and I looked out, and I saw that the fishermen of Mentone were beating the water to drive the fish into the net, or to keep them from leaping out when they had once encompassed them with it. Ah, yes! and you and I will often have to be watching the corners of the gospel net lest sinners who are almost caught should make their escape. They are very crafty, these fish, and they use this craftiness in endeavouring to avoid salvation. We shall have to be always at our business, and to exercise all our wits, and more than our own wits, if we are to be successful fishers of men.

The fisherman is a *very laborious person*. It is not at all an easy calling. He does not sit in an armchair and catch fish. He has to go out in rough weathers. If he that regardeth the clouds will not sow, I am sure that he that regardeth the clouds will never fish. If we never do any work for Christ except when we feel up to the mark, we shall not do much. If we feel that we will not pray because we cannot pray, we shall never pray; and if we say, " I will not preach to-day because I do not feel that I could preach," we shall never preach any preaching that is worth the preaching. We must be always at i t, until we wear ourselves out, throwing our whole soul into the work in all weathers, for Christ's sake.

171

The fisherman is *a daring man*. He tempts the boisterous sea. A little brine in his face does not hurt him; he has been wet thro ugh a thousand times, it is nothing to him. He never expected, when he became a deep-sea fisherman, that he was going to sleep in the lap of ease. So the true minister of Christ, who fishes for souls, will never mind a little risk. He will be bound to do or say many a thing that is very unpopular; and some Christian people may even judge his utterances to be too severe. He must do and say that which is for the good of souls. It is not his to entertain a question as to what others will think of his doctrine, or of him; but in the name of the Almighty God he must feel, "If the sea roar and the fulness thereof, still at my Master's command I will let down the net."

Now, in the last place, the man whom Christ makes a fisher of men is successful. "But," says one, "I have always heard that Christ' s ministers are to be faithful, but that they cannot be sure of being successful." Yes, I have heard that saying, and one way I know it is true, but another way I have my doubts about it. He that is faithful is, in God's way and in God's judgment, successful, more or less. For instance, here is a brother who says that he is faithful. Of course, I must believe him, yet I never heard of a sinner being saved under him. Indeed, I should think that the safest place for a person to be in if he did not want to be saved would be under this gentleman's ministry, because he does not preach anything that is likely to arouse, impress, or convince anybody, This brother is "faithful" ; so he says. Well, if any per son in the world said to you, "I am a fisherman, but I have never caught anything," you would wonder how he could be called a fisherman. A farmer who never grew any wheat, or any other crop,—is he a farmer? When Jesus Christ says, "Follow Me, and I will make you fishers of men," He means that you shall really catch men, that you really shall save some; for he that never did get any fish is not a fisherman. He that never saved a sinner after years of work is not a minister of Christ. If the result of his life-work is nil, he made a mistake when he undertook it. Go thou with the fire of God in thy hand, and fling it among the stubble, and the stubble will burn. Be thou sure of that. Go thou and scatter the good seed; it may not all fall in fruitful places, but some of it will. Be thou sure of that. Do but shine, and some eye or other will be lightened thereby. Thou must, thou shalt succeed. But remember this is the Lord's word, "Follow Me, and I will make you fishers of men." Keep close to Jesus, and do as Jesus did, in His spirit, and He will make you fishers of men.

Perhaps I speak to an attentive hearer who is not converted at all.

Friend, I have the same thing to say to you. You also may follow Christ, and then He can use you, even you. I do not know but that He has brought you to this place that you may be saved, and that in after years He may make you speak for His name and glory. Remember how He called Saul of Tarsus, and made him the apostle of the Gentiles. Reclaimed poachers make the best game-keepers; and saved sinners make the ablest preachers. Oh, that you would run away from your old master to-night, without giving him a minute's notice; for if you give him any notice, he will hold you. Hasten to Jesus, and say, "Here is a poor runaway slave! My Lord, I bear the fetters still upon my wrists. Wilt Thou set me free, and make me Thine own?" Remember, it is written, "Him that cometh to Me, I will in no wise cast out." Never runaway slave came to Christ in the middle of the night without His taking him in; and He never gave one up to his old master. If Jesus make you free, you shall be free indeed. F lee away to Jesus, then, on a sudden. May His good Spirit help you, and He will by-and-by make you a winner of others to His praise! God bless you! Amen.

ENCOURAGEMENT TO SOUL-WINNERS

"Brethren, if any of you do err from the truth, and one convert him; let him know, that he which converteth the sinner from the error of his way shall save a soul from death, and shall hide a multitude of sins ."

James 5:19-20

James is pre-eminently practical. If he were, indeed, the James who was called "The Just" , I can understand how he earned the title, for that distinguishing trait in his character shows itself in his Epistle; and if he were "the Lord's brother" , he did well to show so close a resemblance to his great Relative and Master, who commenced His ministry with the practical Sermon on the Mount. We ought to be very grateful that, in the Holy Scriptures, we have food for all classes of believers, and employment for all the faculties of the saints. It was meet that the contemplative should be furnished with abundant subjects for thought,—Paul has supplied them; he has given to us sound doctrine, arranged in the symmetry of exact order; he has given us deep thoughts and profound teachings; he has opened up the deep things of God. No man who is inclined to reflection and thoughtfulness will be without food so long as the Epistles of Paul are extant, for he fee ds the soul with sacred manna. For those whose predominating affections and imagination incline them to more mystic themes, John has written sentences aglow with devotion, and blazing with love. We have his simple but sublime Epistles,—Epistles which, when you glance at them, seem in their wording to be fit for children, but when examined, their sense is seen to be too sublime to be fully grasped by the most advanced of men. You have from that same eagle-eyed and eagle-winged apostle the wondrous visions of the Revelation, where awe, devotion, and imagination may enlarge their flight, and find scope for the fullest exercise.

There will always be, however, a class of persons who are more practical than contemplative, more active than imaginative, and it was wise that there should be a James, whose main point should be to stir up their pure minds by way of remembrance, and help them to persevere in the practical graces of the Holy Spirit. The text before me is perhaps the most practical utterance of the whole Epistle. The whole Epistle burns, but this ascends in flames to heaven it is the culmination as it is the conclusion of the letter. There is not a word to spare in it. It is like a naked sword, stripped of its jewelled scabbard, and presented to us with nothing to note but its keen edge. I wish I could preach after the fashion of the text; and if I cannot, I will at least pray that you may act after the fashion of it. Downright living for the Lord Jesus is sadly wanted in many quarters; we have enough of Christian garnishing, but solid, everyday, actual work for God is what we need. If our lives, however unornamented they may be by leaves of literary or polite attainments, shall nevertheless bring forth fruit unto God in the form of souls converted by our efforts, it will be well; they will then stand forth before the Lord with the beauty of the olive tree, which consists in its fruitfulness.

I call your attention very earnestly to three matters. First, here is a *special case dealt with.* "If any of you do err from the truth, and one convert him." While speaking of that special case, the apostle declares a *general fact*: "he which converteth the sinner from the error of his w ay shall save a soul from death, and shall hide a multitude of sins." When I have spoken of these two points, I mean, thirdly, to make a particular application of the text,—not at all intended by the apostle, but I believe abundantly justified,—an application of the text to increased effort for the conversion of children.

I. First, then, here is A SPECIAL CASE DEALT WITH. Read the verse, and you will see that it must relate to a backslider from the visible Church of God. The words, "If any of you," must refer to a professed Christian. The erring one had been named by the name of Jesus, and for a while had followed the truth but in an evil hour he had been betrayed into doctrinal error, and had erred from the truth. It was not merely that he fell into a mistake upon some lesser matter, which might be compared to the fringe of the gospel, but he erred in some vital doctrine, he departed from the faith in its fundamentals. There are some truths which must be believed; they are essential to salvation, and if not heartily accepted, the soul will be ruined. This ma n had been professedly orthodox, but he turned aside from the truth on an essential point. Now, in those days, the saints did not say, as the sham saints do now, "We must be largely charitable, and leave this brother to his own opinion; he sees truth from a different standpoint, and has a rather different way of putting it, but his opinions are as good as our own, and we must not say that he is in error." That is at present the fashionable way of trifling with divine truth, and making things pleasant all round. Thus the gospel is debased, and "another gospel" propagated.

I should like to ask modern broad churchmen whether there is any doctrine of any sort for which it would be worth a man's while to burn or to lie in prison. I do not believe they could give me an answer, for if their latitudinarianism be correct, the martyrs were fools of the first magnitude. From what I see of their writings and their teachings, it appears to me that the modern thinkers treat the whole compass of revealed truth with entire indifference; and, though perhaps they may feel sorry that wilder spirits should go too far in free thinking, and though they had rather they would be more moderate, yet, upon the whole, so large is their liberality that they are not sure enough of anything to be able to condemn the reverse of it as a deadly error. To the m black and white are terms which may be applied to the same colour, as you vie w it from different standpoints. Yea and nay are equally true in their esteem. Their theology shifts like the Goodwin Sands, and they regard all firmnes s as so much bigotry. Errors and truths are equally comprehensible within the circle of their charity. It was not in this way that the apostles regarded error. They did not prescribe large-hearted charity towards falsehood, or hold up the errorist as a man of deep thought, whose views were "refreshingly origin al" ; far less did they utter some wicked nonsense about the probability of there living more faith in honest doubt than in half the creeds. They did not believe in justification by doubting, as our neologians do; they set about the conversion of the erring brother; they treated him as a person who needed conversion; and viewed him as a man who, if he were not converted, would suffer the death of his soul, and be covered with a multitude of sins. They were not such easygoing people as our cultured friends of the school of "modern thought" , who have learned at last that the Deity of Christ may be denied, the work of the Holy Spirit ignored, the inspiration of Scripture rejected, the atonement di sbelieved, and regeneration dispensed with, and yet the man who does all this may be as good a Christian as the most devout believer! O God, deliver us from this deceitful infidelity, which, while it does damage to the erring man, and often prevents his being reclaimed, does yet more mischief to our own hearts by teaching us that truth is unimportant, and falsehood a trifle, and so destroy sour allegiance to the God of truth, and makes us traitors instead of loyal subjects to the King of kings!

It appears from our text that this man, having erred from the truth, followed the natural logical consequence of doctrinal error, and he erred in his life as well; for the twentieth verse, which must of course be read in connection with the nineteenth, speaks of him as "a sinner converted from the error of his way." His way went wrong after his thought had gone wrong. You cannot deviate from truth without, ere long, in some measure, at any rate, deviating from practical righteousness. This man had erred from right acting because he had erred from right believing. Suppose a man shall imbibe a doctrine which leads him to think little of Christ, he will soon have little faith in Him, and become little obedient to Him, and so will wander into self-righteousness or licentiousness. Let him think lightly of the punishment of sin, it is natural that he will commit sin with less compunction, and burst through all restraints. Let him deny the need of the atonement, and the same result will follow if he acts out his belief. Every error has its own outgrowth, as all decay has its appropriate fungus. It is in vain for us to imagine that holiness will be as readily produced from erroneous as from truthful doctrine. Do men gather grapes of thorns, or figs of thistles? The facts of history p rove the contrary. When truth is dominant, morality and holiness are abundant; but when error comes to the front, godly living retreats in shame.

The point aimed at with regard to this sinner in thought and deed was his conversion, —the turning of him round, the bringing him to right thinking and to right acting. Alas I fear many professed Christians do not look upon backsliders in this light, neither do they regard t hem as hopeful subjects for conversion. I have known a person who has erred, hunted down like a wolf. He was wrong to some degree, but that wrong has been aggravated and dwelt upon till the man has been worried into defiance; the fault has been exaggerated into a double wrong by ferocious attacks upon it. The manhood of the man has taken sides with his error because he has been so severely handled. The man has been compelled, sinfully I admit, to take up an extreme position, and to go further into mischief, because he could not brook being denounced instead of being reasoned with. And when a man has been blameworthy in his life, it will often happen that his fault has been blazed abroad, retailed from mouth to mouth, and magnified, until the poor erring one has felt degraded, and having lost all self-respect, has given way to far more dreadful sins. The object of some professors seems to be to amputate the limb rather than to heal it. Justice has reigned instead of mercy. Away with him! He is too foul to be washed, too diseased to be restored. This is not according to the mind of Christ, nor after the model of apostolic churches.

In the days of James, if any erred from the truth and from holiness, there were brethren found who sought their recovery, and whose joy it was thus to save a soul from death, and to hide a multitude of sins. There is something very significant in that expression, "Brethren, if any of you do err from the truth." It is akin to that other word, "Considering thyself, lest thou also be tempted," and that other exhortation, "Let him that thinketh he standeth take heed lest he fall." He who has erred was one of yourselves, one who sat with you at the communion table, one with whom you took sweet counsel; he has been deceived, and by the subtlety of Satan he has been decoyed; but do not judge him harshly; above all, do not leave him to perish unpitied. If he ever was a saved man, he is your brother still, and it should be your business to bring back the prodigal, and so to make glad your Father's heart. Still, for all slips of his, he is one of God's children; follow him up, and do not rest till you lead him home again. And if he be not a child of God, if his professed conversion was a mistake, or a pretence, if he only made a profession, but had not the possession of vital godliness, yet still follow him with sacred importunity of love, remembering how terrible will be his doom for daring to play the hypocrite, and to profane holy things with his unhallowed hand s. Weep over him the more if you feel compelled to suspect that he has been a wilful deceiver, for there is sevenfold cause for weeping. If you cannot resist the feeling that he never was sincere, but crept into the church under cover of a false profession, I say, sorrow over him the more, for his doom must be the more terrible, and therefore the greater should be your commiseration for him. Seek his conversion still.

The text gives us clear indications as to the *persons who are to aim at the conversion of erring brethren*. It says, "If any of you do err from the truth, and one convert him." One what? One minister? No, any one among the brethren. If the minister shall be the means of the restoration of a backslider, he is a happy man, and a good deed has been done; but there is no thing said here concerning preachers or pastors, not even a hint is given,—it is left open to any one member of the church; and the plain inference, I think, is this,—that every church-member, seeing his brother err from the truth, or err in practice, should set himself, in the power of the Holy Spirit, to this business of converting this special sinner from the error of his way. Look after strangers by all means, but neglect not your brethren. It is the business, not of certain officers appointed by the vote of the church thereunto, but of every member of the body of Jesus Christ, to seek the good of all the other members. Still, there are certain members upon whom in any one case this may be more imperative. For instance, in the case of a young believer, his father and his mother, if they be believers, are called upon by a sevenfold obligation to seek the conversion of their backsliding child. In the case of a husband, none should be so earnest for his restoration as his wife, and the same rule hold s good with regard to the wife. So also if the connection be that of friendship, he with whom you have had the most acquaintance should lie nearest to your heart; and when you perceive that he has gone aside, you should, above all others, ac t the shepherd towards him with kindly zeal. You are bound to do this to all y our fellow-Christians, but doubly bound to do it to those over whom you possess an influence, which has been gained by former intimacy, by relationship, or by any other means. I beseech you, therefore, watch over one another in the Lord, and when ye see a brother overtaken in a fault, "ye which are spiritual, restore such an one in the spirit of meekness." Ye see your duty; do not neglect it.

Brethren, it ought to cheer us to know that *the attempt to convert a man who has erred from the truth is a hopeful one*, it is one in which success may be looked for, and when the success comes, it will be of the most joyful character. Verily, it is a great joy to capture the wild, wandering sinner; but the joy of joys is to find the lost sheep which was once really in the fold, and has sadly gone astray. It is a great thing to transmute a piece of brass into silver, but to the poor woman it was joy enough to find the piece of silver which was silver already, and had the king's stamp on it, though for a while it was lost. To bring in a stranger and an alien, and to adopt him as a son, suggests a festival; but the most joyous feasting and the loudest music are for the son who was always a son, but had played the prodigal, and yet after being lost was found, and after being dead was made alive again. I say, ring the bells twice for the reclaimed backslider; ring them till the steeple rocks and reels. Rejoice doubly over that which had gone astray, and was ready to perish, but has now been restored. John was glad when he found poor backsliding but weeping Peter, who had denied his Master; he cheered and comforted him, and consorted with him, till the Lord Himself had said, "Simon, son of Jonas, lo vest thou Me?" It may not appear so brilliant a thing to bring back a backslider as to reclaim a harlot or a drunkard, but in the sight of God it is no small miracle of grace, and to the instrument who has performed it it shall yield no s mall comfort. Seek ye, then, my brethren, those who were of us but have

179

gone from us; seek ye those who linger still in the congregation, but have disgrace d the church, and are put away from us, and rightly so, because we cannot countenance their uncleanness; seek them with prayers, and tears, and entreaties, if peradventure God may grant them repentance that they may be saved.

Here I would say to any backsliders who are present, let this text cheer you if you have a desire to turn to God Return, ye back sliding children, for the Lord has bidden His people seek you. If He had not cared for you, He would not have spoken of our search after you; but having put it so, and made it the duty of all His people to seek those who err from the faith, there is an open door before you, and there are hundreds who sit waiting like porters at the gate to welcome you. Come back to the God whom you have for saken; or if you never did know Him, oh, that this day His Spirit may break your hearts, and lead you to true repentance, that you may in real truth be saved! God bless you, poor backsliders! If He do not save you, a multitude of sins will be upon you, and you must die eternally. God have mercy upon. you, f or Christ's sake.

II. We have opened up the special case, and we have now to dwell upon A GENERAL FACT.

This general fact is important, and we are bound to give it special attention, since it is prefaced with the words, "Let him know. " If any one of you has been the means of bringing back a backslider, it is said, "Let him know." That is, let him think of it, be sure of it, be comforted by it, be inspirited by it. "Let him know" it, and never doubt it. Do not merely hear it, beloved fellow-labourer, but let it sink deep into your heart When an apostle inspired of the Holy Ghost says, "Let him know," I conjure you, do not let any indolence of spirit forbid your ascertaining the full weight of the truth.

What is it that you are to know? To know that *he who converteth a sinner from the error of his way shall save a soul from death.* This is something worth knowing, is it not? To save a soul from death, is no small matter. Why, we have men among us whom we honour every time we cast our eyes upon them, for they have saved many precious lives; they have manned the lifeboat, or they have plunged into the river to rescue the drowning; they have been ready to risk their own lives amid burning timbers that they might snatch the perishing from the devouring flames. True heroes these, far worthier of renown than your blood-stained men of war. God bless the brave heart s! May England never lack a body of worthy men to make her shores illustrious for humanity! When we see a fellow-

180

creature exposed to danger, our pulse beats quickly, and we are agitated with desire to save him. Is it not so?

But the saving of a soul from death is a far greater matter. Let us think what that death is. It is not non-existence; I do not know that I would lift a finger to save my fellow-creature from mere nonexistence. I see no great hurt in annihilation; certainly nothing that would alarm me as a punishment for sin. Just as I see no great joy in mere eternal existence if that is all that is meant by eternal life, so I discern no terror in ceasing to be; I would as soon not be as be, so far as mere colourless being or not being is concerned. But "eternal life" means in Scripture a very different thing from eternal existence; it means existing with all the faculties developed in fulnes joy; existing not as the dried herb in the hay, but as the flower in all its beauty. "To die," in Scripture, and indeed in common language, is not to cease to exist. Very wide is the difference between the two words to die and to be annihilated. To die, as to the first death, is the separation of the body from the soul; it is the resolution of our nature into its component elements; and to die the second death, is to separate the man, soul and body, from his God, who is the life and joy of our manhood. This is eternal destruction from the presence of the Lord and from the glory of His power; this is to have the palace of manhood destroyed, and turned into a desolate ruin, for the howling dragon of remorse, and the hooting owl of despair, to inherit forever.

The descriptions which Holy Scripture gives of the second death are terrible to the last degree. It speaks of a "worm that never dies," and a "fire that never can be quenched," of "the terror of the Lord, " and "tearing in pieces" , of "the smoke of their torment which goeth up for ever and ever," and of "the pit which hath no bottom." I am not about to bring all these terrible things together, but there are words in Scripture which, if pondered, might make the flesh to creep, and the hair to stand on end, at the very thought of the judgment to come. Our joy is, that if any of us are made, in God's hands, the means of converting a man from the error of his way, we shall have saved a soul from this eternal death. That dreadful hell the saved one will not know, that wrath he will not feel, that being banished from the presence of God will never happen to him. Is there not a joy worth worlds in all this? Remember the addition to the picture. If you have saved a soul from death, you have introduced it into eternal life; by God's good grace, there will be another chorister a mongst the white-robed host to sing Jehovah's praise, another hand to smite eternally the harpstrings of adoring gratitude, another sinner saved to reward the Redeemer for His passion. Oh, the happiness of having saved a soul from death.

And it is added that, in such a case, *you will have covered a multitude of sins*. We understand this to mean that the result of the conversion of any sinner will be the covering up of all his sins by the atoning blood of Jesus. How many those sins are, in any case, none of us can tell; but if any man be converted from the error of his way, the whole mass of his sins will be drowned in the Red Sea of Jesus' blood, and washed away forever. Now, remember that your Saviour came to this world with two objects: He came to destroy death, and to put away sin. If you convert a sinner from the error of his way, you are made like to Him in both these works; after your manner, in the power of the Spirit of God, you overcome death, by snatching a soul from the second death, and you also put away sin from the sight of God by hiding a multitude of sins beneath the propitiation of the Lord Jesus Christ.

Do observe here that the apostle offers no other in ducement to soul- winners: he does not say, "If you convert a sinner from the error of his way, you will have honour." True philanthropy scorns such a motive. He does not say, "If you convert a sinner from the error of his way, you will have the respect of the church, and the love of the individual." Such will be the case, but we are moved by far nobler motives. The joy of doing good is found in the good itself; the reward of a deed of love is found in its own result. If we have saved a soul from death, and hidden a multitude of sins, that is payment enough, though no ear should ever hear of the deed, and no pen should ever record it. Let it be forgotten that we were the instruments if good be but effected; it shall give us joy even if we be not appreciated, and are left in the cold shade of forgetfulness. Yea, if others wear the honours of the good deed which the Lord has wrought by us, we will not murmur, it shall be joy enough to know that a soul has been saved from death, and a multitude of sins has been covered.

And, dear brethren, let us recollect that the saving of souls from death honours Jesus, for there is no saving souls except through His blood. As for you and for me, what can we do in saving a soul from death? Of ourselves nothing, any more than that pen which lies upon the table could write The Pilgrim's Progress; yet let a Bunyan grasp the pen, and the matchless work is written. So you and I can do nothing to convert souls till God' s eternal Spirit takes us in hand; but then He can do wonders by us, and get to Himself glory by us, while it shall be joy enough for us to know that Jesus is honoured, and the Spirit magnified. Nobody talks of Homer's pen, no one has encased it in gold, or published its illustrious achievements; nor do we wish for honour among men: it will be enough for us to have been the pen in the Saviour's hand with which He has written the covenant of His grace upon the fleshy tablets of human hearts. This is golden wages for a man who really loves his Master; Jesus is glorified, sinners are saved.

Now I want you to notice particularly that *all that is said by the apostle here is about the conversion of one person.* "If any of you do err from the truth, and one convert him, let him know that he which converteth the sinner from the error of his way shall save a soul from death." Have you never wished you were a Whitefield? Have you never felt, young man, in your inmost soul, great aspirations to be another McCheyne, or Brainerd, or Moffat? Cultivate the aspiration, but at the same time be happy to bring one sinner to Jesus Christ, for he who converts only one is bidden to know that no mean thing has been done; for he has saved a soul from death, and covered a multitude of sins.

And it does not say anything about the person who i s the means of this work. It is not said, "If a minister shall convert a man, or if some noted eloquent divine shall have wrought it." If this deed shall be performed by the least babe in our Israel, if a little child shall tell the tale of Jesus to its father, if a servant girl shall drop a tract where someone poor soul shall find it and receive salvation, if the humblest preacher at the street corner shall have spoken to the thief or to the harlot, and such shall be saved; let him know that he that turneth any sinner from the error of his way, whoever he may be, hath saved a soul from death, and covered a multitude of sins.

Now, beloved, what comes out of this but these suggestions? Let us long to be used in the conversion of sinners. James does not speak concerning the Holy Ghost in this passage, nor of the Lord Jesus Christ, for he was writing to those who would not fail to remember the important truths which concern both the Spirit and the Son of God; but yet it may be meet h ere to remind you that we cannot do spiritual good to our fellow-creatures apart from the Spirit of God, neither can we be blessed to them if we do not preach to them "Jesus Christ and Him crucified." God must use us; but, oh, let us long to be used, pray to be used, and pine to be used! Dear brethren and sisters, let us purge ourselves of everything that would prevent our being employed by the Lord. If there is anything we are doing, or leaving undone, any evil we are harbouring, or any grace we are neglecting, which may make us unfit to be used of God, let us pray the Lord to cleanse, and mend, and scour us, till we are vessels fit for the Master's use. Then let us be on the watch for opportunities of usefulness; let us go about the world with our ears and our eyes open, ready to avail ourselves of every occasion for doing good; let us not be content till we are useful, but make this the main design and ambition of our lives. Somehow or other, we must and will bring souls to Jesus Christ. As Rachel cried, "Give me children, or I die," so may none of you be content to be barren in the household of God. Cry and sigh until you have snatched some brand from the burning, and have brought at least one sinner to Jesus Christ, that so you also may have saved a soul from death, and covered a multitude of sins.

III. And, now, let us turn for a few minutes only to the point which is not in the text. I want to make A PARTICULAR APPLICATION of this whole subject to the conversion of children.

Beloved friends, I hope you do not altogether forget the Sabbath-school, and yet I am afraid a great many Christians are scarcely aware that there are such things as Sabbath-schools at all; they know it by hearsay, but not by observation. Probably, in the course of twenty years, they have never visited the school, nor concerned themselves about it. They would be gratified to hear of any success accomplished, but though they may not have heard anything about the matter one way or the other, they are well content. In most churches, you will find a band of young and ardent spirits giving themselves to Sunday-school work; but there are numbers of others who might greatly strengthen the school who never attempt anything of the sort. In this they might be excused if they had other work to do; but, unfortunately, they have no godly occupation, but are mere killers of time, while this work which lies ready to hand, and is accessible, and demands their assistance, is entirely neglected. I will not say there are any such sluggards here, but I am not able to believe that we are quite free from them, and therefore I will ask conscience to do its work with the guilty parties.

Children need to be saved; children may be saved; children are to be saved by instrumentality. Children may be saved while they are children. He who said, "Suffer the little children to come unto Me, and forbid them not, for of such is the kingdom of heaven," never intended that His Church should say, "We will look after the children by-and-by when they have gr own up to be young men and women." He intended that it should be a subject of prayer and earnest endeavour that children as children should be converted to God.

The conversion of a child involves the same work of divine grace, and results in the same blessed consequences as the con version of the adult. There is the saving of the soul from death in the child's case, and the hiding of a multitude of sins, but there is this additional matter for joy, that a great preventive work is done when the young are converted. Conversion saves a child from a multitude of sins. If God's eternal mercy shall bless your teaching to a little prattler, how happy that boy's life will be compared with what it might have been if he had grown up in folly, sin, and shame, and had only been converted after many days! It is the highest wisdom and the truest prudence to pray for our children that, while they are yet young, their hearts may be given to the Saviour.

> "'Twill save them from a thousand snares,
> To mind religion young;
> Grace will preserve their following years,
> And make their virtues strong."

To reclaim the prodigal is well, but to save him from ever being a prodigal is better. To bring back the thief and the drunkard is a praiseworthy action, but so to act that the boy shall never become a thief or a drunkard is far better; hence Sabbath-school instruction stands very high in the list of philanthropic enterprises, and Christians ought to be most earnest in it. He who converts a child from the error of his way, prevents as well as covers a multitude of sins.

Moreover, *this gives the Church the hope of being furnished with the best of men and women.* The Church's Samuels and Solomons are made wise in their youth; David and Josiah were tender of heart when they were tender in years. Read the lives of the most eminent ministers, and you shall usually find that their Christian history began early. Though it is not absolutely needful, yet it is highly propitious to the growth of a well-developed Christian character, that its foundation should be laid on the basis of youthful piety. I do not expect to see the Churches of Jesus Christ ordinarily built up by those who have through life lived in sin, but by the bringing up i n their midst, in the fear and admonition of the Lord, young men and women who become pillars in the house of our God. If we want strong Christians, we must look to those who were Christians in their youth. Trees must be planted in the courts of the Lord while they are yet young if they are to live long and to flourish well.

And, brethren, I feel that the work of teaching the young has at this time an importance superior to any which it ever had before, for at this time there are abroad those who are creeping into our houses, and deluding men and women with their false doctrine. Let the Sunday-school teachers of England teach the children well. Let them not merely occupy their time with pious phrases, but teach them the whole gospel and the doctrines of gr ace intelligently, and let them pray over the children, and never be satisfied unless the children are turned to the Lord Jesus Christ, and added to the Church, and then I shall not be afraid of Popery. Popish priests said of old that they could have won England back again to Rome, if it had not been for the catechising of the children. We have laid aside catechisms, I think with too little reason; but, at any rate, if we do not use godly catechisms, we must bring back decided, plain, simple teaching, and there must be pleading and praying for the immediate conversion of the children unto the Lord Jesus Christ. The Spirit of God waits to help us in this effort. He is with us if we be with Him. He is ready to bless the humblest teacher, and even the infant classes shall not be without a benediction. He can give us words and thoughts suitable to our little auditory. He can so bless us that we shall know how to speak a word in season to the youthful ear. And oh, if it be not so, if teachers are not found, or, being found, are unfaithful, we shall see the children that have been in our schools go back into the world, like their parents, hating religion because of the tedium of the hours spent in the Sunday- school, and we shall produce a race of infidels, or a generation of superstitious persons; the golden opportunity will be lost, and most solemn responsibility will rest upon us! I pray the Church of God to thin k much of the Sunday-school. I beseech all lovers of the nation to pray for Sunday-schools; I entreat all who love Jesus Christ, and would see His kingdom come, to be very tender towards all youthful people, and to pray that their hearts may be won to Jesus.

I have not spoken as I should like to speak, but the theme lies very near my heart. It is one which ought to press heavily upon all our consciences; but I must leave it. God must lead your thoughts fully in to it; I leave it, but not till I have asked these questions:—What have you been doing for the conversion of children, each one of you? What have you done for the conversion of your own children? Are you quite clear upon that matter? Do you ever put your arms around your boy's neck, and pray for him, and with him? Father, you will find that such an act will exercise great influence over your lad. Mother, do you ever talk to your little daughter about Christ, and Him crucified? Under God's hands, you may be a spiritual as well as a natural mother to that well-beloved child of yours. What are you doing, you who are guardians and teachers of youth? Are you clear about their souls? You week-day schoolmasters, as well as you who labour on the Sabbath, are you doing all you should that your boys and girls may be brought early to confess the Lord? I leave it with yourselves.

You shall receive a great reward if, when you enter heaven, as I trust you will, you shall find many dear children there to welcome you into eternal habitations; it will add another heaven to your own heaven, to meet with heavenly beings who shall salute you as their teacher who brought them to Jesus. I would not wish to go to heaven alone;—would you? I would not wish to have a crown in heaven without a star in it, because no soul was ever saved by my means;—would you? There they go, the sacred f lock of blood-bought sheep, the great Shepherd leads them; many of them are followed by twins, and others have, each one, their lamb; would you like to be a barren sheep of the great Shepherd's flock? The scene changes. Hearken to the trampings of a great host. I hear their war music, my ears are filled with their songs of victory. The warriors are coming home, and each one is bringing his trophy on his shoulder, to the honour of the great Captain. They stream through the gate of pearl, they march in triumph to the celestial Capitol, along the golden streets, and each soldier bears with him his own portion of the spoil.

Will you be there? And being there, will you march without a trophy, and add nothing to the pomp of the triumph? Will you bear nothing that you have won in battle, nothing which you have ever taken for Jesus with your sword and with your bow? Again, another scene is before me. I hear them shout the " harvest home" , and I see the reapers bearing everyone his sheaf. Some of them are bowed down with the heaps of sheaves which load their happy shoulders: they went forth weeping, but they have come again rejoicing, bringing their sheaves with them. Yonder comes one who bears but a little handful, but it is rich grain; he had only a tiny plot, and a little seed corn entrusted to him, yet it has multiplied well according to the rule of proportion. Will you be there without so much as a solitary ear? Never having ploughed nor sown, and therefore never having reaped? If so, every shout of every reaper might well strike a fresh pang into your heart as you remember that you did not sow, and therefore could not reap. If you do not love my Master, do not profess to do so. If He never bought you with His blood, do not lie unto Him, and come unto His table, and say that you are His servant; but if His dear wounds bought you, give yourself to Him; and if you love Him, feed His sheep and feed His lambs. He stands here unseen by my sight, but recognised by my faith, He exhibits to you the mark the wounds upon His hands and His feet, and He says to you, "Peace be unto you! As My Father hath sent Me, even so send I you. Go ye into all the world, and preach the gospel to every creature; and this know, that he who converteth a sinner from the error of his way shall save a soul from death, and shall hid e a multitude of sins." Good Master, help us to serve Thee! Amen.

www.ingramcontent.com/pod-product-compliance
Lightning Source LLC
LaVergne TN
LVHW090417090426
835511LV00043B/594